Call Me Gaz

Love,
Gaz Green

Gaz Green

Armadillo Publishing
Corporation

ISBN 13: 978-1-891429-63-7

Library of Congress Control Number: 2007940698

Photo Editing, Graphic Design & Typesetting by Larry Simpson

Published by:
Armadillo Publishing Corporation
Georgetown, Texas
www.fineliterature.com

Contents

FOREWORD

I was always a dreamer. Yet I could never have imagined I would meet the people I have, travel the way I have, and share the love of such a beautiful, wonderful, caring family.

The people I mention in this book are real. Many names might not be familiar to you as they lived in a different era.

My father took me to Yankee Stadium when I was 12 to see Babe Ruth, Lou Gehrig, Bill Dickey, Tony Lazerri beat the Red Sox 4-2. Each time the Babe came to bat everybody in the stadium stood up so show their respect. That day he did not let us down. He got two hits and drove in the winning runs.

My brother took me to see the Lincoln Memorial the morning Marian Anderson was denied the right to perform in Constitution Hall. She got out of the car in front of us to make plans to sing at the Lincoln Memorial instead.

A little boy took me inside the White House grounds. He needed a "grownup" so he could get in for the Easter Egg Roll. There, in front of me, big as life was Eleanor Roosevelt, the First Lady.

Who would ever believe that I would meet John D. Rockefeller Jr. and be invited to his Memorial Service at the Riverside Church in N. Y., be asked by Laurance Rockefeller to deliver the lay sermon in the Union Church of Pocantico Hills, become Board of Trustees President in that church and preside over a meeting with the Governor and future Vice President of the United States Nelson Rockefeller on the Board.

David Rockefeller enabled me to spend an hour with Marc Chagall, serving as our interpreter as we discussed the creation of the "Good Samaritan" Memorial Window honoring "Mr. Junior" at the rear of Union Church.

We were invited to Rockefeller wedding receptions, private memorial ervices, to play tennis in their famous million-dollar playhouse, and to their private homes. We taught their children in Sunday school, sat across the aisle from them in Church, and visited informally on the church lawn.

After living 10 years adjacent to the Estate I probably had enough material to write a book just about the Rockefeller Family.

I met and shook hands with Presidents Harry Truman and George Herbert Walker Bush; knew Secretary of State Jim Baker, Secretary of Energy Charles Duncan, Secretary of Defense Neil McElroy, and met Senators Walter Kerr, Jim Buckley, John Tower, Phil Gramm and Alan Simpson.

Cab Calloway and I attended homeroom parents' meetings together; Victor Mature and I ate ice cream on the deck of my ship in Greenland. I've had dinner with Desi Arnaz and Lucille Ball, introduced Dr. Deepak Chopra, Dr. Wayne Dyer, Dr. Bernie Siegel, Og Mandino and Alex Haley to audiences.

I met Ted Williams and Johnny Pesky the day they joined the Navy Flight Cadet Program; Otto Preminger invited Doc. Straub and me to visit him on the set of "Centennial Summer" that he was directing and asked Cornell Wilde and Linda Darnell to be our guides.

I have sat in the Houston Astros broadcast booth with Gene Elston, Harry Kalas and Lowell Paas, been told an unbelievable story about Jack Kemp by Ray Scott, Voice of the Green Bay Packers, and, with baseball Hall of Famer Joe Morgan, watched Muhammad Ali prepare for a World Heavyweight Championship Fight.

The Houston Oilers drafted their first soccer-style kicker after I gave the General Manager a demonstration of why they should; I conducted a press conference with Paul Richards, Astros GM, with Arthur Daley of the NY Times, Jack Hand of AP, and the leading baseball writers participating.

I visited the Baseball Hall of Fame in Cooperstown and saw the plaques honoring many of the all time greats I had seen play. Additionally, I visited the Football Hall in Canton where I saw honored among others, Clarke Hinkle the great Green Bay Packer whom I met as bat boy for his Bucknell baseball team. I kept his broken bat for years.

At Chautauqua my good friend, Jim Roselle, who has conducted live interviews of the featured lecturers for 33 years introduced me to such people as historians Michael Beschloss, Doris Kearns Goodwin, and her husband, Richard, speech writer for Lyndon Johnson; Columnists David Broder and E. J. Dionne; Bishop John Shelby Spong; Prosecutors Ken Starr and Elliott Spitzer; Poet Laureates Stanley Kunitz and Robert Pinsky; and, last but not least, satirist Mark Russell who became a good friend.

Having completed one lap around the famous Indianapolis Speedway, I was thrilled to meet A. J. Foyt, Mario Andretti and other Indy Drivers. I also met Evil Knievel, the most famous daredevil of all time.

I know nothing about horse racing but I did know Bill Young, whose horse won the Kentucky Derby, and Frederick J. Lennup III, who was principal owner of the Wolverine Raceway in Detroit and the Track in Ft. Lauderdale. He had to be one of the most unusual persons I ever met.

My sister Adelaide, four years older, let me ride in the rumble seat when she went to dance to the Big Bands at Hecla Park. There I saw Louis Armstrong, Horace Height and the King Sisters, whom I would meet in Syracuse many years later.

I've been a sports fan all my life. I have had so many thrills. I saw Cooper French throw the lateral pass to Yutz Dietrich on a punt return to enable Penn State to beat Lafayette 6-3 after their 1932 game had ended.

I was in the Astrodome opening night in 1965 when the first baseball game was played, President Lyndon Johnson was there. The NY Yankees were the Astros' opponent and Mickey Mantle hit the first home run.

While in high school I saw Bill Tilden play. When we lived in New York I saw great matches at Forest Hills. I have been to Newport RI., home of the Tennis Hall of Fame. In Bradenton FL, Andre Agassi and Monica Seles were at Nick Bollettierri's Tennis Academy just down the street from us. We saw Bill Cosby and Robert Redford at John Newcomb's Tennis Ranch in New Braunfels.

My original title to my memoirs was to be "SHAKE THE HAND THAT SHOOK THE HAND OF, OR ALMOST DID" of interesting people I have met in my lifetime. But my wife Pat convinced me they are only incidental to this book.

This collection of vignettes is dedicated to my children, grandchildren and great grandchildren so that they may have an intimate portrait of my life and share some of the experiences I had

While in high school in State College, Pennsylvania, I was a part-time sports reporter for the *Centre Daily Times*. My pay: 2½-cents per column inch for every story I got published. For a one-column, ten-inch article I could earn 25 cents.

I worked my way through Penn State as assistant to the Sports Information Director, Ridge Riley. Also, I had the good fortune to play left halfback on two undefeated national championship soccer teams in 1939 and 1940. That was good enough to get me into one of the best fraternities (Phi Gamma Delta) and a couple of honor societies, Friars and Parmi Nous.

I loved college—so much in fact that it took me nine years to get through. I met and married my college sweetheart, Deenie Wickersham, and we had almost 60 years together before she passed on after we moved to Sun City.

I joined the Navy just before Pearl Harbor, served as an enlisted man for 15 months before being selected to go to Midshipman School at Notre Dame where I received my Deck Officer Commission. My first ship was the *USS LARAMIE* (AO16), an old World War One tanker carrying aviation gas and bunker fuel to Greenland.

On my second ship, the *USS MANATEE* (AO58), we earned eight battle stars in seventeen months helping Admiral Bull Halsey's Fast Carrier Force reclaim all the lost territories in the Pacific and were 200 miles from Tokyo when the war ended.

After the war I had one semester to go for my BA in Business before I began a wonderful 25-year career with Procter & Gamble and the Coca-Cola Company in Sales and Marketing, including ten years as Sales Manager in New York for P&G.

At age 52 my wife, Dee, and I decided literally to take a year out of our lives to see what we wanted to do. We looked into the Peace Corps and lay church work. While we had other ideas, our kids thought we were going to become hippies and applauded.

For 15 years we operated our own real estate company in New Braunfels as entrepreneurs and developers. At the top we had six offices from San Antonio to Austin. Profitability was like a giant roller coaster, but we had fun.

Our company name was Gaz Green Real Estate and Investments. We had four company cars with license plates, GAZ 1, GAZ 2, GAZ 3 and GAZ 4. I wanted everyone to "Call me GAZ." Our office in the historic Village of Gruene was, naturally, "Gaz Gruene Real Estate." I figured that every time someone called out my name in public it was free advertising.

After one year in Kansas City studying at the Unity School of Christianity, Dee and I retired to the Sarasota, Florida area for ten years, then came to Sun City in March 1997 to be near our daughter Lois, who with her husband, Scott & White Surgeon Dr. Charles Reiter, lives in Temple. As it turned out Dee received the best possible care at Scott & White before she died.

My wife Pat's deceased husband of 23 years, Bob Cords, was a dear friend of mine in the Coca-Cola Company. Pat discovered I was here when she read my "Gaz Green Recommends" column in the Stacy Letter while looking for a home in Sun City.

Now, at Age 87, as I finish my memoirs, I have started a new career writing a weekly "Profile" column for *City Week*, the new Community Newspaper for Sun City Texas.

I got the idea for writing these Profiles from reading obituary notices. I would read about somebody who had lived here and passed on and say to myself, "I wish I had known that person."

There are so many interesting people here that I will never run out of subjects. I tell my friends I plan to do this for three years, until I am 90, and then I will decide what I really want to do with my life.

At this age, can you imagine someone having this much fun and getting paid for it?

This is the story of my life.

CALL ME GAZ

—Gaz Green

CHAPTER ONE

MY FIRST MEMORIES

I was born March 29, 1920 in the Lock Haven, Pennsylvania Hospital, although I don't remember much about that phase of my life.

When I was about three years old we moved from the corner of First and Church Streets into the old Kreamer home one block away at Second and Church, next door to my maternal grandmother, Adelaide Kreamer Stevenson, widow of William Stevenson who had died before I was born.

This area was almost like a family compound. On the second floor above Grandmother lived Mother's youngest brother, George Stevenson, his wife Mary and her mother, Mrs. Jesse Duncan. Across the street lived Grandmother's brother, Fred Kreamer and his wife Lena, with their son, Bruce, his wife, Ruby, and daughter Betty next door.

We had the entire first floor of the old family home that still stands. Our family consisted of Mother, Dad, brother Bill, sister Adelaide and me, plus Mary Redding, who took care of us children and our airedale dog, Laddy.

Upstairs lived a great uncle, chiropractor John Stevenson and his wife Martha, plus Grandmother's older sister, Aunt Clara, a maiden lady who, it seemed, always wanted to tell everyone how they should raise their children.

My early memories include being tied up to a long rope so I would not wander out of the front yard: all the excitement when we learned that Charles Lindbergh had flown non-stop from New York to Paris; watching the pilot drop sample bars of Baby Ruth candy with little parachutes attached from a low flying airplane.

I also loved my grandmother and would go with her when she played the chimes in the tower of the Methodist Church nearby. Then we would walk three blocks to Main Street where she would let me look at the bicycles and motorcycles.

Cousin Betty was my constant playmate until I started in school at age five. While I was only six weeks older, her parents held her back until she was six. At first I thought I was a real "smarty pants" but as I got older I was sorry I started at such an early age.

WILLIAM STEVENSON GREEN

The Stevenson ancestors came from Scotland, the Kreamers from Germany. Both were prominent and highly respected families in Pennsylvania, active in the lumber and brick businesses. Lock Haven was on the West Branch of the Susquehanna River.

Grandfather Stevenson was said to have lost more than $100,000 (a huge amount then) when flooding caused the boom to break in 1889, and logs about to be converted to lumber were swept down stream. However, he also had extensive timber holdings near Florence, South Carolina where my father, after finishing business school, advanced to become superintendent of the large lumber camp in Pee Dee, South Carolina. Dad also was postmaster and ran the general store.

Mabel (our mother) was a pianist and planned to attend the prestigious Peabody Conservatory in Baltimore after she completed her preparatory courses at Dickinson Seminary in Williamsport. However, while home on vacation a boy pulled a piano stool out from under her as she was about to sit down. She fell and injured her spine so severely it was necessary to spend two years in the Clifton Springs, New York Sanitarium.

At first doctors were fearful she might never walk again. However, through sheer determination she persevered. To help her rehabilitation her father took her to the warmer climate of South Carolina for one winter.

Mabel Adelaide Stevenson, from Pennsylvania, met Gazexer Graham Green who had grown up on a farm near Durham, North Carolina.

The romance flourished and, after a lengthy courtship, they were married on April 14, 1910 in Lock Haven. After the wedding they moved back to South Carolina, where exactly nine months and six days later their first son, was born in Florence. They had planned to name him after his father.

However, when they sent a telegram to Lock Haven announcing the birth, they received a return reply, which stated: CONGRATULATIONS TO WILLIAM STEVENSON GREEN! Had there not been this telegraphic exchange, I would not have been named Gazexer, Jr., who wants to be called Gaz. I would be Just Plain Bill.

MOVE TO STATE COLLEGE

My father had become a successful businessman and highly respected man in the community even though he had never completed high school.

Dad was a 32nd degree Mason, a member of the official board of the Methodist Church, and president of the Lock Haven Rotary Club, probably the most prestigious organization in a town of 12,000.

Another of my earliest memories was going with my father in the car to take a crippled child to a doctor. I learned early in life about Rotary's humanitarian efforts and was delighted that, as an adult I could follow both my father and my son Graham and become a Rotarian myself.

Dad and Mother were determined that their three children would be able to get a college education. Lock Haven Normal School, a two-year post-graduate program, produced elementary school teachers, mostly women. Penn State, 40 miles away with an excellent reputation, offered a wide variety of undergraduate and graduate programs.

In 1927 we moved to State College, the town where Penn State was located. Bill had one year of high school left, Adelaide was in her first year of junior high, and I entered third grade with a bunch of the brightest kids you would ever meet. Many of my best friends to be were sons and daughters of faculty members. This was a "College" town and everything revolved around it.

Dad rented a big, old three story house at 105 E. Fairmount Avenue that had eight bedrooms, four on the each of the second and third floors. He set up one for his office, one bedroom for Mother and Dad, one for Bill and me and Adelaide had her own. The four rooms on the third floor were rented out to a total of eight college students.

It was several years before I realized the sacrifice our parents had made for our education. In Lock Haven they belonged to the country club, couples bridge and dance groups, and led a very active social life. In State College they were starting anew, and operating a "rooming house".

However, in accordance with the old adage, cream comes to the top, in short time Mother was vice president of the PTA and Dad was on the church board.

EARLY SCHOOL YEARS

Our home was ideally located. Bill's high school was a block away, Adelaide's two blocks, and mine was three, all within easy walking distance. The three schools abutted a sink hole the size of a football field. It was called "The Hollow." Attempts had been made to fill it in on the bottom and level it for a playing field.

It was not regulation length and wasn't very level, but we used it for an athletic field. My school only went through fourth grade. When I entered the fifth grade in the Nittany Avenue School, "the Hollow" is where I first learned to play soccer. We had a pickup game every morning and every afternoon before class. The first ones there would start, and each two who came and joined would go to opposite teams. We might have had 20 kids on each side by the time school stated.

After Franklin D. Roosevelt was elected President in 1932 and started the Works Progress Administration (WPA), one of the first projects in State College was to convert "The Hollow" into the beautiful State College High School Football Field, shaped like an open sided bowl. They closed off Foster Avenue between the Frazier Avenue and the Nittany Avenue Schools to have an ideal field for football and soccer, with entry from street level.

William Foster, President of the First National Bank lived next door to us and had a private tennis court which became an important part of my life. His three children had all married and left home. Their daughter Mary lived in East Lansing, Michigan where her husband, Bill Ball, was a professor and coach of the Michigan State tennis team. He came back to Penn State every summer to complete his PhD,

The Balls had two daughters, the older, Peggy was my age. So, when we were seven years old her father started teaching us to play tennis. As I got older I took care of their court for the privilege of using it any time. I continued to play tennis until 70 years later when I tripped, fell and broke my hip on a hard surface court.

A watercolor of Gaz at age 14 that would reappear later in life.

GEORGE WASHINGTON'S BIRTHDAY

First in War, First in Peace, First in the Hearts of His Countrymen!

That was George Washington. No, I never met the "Father of our Country," but in 1932, after we celebrated the bicentennial of his birth, I felt like I knew him.

We were no longer in elementary school. I had entered seventh grade in the new junior high school building that was added to the high school. In junior high we were no longer confined to one room, with one teacher. We changed classes every hour, passed high school kids in the hallways and sometimes even tried to act like we were grown up.

The new building addition had a gymnasium for basketball and indoor phys ed. Because State College now had an official junior high school they had to have football and basketball teams to represent the school. And, of course, I tried out for both.

Football. They bought 22 new uniforms for the first and second teams. There was no platooning or special teams in those days. Then they used discarded uniforms from the high school team for the rest of the squad.

I remember at the initial team meeting the coach told us all to buy an athletic supporter, commonly known as a jock strap. I was only 11 years old, not very tall and probably weighed 50-60 pounds. I had never heard of a jock strap. When I got home, Dad was away and brother Bill thought it was the most hilarious thing he had ever heard.

"Gazzy needs a jock strap, ha, ha, ha," Bill would say laughing. Mother never could get it straight and always referred to it as a Jack Strop.

We all dressed for the first game, me in my discarded uniform that was way too big. I remember when the coach taped my wrist; he commented it was the tiniest wrist he had ever prepared for a football game. I never got to play.

Basketball was almost the same story. I tried out for the team and got cut every year until I grew almost six inches in one year and finally made the State College High School varsity in my junior year.

MY MUSICAL CAREER

Because I have been honored as the founder of The Georgetown Symphony Society people assume that I know a lot about music and probably played one or more instruments.

Here is my miserable unabridged record, along with my excuses:

Piano – I took lessons for about six months from Eleanor Musser. She got married and moved away.

Cornet – I could not learn to "spit" instead of blow to make a sound.

Violin – I probably could have been a virtuoso, but my mother could not stand the squeaking and sent me down to the basement coal bin to practice.

Is that any way to encourage young talent? I was taking weekly $1.00 group lessons from a WPA subsidized teacher. He supplied everything and if you took all 60 lessons you were allowed to keep the violin.

Voice – As a boy soprano I sang in the junior choir at our church. I sang in the glee club and the acapella choir in high school. Dick Detwiler, director of the Glee Club told my father he was going to have me do some solos. Unfortunately, he took his own life shortly after. I have often wondered if he just couldn't face fulfilling his promise.

Cello – Deenie taught piano, our oldest daughter Marianne played the cello, Adene the violin, Graham had started the piano and Lois was destined to be a violinist. I did not want to be left out so I decided at age 35 that I would take up the cello. I got a self teaching book, practiced every day and actually made one public appearance. During Chuck & Jane Post's New Years Eve party next door in 1955, I went home, got my cello, came back and played AULD LANG SYNE!

While I received a favorable response, I gave up the cello, determined to work even harder to keep my day job. We were about to introduce our first important new product, JIF PEANUT BUTTER, into the New York market and this was a tremendous challenge.

Besides, I did not think I could ever replace Pablo Casals.

MEET MR. ROEBUCK

My grandmother had given me her cornet when I was about 10 years old. It had no lyre to hold marching band music.

I found exactly what I needed in the Sears Roebuck catalogue for 29 cents. In those days it was customary to send postage stamps to pay for purchases which cost less than $1.00.

I dutifully sent 29 cents worth of stamps to buy the lyre.

A few days later my first mail order purchase arrived. However, inside the package was a letter stating that the price had been increased from 29 cents to 32 cents, and that I should please remit stamps for the additional three cents.

Like most kids, I guess, I promptly forgot about the letter.

Periodically my Dad would ask me if I had sent Sears Roebuck the money I owed them.

When I would say no, he would always respond, "You had better do it or you are going to find yourself in trouble."

One afternoon when I came home from school my father called to me as soon as I walked in the door to come into the living room. There he sat with some man I had never seen.

When I responded again that I had not paid Sears Roebuck, Dad stated in a stern voice, "This is Mr. Roebuck. He is here to collect the money you owe him."

It turned out to be Malcolm Stevenson, an adult cousin I had never met.

MY FIRST MARKETING LESSON

Perhaps it was prophetic that one day I would work for the Coca-Cola Company. I got my start selling Coca-Cola at Penn State football games.

I had heard older boys talk about how much money they made selling candy, so when I was about ten or eleven years old, I stood in line with other kids hoping to be picked. Then one day I got my chance.

To get started you had to prove yourself by carrying bottles of Coke in a galvanized bucket up into the stands and hollering, "ICE COLD COCA-COLA." They sold for 10 cents; you would get one penny. A full bucket was very heavy, and the wire handle cut into your fingers. You got your chance because the dropout rate with kids was high.

If you did a good job, the reward was promotion to sell candy bars which were much more popular. That is where I got my first lesson in marketing.

My favorite candy bar was Milky Way, so when I was getting my supply the first day, I told Bob Graham (the owner), to give me three (boxes) of Milky Ways and one Hershey Bars. He told me I should have just the opposite proportion but I would not listen.

Finally, he said, "OK Smart Kid, go ahead."

I came back three times for more Hershey Bars and still had two full boxes of Milky Way at the end of the game.

MY FIRST LESSON IN MARKET RESEARCH: Listen to what the customer prefers. Don't make decisions based on what you like.

ANOTHER IMPORTANT LESSON LEARNED – I would never have to pay to see any Penn State athletic event as long as I worked, whether in the stands selling concessions or in the press box as a sports reporter.

And I did not until after I came back from the Navy at age 25 and decided I wanted to become a respected spectator and get maximum enjoyment from the event.

LEARNING THE FACTS OF LIFE

I don't know of any parents of kids my age who talked about sex to their children when we were growing up. I was more fortunate than most. Brother Bill was five years older than sister Adelaide who was four years my senior. They both tried to educate me.

I believe nearly every boy in the Methodist Church within five years of me, older or younger, was educated by a church employee in private or small group (2 or 3) meetings. I assure you none of our parents knew or the employee would have been fired.

This was 70 years before the pedophile scandals of the Catholic Church, and I don't think any boy was ever molested. The church sexton, "Pop" Snyder, was married and had two sons between five and ten years older than I.

St. Paul's Methodist Church was heated by a coal burning furnace. A large area in the basement was devoted to the furnace and the bin for the tons of coal needed during in winter months.

Pop had a supply of French girlie magazines that he kept under an old broken down sofa he had near the furnace. I never felt he was dangerous. I think he just got a kick out of showing nude pictures to little boys who had never seen them before.

The one thing I remember about seeing these magazines was how unattractive, even ugly, the women were.

I have been told that models who pose for *Playboy* and other magazines that came on the market in the United States 25 years later can sometimes be quite attractive.

POLICE CHIEF YOUGLE

State College, until 1937 with a population of about 5,000, had only one policeman – Al Yougle. Naturally, everyone called him Chief. He was a former state trooper, good-looking, very friendly.

Harlan Hostetter, Hayes Darby and I were 14 years old and members of Boy Scout Troop #1 sponsored by the Methodist Church. We met early in the evening one night each week. The three of us, plus Frank Mitch, had shared a tent at scout camp the previous summer. These were three of my best friends.

After the meetings, Harlan and Hayes, who lived near me, and I would usually stop somewhere and get a coke (for 5 cents) on our way home. We walked up College Avenue along the front of Old Main, the most prominent landmark at Penn State since it was founded in 1855.

Andrew Trish, a 12-year old kid we thought was kind of obnoxious, was walking behind us. Andrew lived in an area behind the campus so when we decided to walk up toward the Old Main flagpole he tagged along. It was twilight, almost dark, on a summer night.

Just as we got to the flagpole one of us (I don't remember who) got the idea. There was no one else around, so we took off Andrew's undershorts, and shorts, and ran them up the flagpole. We tied the ropes so high he could not possible reach them. Then we left, stopped for our cokes and completely forgot about our prank.

UNTIL--Just before we got to my house one of my friends said, "What is Chief Yougle's car doing out in front at your home?" Then, as I went in the front door, Harlan and Hayes disappeared in a hurry.

There, in the living room, sat Yougle talking to my very unhappy parents. When an undressed Andrew, nude below the waist, arrived home, his parents called the chief.

To us it was just a kid's prank. But looking back on it, my conclusion is that if this happened in today's environment Harlon, Hayes and I might have been charged as sexual deviates, adjudged delinquents, and would have brought terrible shame to our families.

LEARNING TO DANCE

When we were in 8th grade, a core group of mothers decided it was time for us to learn to dance. They invited about 10 boys and an equal number of girls from the 7th & 8th grades to take private, group lessons to learn the waltz and fox trot.

The father of one of our boys, Jackie Lee, was the manager of the newly opened Nittany Lion Inn on the Penn State Campus. A Mr. & Mrs. Hanrahan were hired to give us 10 one-hour weekly lessons.

I hate CLIQUES, but I must confess that one of the luckiest things that ever happened to me was to become part of a group who remained close friends all the way through college. After we finished high school almost all of us went on to Penn State and joined fraternities and sororities. If I saw a pretty girl in class or on campus, all I had to do was call a member of "my group" in her sorority to get the inside scoop and an introduction if desired.

Completion of our dance lessons came just before the annual senior-alumni dance which was held in the gymnasium, but open only to freshmen and up. One of my friend's parents pulled some strings and got us invited to our first dance.

When you are a teenager and someone tells you that an attractive girl likes

you, your interest is piqued immediately. Penny Mielenz, daughter of a West Point trained army captain in the Penn State ROTC program, had only lived in State College one year but had been voted most popular girl in our class.

The night of the dance Penny told me to come a half hour early so her mother could teach us another dance step – THE HOP! This was easy to learn. All you did was hold your partner, bounce twice on the left foot, then twice on the right foot and bounce around the room.

If we were not the hit of the dance, we were certainly the most talked about.

Penny's father was transferred after four years and she went to Rhodes College in Memphis where out daughter, Lois, taught violin to some of the Rhodes Scholars.

NEW LICENSE PLATE.

I was about 14 or 15 years old. We had come home from church. Brother Bill was not home. The other four of us sat down to have a chicken dinner mother had prepared for us.

Mother and Dad, Adelaide and I were eating dinner when Mother made this statement. "OK, we have our new license plate to put on the car. It is US 481. How will we remember it?"

We started thinking, Adelaide, Dad and I all made some suggestions, none of which was created any excitement.

Finally, Mother exclaimed, "I HAVE IT!"

US 481.

US FOUR ATE ONE CHICKEN!

I swear I don't remember what year it was.

But I have never forgotten the license plate.

MY FIRST CHECKING ACCOUNT

I started delivering the daily *Philadelphia Inquirer* Monday through Saturday when I was in 9th grade. I had to be at the newsstand by 7:00 AM to have time to complete my thirty-customer route and get to school by 8:00.

The papers came by train to Tyrone, about 30 miles away, then by truck to State College. I delivered them by bicycle. When they arrived late, which was often in the winter, I had to complete my route after school in the afternoon. Since I always played one sport or another I often did not get the morning paper delivered to some customers until 6:00 or 7:00 PM. I had some very unhappy customers. I should have been fired, and I was.

Later, the manager of the Nittany Newsstand, Frank Holmes, who understood my situation and liked me, hired me to assist him on a part-time basis. Thus, in my junior and senior years I opened the store every morning at 6:30, issued the papers to the kids with paper routes and put all the New York, Philadelphia and Pittsburgh morning papers on the rack for sale.

Mondays through Fridays I worked in the morning until school started, came back at noon and relieved Frank for 45 minutes for lunch. On Saturdays and Sundays I was responsible for the store from 6:30 AM until noon. I got paid $2.50 per week for working 18.5 hours. That was 13.5 cents per hour, good pay for a part time high school boy during the depression.

I was envied by many boys. I had money. I felt so prosperous I opened my own checking account. There were no bank charges. Checks were free and No Minimum Balance was required.

One Saturday night, before going out on a date, I purchased three gallons of gasoline, gave the service station a check for $0.50. That is No Dollars and Fifty Cents.

The following Tuesday, Clay Musser, the station owner called me to say my check had been returned by the bank for Not Sufficient Funds. My first NSF check. For fifty cents! Believe me, I have been careful ever since!

HIGH SCHOOL GRADUATION

I almost did not graduate with my State College High School Class of 1937. My grades were not that great, but I never failed a course, and was in the top 80% of my class. That may sound impressive, but what it really means is that only 20% were lower than I.

I just considered myself a well rounded boy. I worked and earned all of my spending money. I won varsity letters in soccer, basketball and tennis. I had started my career as a sports reporter. I was active in the Epworth League at the Methodist church, had a lot of friends, both boys and girls, and, even in the middle of The Great Depression, a very happy childhood.

At 17, I was the second youngest in my class. To be honest with you, I was not a good student. My brother Bill was a straight A student and won a 4-year scholarship to Penn State that he used to get both his bachelor's and master's degrees.

But he had no social life, so sister Adelaide and I felt we had to make up for him.

Our graduation ceremony was held in the Schwab Auditorium on the Penn State Campus. The weather in central Pennsylvania in June is magnificent. During the last week of school we had almost no responsibilities except to attend graduation rehearsal. I ask you. How many times do you need to line up, walk down the aisle and across the stage to remember what to do?

Pete Overholtz, one of my soccer teammates, and I decided we had learned enough. Two days before graduation, on a gorgeous sunny day, we skipped rehearsal and took our girlfriends swimming at Whipple Dam. We had a great time, except, that.....

The next morning my parents received a registered letter from the school superintendent advising them I would not be allowed to receive my diploma with the rest of my class. My mother cried. My father, calm as always said, "You got yourself into this mess. Go get yourself out!"

I went to see Jo Hays, pled my case and, finally, he relented.

It would not be the last time I would have to be responsible for my own misdeeds and have to use the power of persuasion to extricate myself from a difficult situation. It was good training.

BUILDING A ROAD

Immediately after graduation George Zins, fullback on the football team and one of my best buddies, and I started our summer full-time jobs in the Penn State orchards. Immediately I learned a new word. Our boss was a Pomologist. No, he did not make Palmolive Soap. He was a professor of Pomology, the science that deals with fruits and fruit growing.

We worked M-F 7:00 AM—Noon, then 1PM—5:00, a nine-hour day. Saturdays, only 7:00—Noon. Add another hour to walk to and from the orchards. We got 30 cents an hour; $15.00 for a fifty hour week. Nothing was deducted.

Much of the time we harvested fruit, trimmed or doctored trees. When that work was caught up we built a road. I soon learned that using a pick and shovel nine hours a day was not much fun. We slept well at night.

At the end of the summer George and I hitchhiked to New York, a distance of about 275 miles. We left early in the morning, got a series of rides through Pennsylvania to enter New Jersey at Washington's Crossing, the exact spot on the Delaware River that our First President made famous.

Our last pickup drove us to the railroad station in Trenton where we decided to take the train for the hour ride to Penn Station in the Big Apple. From there it was an easy walk to the William Sloan House YMCA. We had confirmed room reservations for 75 cents a night.

The next morning we took a subway to Times Square for breakfast. I wanted to introduce George to a Horn & Hardart Automat. We went into the burlesque show on 42nd St. when it opened at 11:00. By the third show we had moved up to the second row. At 6:00 PM we came out. We were hungry!

We had a great time in New York. We saw a spectacular ice skating review, an all-star college football game, the Paramount and Roxy Theatres, and experienced a "Dime a Dance" joint. We returned home completely happy.

Fifty years later, at our class reunion, I told the burlesque theatre story, thinking everyone would enjoy hearing what two teenagers, loose in the big city, had done. Everybody enjoyed the story except one person. George Zins had never told his wife what we did in New York.

AMOS NEYHART—
FATHER OF DRIVER EDUCATION

In 1934 Amos Neyhart, a professor of automotive engineering at Penn State, became the father of driver's education when he taught the first class ever formed for this purpose, in my State College high school. I was not old enough to be in this class, but I was in the second one a year later;

I have never forgotten his thesis: THERE IS NO SUCH THING AS AN UNAVOIDABLE ACCIDENT.

Neyhart had been given a grant of $500.00 by the American Automobile Association to develop his program. General Motors then supplied him with a dual-control car, with an extra steering wheel and brake on the passenger side.

What makes this so special for me is that Mr. Neyhart also had been my scoutmaster and I knew him really well, and liked him immensely. In 1935, AAA pioneered high school driver education nationwide and published the first course outline for teachers. It was titled "Sportsmanslike Driving."

(Photo Courtesy AAA)

Fifty or more years later I was back for a Penn State Reunion. I had seen Mr. Neyhart's name on the mailbox of a lovely home out in the country. I drove by, and there he was, now in his 80's, with a power mower cutting grass on his very large lawn.

We had a lovely visit. He told me that many millions of students around the world have been trained by his program. He had just come back from Toronto where he had been on national TV. He told me he had speaking engagements throughout the world scheduled for two years in advance.

His parting words to me were, "Gazzy, I figure if I keep busy the good Lord will let me stay around a little longer. If I sit on my butt he may just come and take me away any day."

POOR ADELAIDE

Adelaide didn't stand a chance. In age she was about midway between Bill and me. We harassed her, tormented her, made fun of her, and yet we loved her dearly.

Adelaide's face was covered with freckles. They ran in the family. I had them, too. Mother's arms were covered with them.

There was an "old wives" tale that if you wiped your face in the dew before breakfast on May 1 and did not wash your face, the dew would make your freckles disappear. I have vivid memories of Adelaide coming to the table with mud all over her face several times. The freckles stayed.

A great-aunt and -uncle, Mattie and Burt Sweeney, took Adelaide by train to Atlantic City when she was about 12. They ate in the dining car and the hotel dining room. When Adelaide got home she came to the dinner table with her hat on. When Dad asked her why, she said that is how proper people eat. Dad then said, "She's right. We need to all go put our hats on."

When Mother, Dad, Bill and I all returned to the table properly attired, Adelaide ran to her room crying that we had made fun of her.

Poor Adelaide! When she started dating, she would often sit on the front porch swing with her date. Either Bill or I would turn the porch light on from the inside in the dark where she could not see us. But we could see Adelaide and her boyfriend jump and break apart quickly.

I did not think Adelaide would ever find out how I knew what time she came in every night after the rest of the family was in bed. She had a small electric clock on her dressing table she did not use. When the flow of electricity was broken, it would not function unless started manually.

After she went out in the evening I would activate it, along with a dressing table lamp through to a plug wired to the wall switch by her door and turn it on. Adelaide would come in; turn the switch which would stop the clock. She then would walk over and turn on the light on her dressing table.

The next morning, much to her consternation, I knew to the very minute what time she came home.

MORE FAMILY HUMOR

My whole family had a good sense of humor. Mother loved to take naps after she had eaten a heavy meal, particularly at noon. She would lie down on the couch on her back, arms folded. By the expression on her face you could tell what kind of a dream she was having.

She would have a frown on her face if she were having an unpleasant dream. She would have a big smile if the dream was happy. Then, if you tried to awaken her when she had that smile she would say, "Uh, uh, just a minute. Let me finish this dream."

* * *

Dad was always wonderful with young children. When he was superintendent of the Sunday school, he enjoyed shaking hands with a young boy or girl and asking, "How does your COPPERAUSTAS seem to SAGATUATE today?"

The poor child would look on wide eyed and not know what to say.

* * *

Uncle George Stevenson to a six-year-old boy in Lock Haven, "Gazzy, Do you know why they are not going to have the railroad gates on Bellefonte Avenue any longer?"

My answer, "No, why?"

Uncle George, "Because they are long enough."

STARTING IN COLLEGE

What began in 1855 as the Farmer's High School of Pennsylvania became, after the Civil War, the Pennsylvania State College, a land-grant institution.

The other early land-grant institutions included Iowa State University, Kansas State University, Michigan State University, Rutgers State University, University of Vermont, University of Minnesota, University of Missouri and the University of Wisconsin.

The Land-Grant College Act of 1862, introduced by Senator Justin Smith Morrill of Vermont, provided funding for institutions of higher learning in each state for at least one college "where the leading object shall be, without excluding other scientific and classical studies and including military tactics, to teach such branches of learning as are related to agriculture and the mechanic arts (A&M)."

When we moved to State College in 1927 the community was comprised of about 3,000 Penn State students and an equal number of townspeople. By 1940 the town and student population had more than doubled to about 7,000 each. There was no industry, and everything in the area revolved around the college.

So now, I was ready to enter college myself, or was I?

Since my high school grades were not good enough for automatic acceptance, I had to take an entrance exam about a month before school started. When I learned I had passed and could start college, the only money I had was my $30.00 paycheck for the last two weeks building the road. There was no tuition, so I borrowed a few dollars and then had enough money to pay my fees and buy used books.

There were 1500 of us entered in the Class of 1941. I remember at the first convocation the College President said, "Half of you will graduate in four years. Will you be in that half?"

I thought about that often until I finally got my degree nine years later.

MY FRESHMAN YEAR

I was ready for the excitement of college, but not the discipline required to study. I was just 17 years old. It seems all I did was add 18 hours of class work per week to my already busy life.

The *Centre Daily Times* kept me on as a part-time sports reporter, and I continued the Sunday newspaper route I had developed. I hired a high school kid for $1.00 as my helper and still cleared about $4.00 each week.

Ridge Riley, Sports Information Director for Penn State hired me as his part-time assistant. During the week, between classes, I scanned sports pages and clipped articles about Penn State sports. I was also the football game statistician in the press box and assisted Ridge in filling requests from metropolitan papers for special reports.

In addition I was campus sales representative for the N.Y. Herald Tribune and I had an additional job servicing cigarette machines. I made the freshman soccer team, and, of course, had a girl friend and would allow none of the above activities to interfere with my social life.

Maybe I was spoiled. This was a good life. We were still deep into the Depression, but I had developed a reputation as a hard, dependable worker. My friends would often say how they wished they could do something to make some money. I was turning down jobs.

Midway through my second semester Bill Ulerich, journalism professor and as editor, my top boss at the Centre Daily Times, became so alarmed with my academic record that he arranged for me to be tested by Dr. Robert Bernreuter in his Psychological Lab.

Bernreuter's analysis: There was no reason why I should not have and maintain a B+ average.

My sister Adelaide had her own explanation: If I had just left enough time to go to class, I probably would have been all right.

At the end of the year I received a nicely worded letter from the College stating that they were going to give me a semester off to mature. That was a polite way of saying I flunked out.

TIME TO MATURE

I knew my parents would be disappointed when I told them I had to stay out of school for a semester, but the only admonition from my father was that I would have to start paying room and board to live at home. I readily agreed.

During the summer I organized an eight-team softball league sponsored by five merchants and three college departments: the Ag School, Mineral Industries and the Phys Ed School. The latter was important because we were able to use college athletic facilities and some equipment. We only had to supply the softballs and be responsible for everything.

Games were played four nights a week for four weeks and then playoffs between the two division winners. I was paid by the Centre Daily Times for covering the games with my byline, by Gazzy Green. We got extensive coverage, and one day each week my article was featured under a banner headline across the top of the sports page.

The Phys Ed team was made up of coaches doing graduate work in summer school. They would have walked off with everything except that Mineral Industries had a doctoral degree candidate who had pitched the Armstrong Cork

Company to the state Amateur Softball Championship the previous summer. He was phenomenal and pitched a no-hitter against the Phys Ed team in our league championship game before a huge crowd.

At the end of the season our sponsors were happy and gave me $200.00 for organizing and managing the league.

Then, Jerry Weinstein, my sports editor, took a one week vacation and I filled in for him. I had complete responsibility for the sports page—all content, layout and headlines. I even wrote my own daily column.

I was doing what I dreamed I would do when I graduated from college.

But, when it was all over I found it was not fulfilling.

I decided that when I returned to college I would get my degree in business administration.

I felt very fortunate that I learned this when I was only 18.

BACK IN THE SADDLE AGAIN

I was readmitted to College in February, 1939 after working full time for five months in the mail room of the Penn State Alumni Association. Having satisfied all the requirements of my probation I could not wait until the fall semester so I could play soccer again.

The Penn State soccer team had been undefeated for six straight years and was coached by the legendary Bill Jeffrey, one of the finest men I have ever known. He was in his late 40's but scrimmaged every day, playing center forward on the second team, against the varsity.

I had always played forward in high school and on the freshman team, but, on the first day back, to my surprise, Coach Jeffrey told me to lineup at left halfback with the second team. That was the position the previous year's captain, Fred Spicher played for three years until he graduated.

In the second week Coach moved me up to first team and I remained there for two seasons. The afternoon before our first game my high school coach, John Serf, walked off the field with me after practice and said, "I must admit I am the most surprised person in State College to see you in the

Gaz Green, Left Halfback of Penn State's undefeated National Championship Soccer Teams, 1939 & 1940

starting lineup, but 'Jeff' told me you earned it. That's all the proof I need."

I scored the first goal of the season the next day and when we were ahead 5-0 Al Jones, my replacement, took over in the fourth quarter. Those were the only 22 minutes I was not on the field in either the 1939 or 1940 seasons.

We were undefeated both years and extended THE STREAK to eight years. Also, in both years we were officially declared National Champions.

Making the team opened many doors for me. I was invited to become a member of Phi Gamma Delta, the oldest and most prestigious social fraternity on campus. Friars, a freshman honorary activities society tapped me for membership, as did Parmi Nous, the oldest upper class society.

I was elected president of Parmi Nous at the end of my junior year but could not serve because of being called for active duty in the U.S. Naval Reserves in the fall of 1941, just before we were attacked by the Japanese at Pearl Harbor. The undefeated streak also came to an end that October at West Point.

MASTICATE

Masticate means to chew your food. This vignette is rated PG 17—so if you require parental guidance please skip ahead to the next page.

My first real girlfriend was Dorothy Virginia Long, aka Dot Long. I started dating her when I was a high school senior, and she was a sophomore cheerleader. So, I was already in college when she was ready to enter.

A man who became one of my best friends was Jerry Weinstein, a recent graduate of Penn State handpicked by Bill Ulerich, journalism professor and editor of the of the local daily newspaper, to become sports editor of the Centre Daily Times.

Jerry was a boy from Brooklyn who had won a National AAU Swimming championship in high school. He was just one neat guy who became an award winning editor and married Tomazine Curtin whose grandfather had been Governor of Pennsylvania.

The summer after Jerry graduated from college he was dating a gorgeous blond named Georgia Powers, President of Kappa Alpha Theta, one of the top women's sororities on campus. We cooked up a double date so Dot could get to know Georgia which would give her an edge in rush when school started.

Dot and I tried all evening to impress with our vocabulary. Later, while eating I asked Dot a question. When I realized she was starting to answer with food in her mouth, I blurted out, "Dorothy, didn't your mother ever tell you not to _____ with food in your mouth?"

I meant to say masticate, but a similar sounding word with a completely different meaning came out. I looked across the table just in time to see Jerry put his head down on the table cradled in his arms.

Obviously, Dot did not become a Theta.

RESPECTING BLACK PEOPLE

When I was in college I caused undue embarrassment to a very fine young Negro, one of a handful of carefully chosen black students at Penn State. They had to be good students, and all were athletes. Jimmy Williams was a half-miler of the track team. He was from Philadelphia where his father was groundskeeper at Franklin Field where the Penn Relays are held annually.

Jimmy was elected to Friars shortly after I was, and we attended meetings together. Early on a Sunday evening, after we left a meeting at the Sigma Alpha Epsilon fraternity, four of us were walking home. As we approached the Rea & Derrick Drug Store I said, "Let's go in and have a Coke."

Two of my friends said, "yes," and started to go in. Jimmy said, "You guys go ahead I will see you later."

I then locked my arm inside his and said, "C'mon Jimmy. It's early. You don't have to go home and study yet." And the four of us went in.

When the waitress came three of us ordered our cokes. I looked at Jimmy. He had his head down and just shook it negatively, saying. "I don't want anything."

Suddenly I realized what I had done. I had put him in this embarrassing situation. He was not welcome in this restaurant. They would not serve him.

All I could think from that night on: Why should I be welcome, and Jimmy not allowed to be served? It was wrong, totally wrong. This was in 1940 and I have spoken out about it ever since.

This is a true story that I have told to every Sunday School class I have ever taught.

God has a way of teaching us, if we will just listen.

MEETING MY FUTURE WIFE

At Penn State all freshman girls had to wear a huge nametag for the first month of school. About the second week the school newspaper, the Daily Collegian columnist listed the names of the "10 MOST BEAUTIFUL GIRLS IN THE FRESHMAN CLASS."

As I told the story at Mutti's memorial service, I was no dummy. I was a junior in college so I cut out the list of names and started to peruse the name tags of pretty girls. That was how I spotted DEENIE WICKERSHAM.

One of my teammates on the soccer team, Ned Corman, waited tables in the girls' dormitory, Mac Hall, and knew all the good looking girls. He introduced me to Deenie, but I am sure it did not make much of an impression on her.

However, at the semester break in February, I took a bus to New York to have a job interview for the following summer at a boy's camp in the Catskill Mountains.

At 6:30 AM, as I was about to get on the bus, I noticed that Deenie also was getting on. I let her go first, then took a seat immediately behind her.

As soon as the bus started, I leaned up and told her who I was, and that Ned Corman had introduced us. When I asked if I could sit next to her, she said yes. She was going steady with Garth Dietrick, a handsome Phi Delta Theta junior. She had planned to spend her "break" with him, but they had a fight, and she was going to Harrisburg to visit her aunt Margie.

When she got off the bus in Harrisburg I told her that when I got back from New York I would call her. When I did, she was in the infirmary with a strep throat. After she was released, I called her again, only to be told, "Garth and I are back together again."

There was no contact made by either of us until May when I bumped into her on the walkway leading up to Old Main. We exchanged pleasantries and then I invited to go get a coke. She accepted, so we sat and talked for about two hours.

She told me she and Garth were still going together but that they fought all the time. I asked her if she had a date with Garth the next Friday night. She said, "Yes." I then asked if she had a date with him for Saturday night, and she again said, "Yes."

I responded, "If you have a fight Friday night then you would not have a date with him Saturday night." She agreed.

"OK, I said. "I will call you Saturday noon."

When she answered the phone Saturday her first words were, "Guess what! Garth and I had a fight last night."

"Great," I replied, "I will pick you up at 5:30 to go to my fraternity, Phi Gamma Delta, for dinner."

The date was May 12, 1941 and was the start of a romance that produced four wonderful kids, 13 fabulous grandchildren, and at this writing, seven award-winning great-grandchildren with hopefully many more to come.

Read on, for THE REST OF THE STORY...

HALL OF FAME FOOTBALL COACHES

In my 87-year lifetime, Penn State has had only four head football coaches. All four are already in the Football Hall of Fame, including Joe Paterno, a unanimous choice, who will be installed even before he retires.

Hugo Bezdek, is the only man ever to manage a major league baseball team, the Pittsburgh Pirates, a major college football team, Oregon, Arkansas & Penn State, and an NFL football team, the Cleveland Rams. He coached the Nittany Lions from 1918 through 1929. His 1920 & 1921 teams were undefeated; his 1922 team played Southern California in the Rose Bowl.

Bob Higgins, who was an All-America end playing for Bezdek in 1919 coached for 19 seasons beginning in 1930. His best team, the 1947 edition, was undefeated and tied Southern Methodist in the Cotton Bowl. Some of his teams in the mid-1930's were painful to watch. I saw them lose two years in a row to Waynesburg College, 7-0 in 1934 and 7-6 in 1935.

Bob Higgins's sister, Margaret Sanger, started the birth control movement in the United States and, though she has been dead for many years, her clinics still exist. Higgins is in the Hall of Fame, but I feel his legacy exists through his offspring. Two grandsons, Matt and Paul Suhey, played for the Chicago Bears and a great grandson QB Kevin Suhey is at Penn State now.

Rip Engle took over in 1950 and took Penn State to several Bowls. I had a long talk with Rip one evening after I hired one of his stars,

Bob Higgins

Jack Sherry, as a salesman when I was district manager for Procter & Gamble in Harrisburg.

Engle coached 15 years and never had a losing season. His legacy, however, will forever be that when he came to Penn State he brought with him his young quarterback from Brown University, Joe Paterno, to be his assistant.

Joe Paterno is a great coach. What he stands for is even more important. Now, in his 42nd year as head coach, at age 80, playing student athletes ONLY, insisting they be students first, athletes second. Yet, he has won more football games at one institution than anyone else in history.

Joe Paterno's legacy will be Joe Paterno, himself.

GOING TO WASHINGTON

I had never lived away from home. So, in the spring of 1941, my bother Bill, who had already finished George Washington University Law School, encouraged me to take a civil service examination, come to Washington, get a job in the government and live with him for the summer.

Adelaide and I had spent Easter weekend with Bill two years before, and I was excited at the prospect. We had been there at the Lincoln Memorial Monday morning April 9, 1939 when one of the most famous singers in the world stepped out of a limousine right in front of us.

It was Marian Anderson, who was there to make arrangements for her famous Lincoln Memorial concert that drew 75,000 people after the Daughters of the American Revolution would not allow her to sing in their Hall because she was black.

Later that morning I walked over to the White House hoping that I could see the famous Easter egg roll. As soon as I arrived, a little boy begged me to take him inside. He needed an adult to accompany him to be admitted.

(Photo courtesy US Government)

I have often thought about that incident as an example of my life. I have often been fortunate to be in the right place at the right time. Just as we arrived, Eleanor Roosevelt, the First Lady, stepped up to the microphone and welcomed all of us guests!

In the evening Bill took us to see a D'Oyly Carte Opera Company production of HMS Pinafore. I remember very clearly that I had never seen or heard any musical production so beautiful. It was the start of my appreciation for classical music.

Bill shared an apartment in Buckingham Village in Arlington with a pair of brothers, Bob and Ted Jones. Bob was Bill's classmate and good friend in law school, and his younger brother Ted had recently arrived.

I was excited. I had passed my civil service exam and was about to depart for Washington to begin more new experiences in my life.

JOHN KENNETH GALBRAITH

The first interview I had resulted in immediate employment. "Can you start today?" I was asked.

I reported to work at a newly completed apartment house which the government had leased at 2501 Q Street to house the newly established Office of Price Administration. Leon Henderson, an economic advisor to President Roosevelt, was named administrator I was one of the first fifty employees in an organization that grew to several thousand.

The challenge to OPA was to develop and put in place price guidelines to prevent inflation from hindering our war preparation efforts. By 1945 the Office of Price Administration had branch offices throughout the nation and 90% of all goods sold were under price control.

The deputy administrator was 6-foot, 9-inch John Kenneth Galbraith, an imposing, Canadian-born Harvard professor who was destined to become recognized as one of the half-dozen most famous economists of all time.

Dr. Galbraith had been a student at Oxford when Joseph Kennedy was U.S. Ambassador to the Court of St. James. Galbraith was employed by Papa Joe Kennedy to tutor his young son, Jack. A strong bond developed. Years later, John Fitzgerald Kennedy, President of the United States, named John Kenneth Galbraith, his friend, Ambassador to India.

John Kenneth Galbraith (Photograph courtesy of John F. Kennedy Library)

In the early days at OPA a very informal atmosphere existed. Many newly employed young women in the stenographic pool were from the Midwest and were living away from home for the first time. Many were shy, but all were eager to make new friends.

Dr. Galbraith's office was open to me at all times. I went into his office first thing every morning. He always gave me a friendly greeting. If he was on the phone he would wave, or nod and smile. I can state with absolute certainty that he was always glad to see me.

I spent the summer working with John Kenneth Galbraith. I was important to him. I was a messenger and my responsibility was to fill his carafe with fresh cold water every morning. He depended on me.

THE SUMMER OF 1941

Bob and Ted Jones, and my brother Bill, were great roommates. They introduced me to classical music big time. It was all we listened to in the apartment, and I grew to love it.

Bob and Bill were attorneys and were about 9 or 10 years older than I. Ted was closer to my age, had graduated from college and was in graduate school to get an MA in Liturgical Music. He was bright, disorganized, and absentminded.

Buses ran about every ten minutes from Arlington to Washington. The government had instituted a system of staggered openings and closings to eliminate crowding on commuter lines, so we rarely traveled together.

Ted came home one evening and told us he had met a neat girl on the bus and had been sitting with her every morning. She was the daughter of an army general. It was obvious that Ted was smitten. He told us that he had made a date to play tennis with her the next Saturday morning.

Friday night was always party night to celebrate the end of our work week. Ted loved to drink beer and on occasion drank too much. The night before his tennis date was one of those occasions, and Ted arose Saturday morning bleary-eyed and hung over.

After he left for his match, Bill suggested that he and I walk over to see how Ted was doing. We stood back far enough so that Ted could not see us. We had never seen such a show. Ted couldn't hit anything. He talked to his racquet, yelled at the ball and made a complete fool of himself. Ted then started taking a different bus, too embarrassed to see the girl again.

Seven years later, in 1948, I boarded a train in Newark headed for Philadelphia. When I spotted Ted, whom I had not seen since 1941, I went over and sat down. Without looking at him and with my newspaper shielding me partially, I said, "How are things going, Ted?"

I kept up the banter for about 30 minutes. He could not figure out who I was. Finally I asked, "Did you ever know a guy named Gazzy Green?"

He couldn't believe it was I!

UNCLE SAM NEEDS YOU

In the spring of 1941 I registered for the supplemental draft back in State College. The following summer, while I was in Washington they had the lottery for all those newly registered potential draftees.

I had read when the drawing would take place and that it was open to the public. After work on the given day I sauntered over to the ceremony. Unfortunately I did not have to wait long before Gen. Lewis B. Hershey, Selective Service Administrator, pulled my number out of the fish bowl.

My uncle, George Stevenson, had been an ensign in the U.S. Navy during World War I. All my life I had gazed upon a picture of him in his dress whites hanging in our home.

(National Archives)

Selective Service rules were such that if you wanted to get into another branch of service besides the Army you had to be officially signed up before you received your draft notice. So, I had to act fast.

Within three days I had checked all the branches of service to see what I might qualify for, having completed three years of college. That was LESSON #1 of how important a college degree could be. No advanced placement was assured WITHOUT the degree.

The Navy was my first choice, and fortunately my best opportunity. I could enlist in the U. S. Naval Reserve, be allowed to defer active duty for four months, and be guaranteed that after boot camp I would be sent to storekeeper school. I would be on my way to becoming a petty officer.

I enlisted as an apprentice seaman on August 12 and received my orders to report for active duty November 12, 1941.

By this time, in Washington, I had been promoted to messenger dispatcher. But that was when I also learned LESSON #2 about the importance of a college degree. I was making $90.00 per month. If I had my degree I could go right across the hall and become a Junior Economist at $150.00 per month.

I made up my mind that my number one goal after the Navy would be to complete my college education. I accomplished that in 1946.

THE MEANING OF FILET

Growing up during the Depression we rarely had steak in our home. And when we did, it was always referred to as just beef steak.

I remember when traveling with the soccer team we would take a bus from State College to Lewistown which was on the main line of the Pennsylvania Railroad to go to Philadelphia or New York.

In my sophomore year we played the University of Pennsylvania in Philadelphia one week and Army at West Point the following week. For each of these games we had a private car and ate, as a team, in the dining car.

We were so naïve that when they served us prime rib of beef au jus the second time, some of our team members complained, "Oh, no, they are not serving us that prime rib au jus again, are they?"

My brother Bill took me to restaurant in Arlington a few times for the early bird special, a filet mignon dinner for 75 cents. It was delicious, and I would always tell my friends at work about it.

Then one day I went into a restaurant in Washington alone. I scanned the menu and one item really caught my attention: filet of sole! Yum, yum!

I ordered my dinner, thinking I was getting filet mignon..

When my meal arrived, the filet of sole did not taste anything like I had expected.

Live and learn!

I never made that mistake again.

WASHINGTON FAREWELLS

One of the best parts of my working at OPA was that I found myself working with black people for the first time in my life. There were 12 messengers, including me. Nine were black and three were white.

The nine young black men were quite diverse. One was from Washington and was a graduate of Howard University.

All the others were from New York were high school graduates, and one had finished his freshman year in college.

The nine were as different in temperament as any nine young white men would be. Some tried very hard to please and were hard workers. One or two were either indifferent or indolent.

I developed a very close relationship with a few of them. One confided in me that he wanted to get married but he and his girlfriend had different religious backgrounds, and her parents objected. That was often the case with Caucasian couples, but I would never have thought about that being an issue with blacks.

There was one really outstanding young black, Charlie Nickerson, in the group. He had just finished his freshman year at the University of Wisconsin. He was bright, very industrious, had a great personality and was liked by everyone. I recommended him to replace me as dispatcher, and my boss agreed.

Charlie was also subject to the draft, so I tried to talk him into going into the Navy. "Are you serious?" he asked me. "I am going into the Air Force. That way I can become a pilot and get my commission. If I go into the Navy all I can become is a mess attendant of a cook." Unfortunately I learned he was right, and very sadly, after the war I was told that he had been killed in a plane crash.

Just before I left Washington to go on active duty in the Navy, a group of women in the correspondence section adjacent to where my desk as messenger dispatcher was located gave me a surprise farewell party.

It was a wonderful gesture on their part except that none of the black employees that I had become so fond of were invited.

(Photo: LB Smith)

CHAPTER TWO

FIRST DAY IN THE NAVY

In the afternoon of November 12, 1941 I reported to the U. S. Naval Reserve recruiting office in Washington, took the Oath of Allegiance to the United States and was sworn in. I was now an apprentice seaman making the same pay, $21.00 per month as a new private in the Army.

When I got my first paycheck I was shocked to learn that they had deducted $5.25 for insurance and 20 cents for laundry. I had signed up for the maximum life insurance $10,000.00 which I thought was a good idea in case anything happened to me. Besides, they were furnishing me free room and board.

My first night in the Navy was spent on a ferry that ran from Washington, down the Potomac River, out into the Chesapeake Bay, then on to Norfolk, Virginia. There were probably 15 or 20 of us, and we were assigned cabins two to a room. My roommate was a nice 17-year old kid whose father was a professional waiter in a French restaurant in Washington.

I am happy to report that I did not get seasick my first night in the Navy.

When we arrived in Norfolk we were taken immediately to the Naval base to begin our indoctrination. We had a quick physical exam and were interviewed by a psychiatrist who, I am convinced, was just trying to weed out homosexuals.

After burr cuts (haircuts when they run clippers over your entire head) we joined a long line to be issued our uniforms. A sailor came up to us and barked, "Got a cigarette, Bud?" Three or four of us reached into our pockets immediately to comply.

What we did not know was that the line we were in made a big "U" turn. We went in wearing civilian clothes; we came out in our Navy uniforms.

The "sailor" who intimated us with his request for a cigarette had been in the Navy about 15 minutes longer than we had.

45

MOST UNFORGETTABLE PERSON

Readers Digest magazine for many years has had a feature section entitled "The Most Unforgettable Person I have ever known." When I was in boot camp I was convinced that my drill instructor fit that description. I can't remember his name. Maybe unconsciously I chose not to.

He was a retired chief boatswain's mate who, probably grudgingly, had been called back to active duty. Remember, we were not at war yet. He fit the description of any hardened drill sergeant you ever read about or saw in a movie.

There were about thirty men in our platoon. A few were my age, 21, or older. But the large majority consisted of 17 & 18 year old kids from the mountains of West Virginia and Tennessee, or farm boys from North Carolina, South Carolina and Virginia.

When we made our first formation on the drill field our drill sergeant asked if any of us had had ROTC in college. I made my first mistake. I admitted that I had and was immediately appointed to be platoon leader.

It was pure HELL from that point on. He did everything he could to break my spirit. He called me every name in the book. He repeatedly told the platoon the reason they were so lousy was that their platoon leader was stupid, and he could not expect anything better from them.

But I survived, and at the end of three weeks we were given our first evening of liberty. We had to wear our "boots" (khaki leggings) that identified us as new recruits, were not allowed to consume any alcoholic beverage, and the shore patrol seemed to be everywhere to enforce the rules.

I went into town with a young kid from West Virginia, Charlie Prince, who had dropped out of school and enlisted in the Navy on his 17th birthday. He confided in me that he had gotten a girl pregnant at home and wanted to get out of town. This night, all he wanted to do was get a tattoo. This was my first (and only) visit ever to a tattoo parlor.

Two years later when I saw Prince in Pearl Harbor he was covered with tattoos on both arms.

TIME OUT FOR SOCCER

Gene Tunney

Gene Tunney, the former World Heavyweight Boxing Champion, headed a program to keep Navy personnel physically fit. To accomplish this, athletes, some professional, but mostly recent college graduates, were selected to become physical education and drill instructors.

This group earned the nickname "Tunney Fish." A contingent was being trained at the Norfolk base while I was in boot camp. Bob Feller, one of the greatest baseball pitchers of all time left in the middle of his career with the Cleveland Indians to join this group, and I saw him often.

Dean Hanley, a friend of mine from Penn State who had been captain of football team in 1940 was also in the group. It was very fortunate for me that he learned that I was there in boot camp.

A British aircraft carrier was in port and a group of their sailors challenged the Tunney Fish to a soccer game. Unfortunately the only soccer player in the Tunney program at that time was Bob Partridge, against whom I had played the year before when he was captain of the University of Pennsylvania team.

Hanley and Partridge came over and got permission for me to play on their team. In soccer the center halfback plays both offense and defense and runs almost the entire game. The center forward is the offensive key, but gets some rest when his team is on the defensive.

It did not take us long to realize how badly we were outclassed. Our team was comprised of mostly former college football players. Partridge and I alternated at center forward and center half. My mind has chosen not to remember the score. It was not pleasant. It got me out of drills for one afternoon and was a great experience.

Several years later I met up with Bob Partridge when he was soccer coach at a boys athletic camp Graham attended. He invited Marianne, Adene and me to join Graham's team for a game when we visited.

Adene, who was an outstanding soccer player, took the ball away from a boy on the opposite team, and he was mortified. He fell prostrate on the field, moaning, "A GIRL, A GIRL. I WILL NEVER LIVE THIS DOWN."

PEARL HARBOR DAY

Dr. Seth Russell, my sociology professor at Penn State, was an ordained Methodist minister and a lieutenant commander in the U. S. Naval Reserve Chaplain Corps. He had been called to active duty and was stationed at the Navy base in Norfolk.

I had read in the base newspaper that Dr. Russell was preaching at the morning Protestant chapel service. So, on Sunday morning, December 7, 1941, I decided to walk over from boot camp and go to church.

After the service was over, Dr. Russell offered to drive me back to my barracks. We sat in his car and talked for perhaps a half hour. When I left him and went to my bunk area, it was bedlam. The first announcement had just come over the radio about the Japanese attack on Pearl Harbor.

We had no drills on Sunday. So, to get the latest news,

USS Arizona, December 7, 1941

we stayed glued to the radio the remainder of the day. A couple of petty officers provided good background information to those of us who were not familiar with Pearl Harbor and its importance to the Navy.

Normally we went to bed at nine o'clock. What made this night different was that about an hour after lights out, alarms sounded, and we were instructed to get dressed immediately, bring our ponchos with us and march over to the parade grounds away from any of the buildings.

There was light rain falling, no cover, and no place to sit down. We stood almost all night, not allowed to talk: just stand and wonder what was going to happen.

We learned the next day that there were reports of German submarines in the waters near Norfolk. I guess there was mass confusion, almost bordering on hysteria in some instances, among armed services all along the East Coast.

Nobody knew what to expect. It was like we all might have felt had we been in New York on Nine Eleven.

BOOT CAMP ENDS

President Roosevelt went before Congress on Monday, December 8 and the United States officially declared war against Germany and Japan. The first decision affecting us was that boot camp was reduced by two weeks, and these would be our last seven days. Rumors started to fly.

Individual transfers and assignments for members of our platoon began to be posted on the bulletin board almost nightly. One evening one of our group came in the barracks and yelled, "Hey Green, you have been assigned to a destroyer."

I hurried over to the mess hall where they had just posted a new list, with last name first, followed by first and second names. Everybody was called by his last name, and only those close to you did you refer to by a first name.

There listed was: Meachem, Anthony Green

Thankfully this was not my name, and not my assignment. Instead, I was assigned temporarily to mess hall duty awaiting orders to be transferred to the Navy Storekeeper School at the start of the next class.

Here I got a wonderful break. The men in charge of food service were retired members of the U. S. Navy Band who had been called back to active duty to play for ceremonial events and parades. They were some of the nicest men I had ever known and a stark contrast from my drill sergeant.

When they learned I could type, I was assigned to be the clerk in their office which turned out to be a lounge for all the retired bandsmen. I became friends with all of them immediately.

The chief bandmaster had started the Washington Redskins Band after he retired from the Navy. He told me "Hail to the Redskins" made its debut as the official song of the storied Washington NFL football team August 17, 1938. The original words, since changed slightly, were written by Corinne Griffith, wife of Clark Griffith, long time owner of the franchise.

One last memory about boot camp: I learned in dramatic fashion that the term SOB meant something different down south than it did up north. I called one of the young farm kids an SOB, and he came right over the table after me shouting, "You can't talk about my mama that way."

ARRIVAL IN TOLEDO

In early January, 1942, I was assigned to the Navy Store-keeper School in Toledo, Ohio. We lived and took our classes in the Naval Reserve Armory which was located at the point where the Maumee River flows into Lake Erie. This is also the site where Jack Dempsey knocked out Jess Willard to become Heavyweight Champion of the World on July 4, 1919.

This modern armory had been home base for a large Naval Reserve contingent that had been called to active duty. The gymnasium had rows of triple-decker cots on one side for students in the storekeeper school and an equal number on the other side for the yeoman school.

There were about 400 of us altogether. They were a real cut above my platoon mates in boot camp. Many were college graduates. One of my bunk mates had his law degree.

We arrived barely a month after Pearl Harbor when patriotism was running very high. With so many young native sons off to war in the Navy our arrival was welcomed by Toledo residents in the most wonderful fashion.

We were given liberty every weekend beginning at about 10:00 Saturday morning (after inspection) and ending at 9:00 P.M. Sunday evening. On Saturday night we could rent a cot at the YMCA for 50 cents or, if two of us rented a double room at the Milner Hotel for $1.50, we could stay for 75-cents each.

Bartenders would NOT allow us to pay for a drink. They would ask us what we wanted and then hit on some civilian to pay for it. If we went to church on Sunday morning we could not leave without someone inviting us to go out to eat, or home with them for dinner.

Toledo had a large Navy Mother's Club and a very active USO organization which hosted free dances every Saturday night. We were the first classes there, and sailors had a wonderful  reputation. We could date the nicest girls in town.

Unfortunately, all that changed in less than one year.

STOREKEEPER COURSE COMPLETED

Toledo is the westernmost city in the United States in the Eastern Time Zone. In less than thirty minutes we could cross the Michigan border and be in the Central Time Zone.

During WWII Congress adopted War Time, which was year-around daylight saving time. In January it would not become daylight until between eight and nine o'clock in the morning. What made it even worse was that we went to bed at nine o'clock, had reveille at 5:00 A.M. and calisthenics at 5:15.

I can remember days when we had finished breakfast and been in class for two hours before it was daylight outside. I had not liked accounting in college, but found that these courses were very practical. We were being trained to assist supply officers in inventory control and payroll records.

One of my friends, John Bowden from North Carolina, and I enjoyed the Methodist church. We made many friends there. I remember one banker and his wife who befriended us. One Sunday we were guests for dinner along with her mother and three aunts, all of whom were in their 70's. Now that I have gone past that decade I don't feel it is quite the miracle we thought it was then.

I made two memorable hitchhiking side trips. One was to Lansing, Michigan to visit Dr. Ball, the Michigan State tennis coach who had first taught me to play, and his family. Two weeks later I visited their daughter, Peggy, a student at Oberlin College. I stayed overnight in one of the fraternity houses. Peggy and I first met when we were seven and had not seen each other in at least ten years. We had fun reminiscing.

Upon completion of our course in May several of us received orders to report to the First Naval District Headquarters in Boston for assignment where needed.

Once again, fortune smiled on me and I ended up at the Fargo Building (adjacent to the North Boston Train Station) working for the Flight Selection Board Offices.

I landed a plum assignment. It started me on the path to become a commissioned officer!

FIRST DAYS IN BOSTON

The four of us assigned to the Navy Air Corps recruiting center were: Blair Hagy, a handsome, blond hell-raising

farm boy from Tennessee; Johnny Stefanek, a well mannered Polish boy from Detroit; and a guy named Harry from Taunton, MA who really did not fit in with the others. But he was so delighted to be back where he could go home on weekends that he didn't cause us any trouble.

In addition to having jobs that we liked, we were in much better shape financially. Congress had passed a new pay bill and, as Seamen First Class we earned $90.00 per month. Also, we were eligible for and drew subsistence living expenses.

The four of us rented a one-bedroom basement apartment in a convenient location on the backside of Beacon Hill, not far from Scully Square. It was within walking distance of the Charles River, the Esplanade and the Hatch Shell for the outdoor concerts of the Boston Pops Orchestra.

We had a double bed and a cot in the bedroom and a sofa in the living room. We ate our breakfast and dinner in the apartment. I had done a little cooking in the apartment in Arlington so I said I would cook if one person prepared the vegetables for me and set the table. The other two were responsible for cleanup. My mother sent me recipes to cook my favorite dishes.

It worked! We lived well, worked hard Monday through Friday and then had the weekends off. I made two or three visits to Deenie's home in Rutherford NJ, and our affection for each other continued to grow stronger.

It was a good summer, and it was not yet over.

FLIGHT PHYSICALS

The doctors with whom we worked at the recruiting center were responsible for giving intensive flight physical examinations to the recruits. By July of 1942 we had been at war for seven months, and all branches of service had stepped up their mobilization efforts.

We were busy from the time we opened in the morning until we closed at the end of the day. We were a small unit, about seven or eight doctors, an equal number of male nurses and hospital corpsmen, plus the four of us. It was a friendly, cooperative atmosphere.

The doctors shared unusual cases with us. A pilonidal cyst was cause for rejection. The reason: if it became inflamed it could present a severe problem if it went on to become infected. If surgery were required it could take several weeks for recovery. What, you may ask, is a pilonidal cyst?

It is a sinus or abscess (localized collection of pus) or a chronic draining sinus (canal or passage leading to an abscess) located in the opening between the buttocks muscles. This cyst may have a deep cavity containing hair and may be without symptoms unless it becomes infected.

Rarely did they find anyone with more than one pilonidal cyst. However one of the doctors called us in to see a young man who had six readily identified cysts. The doctors said they had never seen that many on anybody before.

One morning I was told the medical director wanted to see me. "How many years of college have you had?" he asked. When I answered three he said, "I believe I have something interesting for you that just came in the mail."

Instead of requiring a college degree for admission to midshipman school the newly announced changes permitted enlisted personnel with three years college and six months active duty, or two years college and twelve months active duty to apply. All that I needed to qualify was his recommendation and a course in trigonometry.

Boston University, here I come!

MARRIAGE PROPOSAL

I called the registrar's office at Boston University and learned they had a six-week trigonometry class starting in two weeks. It would be from 6:30 – 8:30 P.M. Monday through Thursday, perfect timing for me.

Johnny Currier, a fraternity brother and very good friend from home, was at the Harvard Business School. He had accepted a commission as Second Lieutenant in the Army Supply Corps Reserve, and his call to active duty was deferred until he completed work on his MBA.

Johnny and I had grown up together in State College. After we became Fijis we grew even closer. He was engaged to be married to a wonderful girl, Sally Searle, also from home. Sally had taken a job and an apartment in Cambridge to be near him. Sally told me that anytime I wanted to have Deenie come to Boston to visit she could stay with her.

One of the first things I did after enrolling in night school was to call Deenie's mother to see if she would let Deenie come to Boston for a weekend. I had fallen in love with her mother, Mary Wickersham, on first meeting and knew that she liked me, too. She approved, so we were all set.

Having completed the secretarial course at Katherine Gibbs School in New York City, Deenie was working in New York. She was able to get off early one Friday and came by train to Boston. I cooked a stuffed pork chop dinner for her and the guys in the apartment the first evening, then took her to stay with Sally.

We spent Saturday evening with John and Sally and reminisced until quite late. It was a beautiful moonlight night so I suggested to Deenie that we go for a walk. We walked, and we talked. (Maybe that is where "talk the walk" originated.) We ended up on a park bench on the famous Boston Common.

I then got very serious. I told her I wanted to marry her and outlined exactly how I could do it. I would complete my course, go to Midshipman School and as soon as I got my commission we could afford to get married. I was positive about everything, except I told her I did not want an answer yet.

Deenie said that all her life she had looked forward to a romantic proposal, but when it came, all I did was talk about money.

TED WILLIAMS AND JOHNNY PESKY

After proposing to marry Deenie, I was really motivated. The first order of business was to do well in my trigonometry course. Brother Bill had gone to night school for five years to get his Bachelor of Law and Master of Law degrees. I could certainly go for six weeks.

Ted Williams

Rooming with three other guys who were not in school was not conducive to study. I solved that by forcing myself to go to the library immediately after each class, to do my homework and prepare for the next session. I could then review the material just before going into class.

The doctors told us one morning to expect excitement. That day brought two new recruits to have their physical exams: Red Sox all-star Ted Williams, the leading hitter in the American League, and Johnny Pesky, the rookie short-stop, who was third in the League. Navy recruiters had hit a double home run by signing two of the most popular athletes in the country.

Everybody in the office shook hands with them before we got down to the serious business of typing their medical histories. Hagy, sitting at the desk in front of me recorded Ted Williams's information, while I interviewed Johnny Pesky. I learned very quickly that, by his real name, John Michael Paveskovich, was born September 27, 1919 in Portland, Oregon.

Both Williams and Pesky had outstanding military records. Pesky missed all of the 1943, 1944 and 1945 baseball seasons but returned and played until 1954, He is known today as "Mr. Red Sox" and, after 63 years with the organization was chosen to help raise the 2004 World Series Championship banner up the Fenway Park center field flagpole the following season.

Many consider Ted Williams to have been the greatest hitter in the history of baseball. He hit 405 in 1941, and no one has come close to hitting 400 since then. As good as Williams was, people will always wonder what might have been. What if five of his prime years had not been spent in the Navy in World War II (1943-45) and flying combat missions for the Marines in the Korean War (most of the 1952 and 1953 seasons)?

The most exciting news for me came in September when I received my orders to report to Midshipman School at Notre Dame University.

NOTRE DAME FOOTBALL

I stopped overnight and had dinner with an old friend in Toledo on my way by train to South Bend, Indiana from Boston. That was when I learned the relationship between the Navy and the Toledo residents had deteriorated.

While I was there, all students who failed the yeoman or storekeeper courses or, who were dismissed for disciplinary reasons, were kept on to serve as mess attendants or to do other custodial jobs. They had liberty every night and had developed such a bad reputation that most of the bars in town were now "off limits" to all Navy personnel.

That was sad, because the people in Toledo had been so supportive, so friendly and so hospitable. And they still had native sons serving in the Navy throughout the world. I have always remembered them for the way they treated us.

Can you imagine anything more exciting than to arrive on the Notre Dame campus during football season? All midshipmen whose last name started from A-G lived in Lyons Hall which was next to the Rockne Gymnasium, named for the legendary coach, Knute Rockne.

I roomed with Joe Graham, who had just graduated from Clemson College. We made a good team. He was shy, but was a very serious student; Joe was a tremendous help to me, particularly in damage control class, one of our most important subjects, and I tried to help him get over his shyness.

One of the men rooming across the hall from us was another shy, but very good looking young man from North Dakota, Bill Guy. Bill overcame his shyness to such an extent that he became governor of his native state. Marianne and I saw him riding in President Dwight Eisenhower's Inaugural Parade in 1956. Such irony; North Dakota is the only one of the 50 states I have never been in.

Angelo Bertelli

At the end of the first week in midshipman school we were treated to an unforgettable experience, watching our first Fighting Irish football game in the Notre Dame Stadium.

Who said, "War is Hell"? Not for us at Notre Dame during football season!

NOTRE DAME VS. MICHIGAN

The T-formation was so new in the fall of 1942 that it was difficult to figure out who had the ball. The Notre Dame quarterback, Angelo Bertelli, was like a magician. He managed the "T" so well that he won the Heisman Trophy, the most coveted honor in college football, the following year.

The Fighting Irish had four home games. Two were of special significance, those against Northwestern and against Michigan. The star for Northwestern was Otto Graham, Bertelli's chief competition for the Heisman.

When Paul Brown began organizing the initial Cleveland Browns team the first player he signed was Otto Graham. Brown felt Graham was the perfect T-formation quarterback for his new pro team, even though he played tailback for Northwestern. Graham's record 52-4-3 at Cleveland made him a first round choice for the Football Hall of Fame.

We had seats on the 40-yard line for all games except the one against Michigan, the final contest of the season. This was one of the biggest rivalries in the country, and the game was completely sold out weeks in advance. I really take my hat off to the Notre Dame Administration for the way they accommodated us.

We marched into the stadium carrying wooden folding chairs. Half of our battalion sat behind the south end zone, the other half on the north end.

Everyone anticipated an offensive battle. Bertelli led the Irish, and the Wolverines featured their all-America halfback, Tom Kuzma.

Once again, fortune smiled on me. I was in the front row of the midshipmen seated behind the south goal post. Michigan won 33-20, and I swear, I believe almost all of the points by both teams were scored at our end. On one play Kuzma ended up right at my feet after scoring a touchdown.

Notre Dame was good to us, and I have always appreciated the way we were treated during the four months we were there. Their administration went out of its way to make us comfortable.

Their president greeted us when we arrived and wished us Godspeed when we finished.

ABOUT TO BECOME AN ENSIGN

Deenie had accepted my proposal, her parents had approved of our marriage, and our wedding was scheduled for Saturday, January 30, 1943, two days after I would complete my program at Notre Dame.

January was a brutally cold month in South Bend, Indiana. Once again we were in the extreme western end of the Eastern Time Zone where we did not have daylight until after 8:00 in the morning.

That notwithstanding, we mustered on the Quadrangle Grounds every morning at 6:00 and marched to the university cafeteria for breakfast. We had to be finished and out by 8:00 so the Notre Dame students could eat. We started our classes at 7:30 and went all day, except for a break for lunch,

I had no problem with any of my classes, except damage control, which, as I have noted earlier my roommate Joe Graham helped me understand. I enjoyed the other subjects and felt I learned quite a bit about navigation, seamanship, gunnery and communications.

We were training to become deck officers, meaning we would eventually have responsibility as Officer of the Deck for a ship underway at sea. All of the subjects became relevant.

PT Boats, or "Swift Boats," on which both President Jack Kennedy and Senator John Kerry served, were the "hot" or "glamour" duty at the time. When their recruiters came to Notre Dame seeking volunteers, I listened. But the more I heard, the more I knew that was not for me.

When we finally received our orders, nearly all the members of our class were assigned to amphibious-type ships. I felt I was one of the lucky ones, although some of my classmates disagreed when I told them I would report to a fleet oiler, commonly known as a tanker. The *USS LARAMIE* (AO16), would be my new home.

I was on "cloud nine" January 28, 1943, when, as Ensign Gazexer G. Green, Jr. USNR, I boarded the train for New York. I was about to be married in Rutherford, New Jersey, to the most beautiful girl in the world.

OUR WEDDING

When my train pulled into Grand Central Station in New York City the next morning, Deenie was waiting for me. We had not seen each other for more than four months, so it was a happy reunion.

The area was digging out from under a blizzard that had hit the area and deposited thirty or more inches of snow. We were able to get a bus to Rutherford, New Jersey that stopped a block from Deenie's home. My parents were there, having come from Pennsylvania, as had two of Deenie's aunts who lived in the Harrisburg area.

My mother was famous for getting names confused. She was meeting Luther and Mary Ann Wickersham, Deenie's parents, for the first time. As she approached the front door Mother kept repeating, "It's Mrs. Wickersham, and she lives in Rutherford. It's Mrs. Wickersham and she lives in Rutherford." Upon meeting her, Mother blurted out, "How do you do, Mrs. Rutherford?"

Even though the service was in the First Presbyterian Church of Rutherford, this was wartime, and we did not want to have a large wedding. Johnny Currier was my best man; Deenie's sister Winnie was maid of honor. Deenie looked absolutely gorgeous in a long, flowing white wedding dress as the Rev. Dr. Fred Holloway pronounced us man and wife.

Lois Adene "Deenie" Wickersham becomes Mrs. Gazexer "Gaz" Green, Jr. on January 30, 1943.

After the wedding we had a small reception at the Wickersham home. Sally Currier (née Searle) helped Deenie change into her traveling clothes. When Sally asked where we were going on our honeymoon, Deenie said she wasn't supposed to tell anyone, but "I know I can trust you."

We took a cab into the Statler Hotel, now the Pennsylvania Hotel, near Pennsylvania Station in New York. We left word not to be disturbed.

At about 11:00 there was a knock on the door saying it was "Room Service." I got up to tell them we had not ordered anything.

Standing there were John and "you can trust me" Sally Currier. They had been married about six months and just wanted to make sure we were OK.

REPORTING TO THE USS LARAMIE

We spent the first weekend of our honeymoon in New York City. The Statler was a lovely hotel. I guess it was the first hotel I had ever stayed in where a maid came in early in the evening, turned the sheets down and put a piece of candy on the pillows.

It also had a large well-appointed dining room just off the main lobby. It featured a large dance floor where Charlie Spivak, one of the most popular band leaders of the time, and his orchestra played every evening. Deenie and I loved to dance so this was an added feature for us.

We had a wonderful and memorable few days together, except that the cloud of war and our impending forced separation hung over us at all times.

Before the wedding we had decided to go to State College, Pennsylvania for a few days. We had only ten days from my graduation until I had to report to the *USS Laramie* in Norfolk, Virginia on Monday morning, February 8, 1943.

That meant I had to leave New York by train on Sunday evening, February 7. It was typical of most trains during the war, full of military personnel trying to sleep sitting up all night in a very uncomfortable coach. The train went only as far as Newport News where I caught a ferry to complete my journey.

Upon arrival in Norfolk I caught a bus from the ferry dock to the Naval Base and reported as instructed. I was told that the *USS Laramie* was not in port at Norfolk, and I was to wait until they could determine its location.

There was a very popular expression in the war—SNAFU. The polite translation is Situation Normal, All Fouled Up. That is what I felt when I got the news and was told to go back on a ferry and get on an overnight train for New York that evening. The *USS Laramie* was in Brooklyn.

So I tried to sleep sitting up on the train for the second night in a row, without much success. I was dead tired, and honestly quite relieved when I found my ship was in dry-dock, in the Brooklyn Navy Yard.

At least I could get some rest before we went to sea.

MEETING MY NEW SHIPMATES

After presenting my orders to the Officer of the Deck (OOD), I was taken to my quarters and met my new room-mate, Lieutenant Emmett Davis of Asheville, North Carolina.

Emmett had the largest stateroom on the ship, other than those of the Captain and the Executive Officer. Emmett could have had a private room, as most of the other Senior officers had, but said he would rather have a large room with a roommate.

Our room was actually designed for four officers with built in double-decker bunks on the outside side walls, with drawers underneath the bottom bunk. We also had built in desks against the front wall. The entry door was located in the middle of the back wall separating two large, comfortable lounge chairs.

Emmett was a very accomplished pianist and organist who kept an accordion with him and loved to entertain. He was bright and very literary. After the war was over he became an editor at Town and Country Magazine.

The first thing I learned from Emmett was he was on the ship, the *USS Laramie*, six months before, on August 27, 1942 when she was hit by a torpedo fired from a German submarine near Newfoundland. Here is a first hand account by one of the seamen who also survived the attack:

"On the evening of August 27, 1942 we were torpedoed in the Belle Isle straights off the Coast of Newfoundland. I was on watch on the forward 5-inch gun when we were hit by the torpedo between the food locker and the crew's quarters. It ruptured the bulkheads and killed four of my shipmates.

"The damage control gang was credited with saving the ship along with the skipper by using evasion maneuvers. Why the ship didn't blow us all to Kingdom Come is one of the miracles of the war. We limped into the Boston Navy Yard for repairs.

"We buried our shipmates at sea on September 2. That was the saddest moment of my life--watching them go overboard," Emmett concluded.

MY FIRST DAYS AT SEA

After completing Midshipman School and getting my commission I reported to the *USS LARAMIE* (AO 16) in dry-dock in the Brooklyn Navy Yard. Two weeks later, repairs completed, we went down the East River around lower Manhattan to Bayonne NJ to take on a load of Aviation Gasoline.

Then on February 22, 1943 we sailed out of New York Harbor as part of a huge 78-ship convoy consisting mostly of merchant ships bound for England and Russia. This was during the height of the German Submarine menace in the Atlantic. Yet, we had only two (2) escort vessels to protect 78 SHIPS!

My roommate, Emmett Davis, as well as other officers who had lived through the torpedoing of the *Laramie*, had already told me many bone-chilling stories of what actually happened that night, and how lucky they all were to be alive.

I could not help but be apprehensive.

An emergency call to go to our battle stations was called

Ensign Gaz Green on deck of USS Laramie *off Greenland in 1943.*

"general quarters." It was nothing like any fire drill I had ever participated in. The instant the alarm sounded we put on our life jackets and went as fast possible, in an orderly fashion, to our assigned positions.

My assigned station was to be in charge of a battery of 20-millimeter anti-aircraft guns on the starboard side of the ship above the engine room. Our main firepower: two five-inch guns, one in the bow and one in the stern,

We had several drills and then, the second night at sea, the alarm sounded. It was the real thing. We kept our life jackets next to our beds and were trained not to turn on any lights. So, in total darkness, I made my way down the outside ladder from our room, across a long catwalk over the huge gasoline tanks to the aft part of the ship, and up a ladder to my station.

Though there were no lights on any of the ships, I could make out the silhouettes of the closest ones. In addition to the sounding of the general alarm, we could hear the explosion of depth charges being dropped. The concussions reverberated throughout our ship.

For the first time I fully understood I WAS IN THE WAR.

TURNING TO GOD

I was scared. That is the only way I can put it.

Yes, I was really SCARED, I believe for the first time in my life.

The picture of what I did has flashed across my mind a thousand times during my lifetime because that is when I turned to God.

I looked up toward the heavens and I prayed. I asked God to protect me. I asked God to help me. I asked God to make me strong, to give me the strength to be a leader, not a coward.

It seemed like everything I had been taught in Sunday school, in church, and at home all came to mind in that instant. And it has never left me.

That night, after we were secure to go back to our quarters, I got into bed, and I prayed for the first time in years the child's prayer we were all taught:

Now I lay me down to sleep
I pray the Lord my soul to keep.
If I should die before I wake,
I pray the Lord my soul to take.

I prayed that prayer, or a similar one, every night I was in the Navy.

Most importantly, when I returned home safely at the end of the war, and learned so many of my friends had died; I decided God must have saved me for a reason.

I had to make my life worthwhile.

ST. JOHN'S, NEWFOUNDLAND

The top speed of the *USS Laramie* was 10½ knots. However, a convoy can go only as fast as the slowest ship. Our first convoy traveled at 7 knots; 78 ships creeping along at 7 knots with 2 escort vessels. Sitting ducks? YES.

It is no wonder the German submarines were able to sink so many ships from 1940 to 1943. The United States was woefully unprepared.

After about a week we were close enough to Newfoundland to break off from the convoy and go into the St. John's harbor where we would join other ships bound for Greenland, our ultimate destination.

During WWII the US Air Force built an airbase in Narsarsauq, Greenland, as a weather forecasting station and a stopping off point for planes flying to and from Europe. This was on the west coast of southern Greenland and accessible by ship through the Narsarsuaq Fjord.

The *Laramie* was a key part of the regular supply chain bringing personnel, food, fuel and other supplies to the base. Three former luxury cruise ships, which had been converted to troop carriers, were also part of this chain.

One of these, the *USAT Chatham*, was torpedoed and sunk in the Belle Isle Straights the night *Laramie* was hit. The *USAT Fairfax* was in this convoy with us.

Upon arrival in St. John's we learned for the first time that the *USAT Dorchester* had been torpedoed and sunk in the last convoy trying to reach Narsasssuaq. Of the 902 passengers and crew on board, US Coast Guard Escort Ships *Escanaba* and *Comanche* rescued 229.

On board the Dorchester were four Army chaplains of different denominations. When the life jacket storage locker was empty the chaplains removed their own and handed them to the next men in line. As the ship went down, survivors in the water could see the four chaplains standing on the sloping deck, arms linked and praying while awaiting their fate.

A special Medal for Heroism was authorized by Congress and along with the Purple Heart and the Distinguished Service Cross, was posthumously awarded to the four chaplains.

MY FIRST TRIP TO GREENLAND

With our hearts saddened by news of the sinking of the Dorchester, we departed St. Johns along with the *USAT Fairfax*, two merchant vessels and three Coast Guard cutter/ice breakers as escorts.

Winter weather in the North Atlantic, particularly in the vicinity of Newfoundland, Greenland and Iceland was usually very rough and extremely dangerous because of the German submarines. It was so rough that once we were underway, all we were required to do was stand our watch duties, usually four hours on and eight hours off, and then we were free.

The farther north we went, the shorter the days and longer the nights became. The Coast Guard cutters tossed around in the heavy seas like tops. The old *Laramie* groaned a lot, but held up pretty well until we entered into the Narsassauq Fjord, which was frozen solid.

The Coast Guard cutters, which were designed as icebreakers, would then cut a narrow path for us. This path was probably 25 to 30 feet wide while the *Laramie* was 68 feet.

This was bad, but good; bad because the *Laramie* was not a welded ship, but rather was held together by rivets and bolts; good, because plowing through the ice would destroy so many bolts we would have to go into dry-dock in either Boston or Brooklyn for repairs. This meant extra liberty for us.

The two things I remember most about this first trip are, (1) that survivors from the *Dorchester* had been taken to the air base here. We talked with several of them. They told us that most who lived were the ones who stayed in the 27 degree water until they were rescued. Those who got out of the water and up onto life rafts froze to death in the near zero temperature air. (2) That there was a plane down somewhere on the ice cap, and they were sending search planes out to look for it. They invited any of us who wanted to go along to do so. When I learned they had only four hours of daylight to search, and fog could roll in at any time, I said, "Thanks, but no thanks."

I had been married less than two months and wanted to return to Deenie and start our family. I have never regretted that decision.

PLAYING BRIDGE

I mentioned that because of the inclement weather in the North Atlantic we would fulfill our duty-watch requirements and then have much leisure time.

By the time we arrived in Newfoundland I had discovered that bridge was the favorite game of many of the officers on the *Laramie*. It almost became a cliché: If you were a deck officer you left the "bridge" to go play "bridge" in the wardroom. This suited me just fine.

My parents loved to play auction bridge and had taught Adelaide, Bill and me when we were very young. In fact, when I was just beginning, and they needed a "fourth," they would roll up the piano stool and make me the rotating "dummy." I did not bid, but watched, and played the "dummy" hand whose cards were face up.

Contract Bridge in 1943 was not nearly as complicated (or sophisticated) as it is today. Everybody played the Culbertson System, as developed by Eli Culbertson. Also very popular was the Blackwood Method which, in bidding, you asked your partner how many aces and kings in his hand.

We had a bridge game going in the wardroom 24 hours a day when we were underway. Every four hours we recorded each player's individual score, and an officer would leave to go on watch duty. Often, someone coming off watch was ready to join the game. We rarely lacked four ready to play.

We played for very modest stakes, 1/10 of a cent per point. We settled the score and paid off each time the ship dropped anchor or went alongside a dock. Nobody got hurt financially, nor do I remember anyone ever having bad feelings about losing. It was friendly, fun and a great way to pass time.

When we came into Boston, which we did about every two months, our wives could come aboard and spend the evening with us when we had the duty watch. We would usually play two officers against two wives. The wives could never understand how we always won.

The answer was simple. We men had played bridge so many hours with, and against each other, we almost knew before we started exactly what our partner was going to do.

RANK HAS ITS PRIVILEGE

Our skipper on the *USS Laramie* was Commander Walter Keller, a Naval Academy graduate who "messed up" early in his career and was relegated to a fleet oiler rather than one of the capital ships like an aircraft carrier, battleship, cruiser or destroyer.

I was told he had been navigator on a destroyer during peacetime that went aground, a major "No-No" for a career Navy officer. Anyhow, he wasn't happy, and that was evident.

Lt. Commander Earnest Holdorff, a Merchant Marine captain with many years experience, was the executive officer. Three other reserve officers from the merchant fleet were Communications Officer Frank Phillips, First Lieutenant Mick Brower, and Chief Engineer Charlie Davis.

Then the group, mostly younger, who had come from civilian life, included Dr. Chris Bitner from Nebraska, Supply Officer "Sunshine" Powell and Emmett Davis from North Carolina, Assistant Engineer Frank Hannigan and Ed Banagan from NY State, "Spence" Spencer from Ohio, Ivan Coler-Dark, "the mad Russian" who was assistant supply officer, and five young ensigns who came aboard after I did.

Some individual memories: Emmett Davis started getting seasick as soon as he heard them pulling up the anchor; Sunshine Powell was the cheapskate; Spence became uncontrollable when he drank; Charlie Davis was a "Southern gentleman"; Frank Phillips was a voracious reader and self taught; Ed Banagan was a graduate of Villanova and became a good friend.

Lt. (JG) Frank Hannigan and I were down in the bowels of the ship inspecting the forward ammunition storage when an escort began dropping depth charges. The concussion was so loud, so dramatic, it scared the hell out of me and left an indelible impression. I was sure a torpedo was coming right through the side of our ship.

When I grabbed the bottom rungs of the ladder to go topside, I heard Hannigan's booming voice shout, "Atten-SHUN!"

Ensign Green had to step back and allow Lieutenant Junior Grade Hannigan up the ladder first. Yes, rank has it privilege!

FIRST RETURN FROM SEA

Our return trip from Greenland included a stop in St. John's, Newfoundland to meet up with a larger trans-Atlantic convoy bound for Boston.

It is a good thing there were no suicide terrorists in the harbor because the St. John's port was full of "bum boats," small open motorboats that served as water taxis. I made my first and only visit to St. John's. I had to see for myself what the other officers told me. There was no reason to go into town.

Before we arrived in Boston we were told that the *Laramie* would go into dry-dock to inspect the hull for damage caused by plowing through the ice. We knew from that we would be in port a minimum of ten days to two weeks, and we could have our wives come to Boston to join us.

Deenie, who was working in New York City, had an arrangement with her employer that she could take unpaid leave anytime I was in port. I was told that I would be sent to a two-day firefighter's school in Newport, required for all officers serving on tankers.

We worked out the details that she would come to Providence on the New Haven RR and that I would meet her upon arrival. So there I stood on the platform as her train from New York arrived, expecting to embrace my bride of a few weeks as she stepped off the train. So what did I see?

Here came Deenie walking down the platform, more beautiful than ever, busily talking to a soldier who was carrying her suitcase. I had my arms practically outstretched for her, and she walked right by me. I knew she sometimes wore glasses, but I did not think her eyesight was that bad.

She stopped when I called to her, and it was a very loving, emotional reunion.

Her excuse for why she did not see me was that she had never seen me in khakis uniform before and was looking for me in my Navy blues.

She was forgiven unconditionally. We took the bus to Newport and had a wonderful, exciting first night back together at the Viking Hotel.

FIREFIGHTERS' SCHOOL

The purpose of firefighters' school was to teach us not to panic in the event of a fire aboard ship. I must tell you, it was a memorable experience.

Let me set the scene.

Picture a steel tower with catwalks and ladders going from one level to the next. On the lowest level there was an oil fire about to start burning on both sides of a metal catwalk as we crawled along cradling a high-pressure fire hose.

They divided us into teams of four men assigned to each team. Positions on the team were labeled A, B, C and D. Position A was the lead person on the nozzle of the fire hose. Positions B, C and D were on the hose behind the man in position A.

For each drill the positions rotated so that at the end of our drills each team member had been in every position, ESPECIALLY POSITION A.

The first man in Position A was lucky. He was merely encouraged by the three guys behind him to get closer to the fire. Each succeeding man received stronger urging from his teammates who had already gone through the Position A experience.

Pity the poor guy who started out in Position D. By the time he got to Position A, all three of his teammates had been there and wanted to make sure he has an opportunity to learn as much, if not more than they did.

So he got the GOOSING TREATMENT!

I can assure you there is nothing that will motivate a man to move forward more quickly than that.

MOVIE ACTOR VICTOR MATURE

On my second trip to Greenland I learned that Victor Mature, a leading movie actor in the era just before the start of WWII, was a member of the crew of the *USCG Storis*, one of our escort vessels. When we arrived at our destination, Bluie West One in Greenland, the *Storis* tied up alongside us.

The captain of the *Storis* told Emmett Davis that they were showing a movie that night featuring Victor Mature and invited us to be his guests. Emmett and I went. It was hilarious. Mature was the star with Carole Landis as his romantic attraction.

Mature was also the Master at Arms in charge of discipline of the crew during the movie. Every time he would kiss Carole Landis, the sailors would explode, cheering their hero. They had discovered he was a regular guy, and they loved him.

Victor Mature

We had an ice cream machine on our ship so that night after the movie, Emmett and I sat on our deck with Mature and ate ice cream cones.

The next afternoon Victor came over to our room and the three of us talked about Hollywood for about two hours.

Victor Mature was born in Louisville, Kentucky. His some 70 films include John Ford's "My Darling Clementine" (1946), "Kiss of Death" (1947), "Samson and Delilah" (1949), "The Robe" (1954) and "The Egyptian" (1954).

Mature enlisted in the Coast Guard in 1942 as a seaman recruit and immediately reported to the cutter *Storis* in Boston Harbor. Known in Hollywood as a "beautiful hunk of man," his Coast Guard shipmates, who took an immediate liking to the unpretentious actor, dubbed him "hunk of junk." Mature worked hard, eventually working his way up to chief boatswain's mate and survived most hazardous duty.

He never asked for any soft duty. Between tours of sea duty, Mature appeared at Bond rallies for the Coast Guard and eventually starred in the Coast Guard show "Tars and Spars," a morale building show which toured the country during WWII. After the war he returned to acting and was always proud of his Coast Guard service. He died of cancer in 1999 at age 86.

SINKING OF THE ESCANABA

On the morning of June 13, 1943 I was Junior Officer of the Deck on the 0400 to 0800 watch. We had left Greenland a couple of days earlier enroute to St. John's, Newfoundland.

From the time our ship departed Greenland we had encountered extremely bad weather, dangerous icebergs and fog. There also had been reports of submarine soundings, and we could not travel under the cover of darkness.

After the period of midnight twilight, it had become daylight at about 2:00 A.M. Our escort screen included the Coast Guard cutters *Mohave*, *Tampa*, *Escanaba*, *Algonquin* and *Storis*, with Victor Mature on board.

I was on the port wing of the bridge scanning the horizon with my binoculars when I heard a loud explosion. I turned and looked just in time to see the bow of one of our escort vessels slip back into the water and sink.

The *USCG ESCANABA*, whose officers and crew had acted so heroically in rescuing 133 survivors when the Dorchester (with the four chaplains) was sunk in February, had been hit by a torpedo from a German submarine at 0510. It sank within three minutes. Only two of the crew of 103 survived.

The two survivors were, it is believed, on the bridge and either were blown free, or were able to get off the ship before it sank. The only body found was that of Lieutenant Robert Prause, the executive officer.

Melvin A. Baldwin and Raymond R. O'Malley, the two lone survivors of the sinking of the USS Escanaba, June, 1943.

Lt. Prause had gone into the icy water off the dock at Bluie West One in Greenland in a rubber suit with a line attached to develop the retriever method of rescue that proved so successful in saving lives after the *Dorchester* disaster.

USS Escanaba *Memorial in Grand Haven, Michigan, her home port.*

While we did not know any of the *Escanaba* crew personally, they were like family to us. They had traveled with us and protected us. We owe them forever, a real debt of gratitude. Lt. Prause received special commendation for his work in planning and executing this method.

Five out of every six of the 231,000 Coast Guardsmen serving during WWII, were reservists. 1,918 men paid the ultimate sacrifice. In my opinion this was the most hazardous, least recognized service.

MEMORIES OF THE LARAMIE

During the fifteen months I was on the *Laramie* we made trips to Greenland in all four seasons of the year. I experienced the shortest days (about four hours daylight), the shortest nights (the midnight twilight), and trips in the spring and the fall when massive icebergs are a menace. Here are some of my lasting memories:

Captain Keller holding a silk stocking he had found in his cabin, screaming, "What was going on in my quarters while I was gone?" Answer: While we had been playing bridge there, Deenie took off her stockings to get comfortable. She forgot she had put them behind a pillow on his couch.

Executive Officer Ernie Holdorff, a man in his 50's, dives off the wing of the bridge down into the ice-cold water 40 feet below. And then, his sharing with us for breakfast the fresh cod he caught fishing off the fan tail.

Sunshine Powell, the cheapskate supply lieutenant who would get out of a taxi and escort two wives into a restaurant while we paid for the cab. Then, when we got the check, he would give us exactly what his meal cost and would never contribute to the tip unless we asked him specifically for it.

The time we came through the Cape Cod Canal with vacationers waving at us on our way to refuel at the Bayway Refinery in New Jersey. Ed Banagan went home with me to Rutherford to enjoy the hospitality of the Luther and Mary Wickersham family. On Saturday night Ed and I took Deenie and her sister Winnie to Coney Island, and we acted like kids again.

The night Spence got drunk at the staid Fox and Hounds Club in Boston where we had guest privileges. The manager threatened to call the Shore Patrol. Finally, Spence's wife asked me to do whatever I had to do to get him into a taxi, even if it meant hitting him. Spence became the only person since I was a kid that I ever hit with my bare fist. Fortunately I only stunned him. We got him back to the hotel. Next day he apologized to us.

Spence became a Lieutenant Commander and Skipper of a Navy Cargo ship. Two years later we met up again half a world away at the Ulithi Atoll in the Western Caroline Islands. He sent his Captain's Gig over to get me to have dinner with him and spend the night. The Boston incident was not mentioned.

ORDERS TO TRANSFER

When we arrived in Boston, Emmett Davis and I were notified by Captain Keller that he had received orders to transfer the two of us to Newport, Rhode Island for pre-commissioning duty for the *USS MANATEE* (AO58), a new, fast fleet oiler under construction.

Deenie and I had been married a little more than a year. The few times we had been together were limited to two or three days up to about ten when we were between trips to Newfoundland and Greenland.

Now I had received orders to proceed to the Naval Training Station. We did not know how long we would be there but were told we would receive a per diem allowance and, those of us who were married, could have our wives there with us.

That was about the happiest news I could have received other than that the war was ending. But, that was still a long way off.

I saluted the American Flag on the fantail of the *Laramie* for the last time in the Boston Harbor on February 18, 1944 and took a train to go meet Deenie when she arrived in Providence. We were a happy and very excited young couple when we checked into Newport's famous Viking Hotel that evening.

Because Newport had been an established base for the U.S. Navy since it was opened as a torpedo base in 1869, it had plenty of accommodations for personnel on assignment for short or long periods of time.

We were fortunate to find a lovely room in the private home of a widow on John Street. I could say it was in the historic district, but the whole town is the historic district. We shared kitchen privileges, bathrooms and laundry facilities with two other Navy officers and their wives.

This was a wonderful break in the war for us. We began the development of lasting relationships with some of the officers we would be with for almost two years. But, most important, Deenie and I could seal our own bonding in cement and start our family.

And we did.

NEWPORT

The few weeks we were in Newport went by quickly, too quickly. We were so happy to be together to get a taste of what life would be like for us after the war.

We were welcome at the famous old Newport Casino, now the site of the Tennis Hall of Fame. It was a private club that could very well have been our own Navy Officers' Club.

There was no gambling in the "Casino". There was a lovely dining room, a lounge, and a card room, which we used on more than one occasion to have spirited bridge games. It was famous for its tennis, but in the winter months the weather rendered the beautiful clay courts unusable.

It was a relaxed time for us. I did not have to stand any watch duty so I was home with Deenie every night. We were "getting acquainted" with the crew so there was no pressure in our work

The *Manatee* was designed for fueling major warships at sea as part of the support group of the Fast Carrier Forces. These included our largest and most modern aircraft carriers, battleships, cruisers, destroyers and destroyer escorts. We had a top speed of 18 knots, or about 30 MPH.

The *USS Manatee* (AO58) was being built by the Bethlehem Steel Shipbuilding Company in Sparrows Point near Baltimore. Much of our time in Newport was spent learning everything we could about our ship and the fueling at sea operation before we actually went aboard the ship.

Just as we officers were transferred from ships on active duty, many of the crew also came from other Navy ships. Each department had a nucleus of petty officers, a rank similar to corporal and sergeant.

Crews were being assembled at Newport for several other ships under construction at various shipyard around the country. One was a sister ship AO59, the *USS Mississinewa*. We became friends with their officers in Newport as we trained for similar missions. More about that ship's fate later.

Finally, the word came that the *Manatee* would be ready May 6, 1944.

CHAPTER THREE

USS MANATEE *COMMISSIONED*

There is probably no greater thrill than seeing the commissioning of a U.S. Navy ship that is to become your new home away from home.

Our wives left Newport for Baltimore early the day before so they could be with us and witness the ceremony on the morning of April 6, 1944.

There were about 300 of us, counting all the officers and crew who traveled overnight on a troop train, sitting up in coaches, trying to catch any sleep we could. We arrived early on the clear, crisp morning of the big day.

After brief remarks the traditional bottle of champagne was smashed over the bow by Mrs. Paul McNutt, wife of the former U.S. high commander of the Philippines (1937-1939).

We said tearful goodbyes to our wives and then set sail under the command of our new ship's captain, Lt. Commander Joseph B. Smyth, a Merchant Marine veteran of some 40 years at sea. He had been in the U.S. Naval Reserve and was called to active duty.

USS Manatee *AO58*

We had ten days of sea trials in the Chesapeake Bay, followed by a couple of days in the Navy Yard to "tighten a few bolts." Most of our sea trials were spent learning fueling at sea techniques. It is quite different putting into operation what you have gleamed out of books. Particularly since only one officer had ever done it before.

We then took off for Aruba, an island in the Dutch West Indies. I will never forget how hot it was there. The *Manatee* was not air conditioned, of course.

We were moored to the dock for several hours while we took on about 120,000 barrels of oil. There was no breeze and the hot sun made the decks so hot we could have fried eggs on any one of them.

Next came a most exciting adventure—passage through the Panama Canal from the Atlantic Ocean to the Pacific. You can see pictures, even movies, but there is nothing like the first time real life experience of going through the locks.

Pearl Harbor, Here We Come!

PEARL HARBOR, WAIKIKI BEACH AND HONOLULU

Our first impression on entering Pearl Harbor was instant reminder of the devastation caused by the sneak attack by Japan on December 7, 1941.

The surprise bombing that Sunday damaged or destroyed twelve U. S. warships and 188 aircraft, and killed 2,403 servicemen and 68 civilians. Wrecked hulls of sunken ships were clearly visible and oil droplets still bubble to the surface from the *USS Arizona*, where 1,177 men are entombed.

Today, visitors come from around the world come to see the *USS Arizona* Memorial, which spans the mid portion of the sunken battleship resting on the bottom of the harbor. This national memorial is designed to encourage quiet contemplation and to appeal to our memory and sense of sacrifice.

Upon arrival we were told that we would be in port for a few days while our task group was being formed. Pearl Harbor had been the staging ground for all the fleet activities so we assumed we would be returning on a regular basis and would have plenty of time for sightseeing. Besides, we were all broke after having lived in Newport with our wives for several weeks.

I did go into Honolulu one day just to look around and on another occasion to try surf boarding at Waikiki Beach. Did I get a rude awakening? I had never been swimming at a coral beach before and had no idea how difficult is was to walk once I got into the water. (No, I could not walk on the water.)

We visited the famous Mauna Loa Hotel which had been taken over by the Navy and was being used for R&R (Rest and Relaxation) for sailors to have a few days recreation away from their regular duties.

I also had a chance to play a little tennis and visit some of my old buddies from storekeeper school in Toledo who were stationed at supply depots.

Finally, the day came to proceed to Eniwetok Atoll in the Marshall Islands in company with several other oilers, representing a sizeable portion of the logistics support group preparing to support the invasion of Saipan.

This voyage was our first chance to practice fueling at sea in the open ocean.

We were making progress but had a lot of work to do to become proficient.

ENIWETOK ATOLL

Eniwetok was one of the Marshall Islands captured from the Japanese in the spring of 1944 as the United States began its offense campaign westward from Hawaii across the vast Pacific Ocean toward Japan.

An atoll is a ring of coral islands and reefs surrounding a central lagoon. The Eniwetok Atoll was critical to the success of the Navy as it prepared for the recapture of the Marianna Islands, Saipan, Tinian and Guam. This atoll was large enough to accommodate a large number of ships at one time.

Between Pearl Harbor and Eniwetok I did something that, in retrospect, surprises me. Having been in the North Atlantic for so long my blood had thinned out. So when we got into the warmer climates I had a very difficult time wearing long sleeve shirts and long trousers every day.

I knew we had a tailor on the ship so I asked him to cut off the sleeves of my khaki shirt and make a pair of trousers into shorts. By this time one of my primary duties was to be the officer of the deck (OOD) when the ship was underway. Unless or until I turned control of the ship over to the captain, or another officer, I was responsible for the safety of every man on the ship.

So one day I very brazenly appeared on the bridge for duty in my shorts and short sleeved shirt. Captain Smyth had been a Merchant Marine Captain, and all he really cared about Navy regulations was that he would not do anything to get into trouble.

Captain Smyth came to the bridge greeted me and walked away. I could see him eyeing me. He came back over, cleared his throat and asked, "Mr. Green. Is that uniform regulation?" "Yes, sir," I replied positively. He walked away, then came back and asked in a very polite tone, "Where did you get it?"

After I told him the ship's tailor had made the shorts and short-sleeved shirt, he asked, "Do you suppose I can get one of those?" "Yes, sir," I assured him, saying I would have the tailor come to his quarters and measure him.

Three days later Captain Smyth made his sartorial debut. Within a week nearly every officer had adopted the casual attire as his standard uniform for the duration of the war.

Marines landing on Saipan, June, 1944.

MY MEMORIES OF WAR IN THE PACIFIC

From our entry into Eniwetok June 16, 1944 until the Japanese surrendered in late August 1945 the *Manatee* earned eight battle stars and two bronze stars. And there was not a man killed or seriously injured on either the *Laramie* or the *Manatee* in the almost 33 months I was aboard those ships.

Probably 90% of our days at sea were routine after we became proficient and experienced at fueling at sea, our main mission. My intent, therefore, will be to highlight those experiences that were etched into my memory.

The day after our arrival in Eniwetok we were part of a group of oilers ordered out to refuel the amphibious forces then busy with the landings on Saipan, the first island to be captured in the Marianas Campaign.

Our first day of fueling was a difficult one. It started at 0900 and lasted for more than ten hours, hampered by darkness and damage to our fueling rig from when we suffered a steering casualty. Also, let's face it, we were novices.

The official Navy record states, "Several days later another fueling took place that gave the *Manatee* crew confidence to perform this task as efficiently as any of the more experienced sister ships. A new battleship in Task Force 58, the *USS Indiana* BB58, came alongside, was fueled, and departed in a minimum of time, without incident."

Over the next 17 months the aggressiveness of Admiral "Bull" Halsey changed the strategy of fueling at sea completely. Initially, the Fast Carrier Force would fuel about every third day and would do nothing else on that day until the fueling was complete.

Before the war ended we still fueled every third day, but the aircraft carriers would launch and land aircraft while they were

Officers of USS Manatee *A058 in South Pacific, 1944. Lieut. (jg) Gaz Green is standing at back on right.*

alongside us fueling. We would head into the wind for about an hour while they launched, then reverse course and go downwind while the planes were gone. We usually fueled a carrier and another fighting ship at the same time.

When it was near time to retrieve planes we would again head into the wind and complete the fueling. One bit of excitement of which I never grew tired was watching, through binoculars, fighter or torpedo planes take off and land while their landing field, the carrier deck, was right alongside us.

LEARNING TO PLAY POKER

You will recall that when I was on the *USS Laramie* we had a bridge game going sometimes 24 hours a day in the wardroom. On the *Manatee* we could not find a fourth for bridge, no matter how hard we tried.

The card game of choice, in the Manatee wardroom, was POKER. I was raised in a pretty strict Methodist home and GAMBLING of any kind was absolutely forbidden. In fact, I almost believed you would go to Hell if you gambled.

Every night a spirited poker game began shortly after the dishes had been cleared from dinner, usually led by Bill Yourdan, our executive officer who did not have to stand any regular watches.

My roommate, Walt Krumweide, was a regular player, so I had him make a chart for me showing the basics of poker – what beats what. Honestly, I did not know the first thing about poker, so I took my little chart, sat and observed night after night when I was not on watch and studied how

everybody played.

Finally, I got up my nerve. I decided I would invest $10.00. If I lost that I would quit, agree that my mother was right, and never play again. The game they played was dealer's choice, with a 25-cent limit, and a limit of three raises. Over time, seven-card stud, with the joker wild, became so popular that it was played almost every hand.

Marines shelling in Guam, 1944

I developed a very conservative system, and kept a record after every time I played of how much I won or lost. Over the next 17 months I sent money home to buy:

• A lifetime membership to the Penn State Alumni Association.

•   A lifetime membership to Phi Gamma Delta.

•   Initial membership dues to become a Mason.

But the best investment of all was the $25.00 lifetime subscription to *Reader's Digest* magazine for daughter Marianne's first Christmas when she was seven weeks old. She received the magazine for many years in Switzerland when the cost for one year would have been more than I paid.

RINGSIDE SEAT TO THE WAR

Throughout the campaign for Saipan, Tinian, and Guam, the *Manatee* shuttled from Eniwetok, where we were replenished with oil, aviation gas and provisions brought out to this atoll by merchant ships, either from Pearl Harbor or directly from the States.

Fueling the largest and most famous fighting ships in the world was exciting: standing on our deck or on the bridge less than 50 feet from a giant aircraft carrier or a behemoth battleship. Our 550 ft. ship was dwarfed alongside these.

A battleship like the *USS Iowa* or *USS New Jersey* was 887 ft. long. An Essex Class Carrier was like a city unto itself, 820 ft. long, 93 ft. wide and extended in height to 147 ft. It carried a crew of more than 3,000 officers and men.

After Saipan was secured and the Tinian invasion was underway, we were ordered to proceed to Garapan Bay, a small body of water separating Tinian from Saipan. Our assignment was to refuel the ships supporting the invasion.

Half of our crew manned their battle stations the entire time we were in the bay. I was at that time the gunnery officer. My command post was over the roof of the bridge. I had a ringside seat to the war.

Our battleships and heavy cruisers fired continuous rounds from offshore at Japanese troop positions on Tinian. Planes flew over and drop bombs. But the most exciting part for me was to watch the U.S. Army heavy artillery firing from Saipan onto Tinian. I could put on earphones and hear the instructions from the spotters in a piper cub back to the artillery.

We saw Japanese soldiers running up hills, trying to hide in caves, being chased by U.S. Infantrymen with flame throwers.

No more details.

This was witnessing the ugly side of war. I don't want to give anyone the impression that war is glamorous. It is NOT.

USS Manatee *fueling a destroyer in Pacific somewhere off the China Coast in 1945.*

FROM POLYWOG TO SHELLBACK

On the 20th of August 1944, about the time Guam, the last island in the Marianas, was secured, our base of operations shifted to Manus, one of the Admiralty Islands. This was considerably south of where we had been operating and meant that we would, for the first time, cross the equator.

The ceremony of Crossing the Line is an initiation rite in the U.S. and other world navies which commemorates a sailor's first crossing of the equator.

Originally the tradition was created as a test for seasoned sailors to ensure their new shipmates were capable of handling long rough times at sea. Sailors who have already crossed the equator are nicknamed (Trusty) Shellbacks, often referred to as Sons of Neptune; those who have not are nicknamed (Slimy) Pollywogs.

King Neptune and his court provide a lighthearted ceremony that all members of the crew look forward to. When we crossed the line, our First Lieut. J. J. Huml, a crusty sailor who came up through the ranks, played the part of King Neptune. His court included Assistant Engineer Lt. Lenny Long as her Highness, the buxom Amphitrite. Long, a graduate of Cal Tech, was made up to perfection and looked beautiful.

King Neptune presided over the ceremony, during which we Pollywogs underwent a number of increasingly disgusting ordeals, largely for the entertainment of the Shellbacks. Once the ceremony is complete, a Pollywog receives a certificate declaring his new status.

Another common status is the Golden Shellback, a person who has crossed both the equator and the International Date Line on the same ship. We had already crossed that line so we automatically became Golden Shellbacks.

While that was the first time we crossed the equator, we did it many times after that. I remember one day, in particular, when we were fueling right on the 180 degree parallel, traveling north for an hour, then south for an hour as the carriers launched and landed their planes.

No extra credit was given for the number of times we crossed the imaginary line.

Just satisfaction!

ISLAND HOPPING STRATEGY

We often wondered why the U.S. military skipped over certain islands that still contained Japanese troops. According to the historian Edward Drea, this strategy was developed many years before the attack on Pearl Harbor.

The U.S. island hopping approach was one imposed by enormous distances across the Pacific Ocean and the technological restrictions of the mid-1940s. The Japanese had strong carrier- and land-based air units protecting the approaches to Japan.

The United States had to reduce this defensive perimeter by seizing key bases and bypassing (or hopping over others). The strategy depended on isolating the Japanese defenders from reinforcements and controlling the skies about the contested island.

Because the range of fighter aircraft was limited in the mid-1940s, operations were planned around this factor. Once U.S. forces captured an island, they built forward logistics bases to support the next invasion.

The South Pacific and Central Pacific were the main approach routes to Japan. The U.S. Navy had studied the Central Pacific route since the 1920's, and their World War II campaigns generally followed the outline of the prewar studies.

Manus was the first big 'leapfrog' landing in the Pacific war. The original target for the Manus landing was to have been Rabaul in New Britain. Rabaul was the major Japanese base in the area and was the staging ground for their Solomon Islands invasions.

It was from Rabaul that the Japanese sortied to Guadalcanal and the Coral Sea. The Manus substitution cut the Philippine resupply line for the 10,000 man Japanese garrison at Rabaul.

Seadler Harbor in Manus proved to be a better staging site for the fight to follow than Rabaul would have made. It was closer to Japan and the Philippines. B-24 liberators stationed there provided a 1,100-mile search radius into the surrounding ocean.

SECOND BATTLE OF THE PHILIPPINE SEA

Manus was home base for us for about three months. We were part of the support group for the Pelilieu Island campaign and the first phase of the Battle of the Philippines.

On October 20 we left Manus for the last time and proceeded northward to join the forces of Admiral Halsey covering the landings at Leyte. It had become customary for us to fuel the fleet every third day. Then, usually the next day, we would consolidate fuel; fully loaded tankers would stay on the line, empty tankers would be relieved by full tankers returning from base.

We were a true SUPPORT GROUP. In addition to tankers, our group included light aircraft carriers carrying replacement planes and crews, ammunition ships, dry cargo and fresh provision ships and ocean going tugs.

One of the biggest scares we ever had took place during a consolidation operation when a destroyer in our protective ring identified a dive bomber from a Japanese Aircraft Carrier approaching our group from the north.

Next, we received an URGENT message that the Japanese fleet had been spotted COMING DUE SOUTH directly toward us and we were traveling DUE NORTH!

Our Fast Carrier Force was DUE SOUTH of us COMING DUE NORTH AT FLANK SPEED to meet the Japanese fleet.

Our support task group, the most vulnerable part of the entire Navy, presented sitting ducks on the sea about midway between the two most powerful navies in the world about to become engaged in battle.

Our task group was ordered to change course immediately and precede DUE EAST at top speed attainable to "get out of the way." Fortunately, U.S. carrier-based planes began their attack on the Japanese fleet which then became so absorbed in defending itself it could not come after us.

This engagement, officially labeled THE SECOND BATTLE OF THE PHILIPPINE SEA was one of the turning points in the war. It ended the Japanese Navy's effectiveness for good.

MY DAILY NEWSPAPER

One of the true joys I had aboard the *Manatee* was creating and editing a daily newspaper which I called the *MANATEE TIMES*. I guess it started sometime after we left Pearl Harbor and resulted from a casual conversation with Captain Smyth while standing an uneventful watch on the Bridge.

I think I have always been interested in people (but then, who isn't?). I had asked the captain where he grew up and how he first became interested in joining the Merchant Marine. When I learned that his father owned three weekly newspapers in California, I mentioned to him that I had started out in journalism in college.

We talked about having a newspaper on the *Manatee* to provide some information and humor for our crew of about 350. He liked the idea, asked me if I would do it and pledged his full support.

We had about ten men who manned the "Radio Shack," sending and receiving messages in code 24 hours a day. It was very important that this discipline be maintained and perfected so our enemy would not be alerted if we needed to send or receive urgent information.

Our radiomen had access to world and sports news, feature stories and were already typing this information. All I had to do was edit and reproduce copies for distribution to our crew. I got some joke books, inserted officers and sailor names to localize the jokes and wrote a daily column "STRICTLY SCUTTLEBUT."

All mail leaving our ship was censored so I could write anything about where we were or what we were doing. Our battleships and carriers all had shipboard newspapers so, while fueling, I would get on a hand held phone, talk with one of their officers, find out everything exciting, and get copies of their newspapers to plagiarize.

The daily *MANATEE TIMES* became so popular that the chow line for breakfast formed, not in front of the mess hall at 0630, but at the door leading to the Radio Shack where the paper was distributed.

Radio Shack—now there is a good name. I wish I had thought to get the copyright for it.

MOG MOG ISLAND

After Leyte was secure we changed our base of operation from Manus to Ulithi Atoll in the Western Caroline Islands.

As a deck officer I was required to read the port instructions prior to entry of each new area. Upon entering Ulithi

Atoll, I was surprised to learn that the officer in charge of the designated recreation facility for our armed forces, Mog Mog Island, was a long time friend, Lt. Comdr. Charles M. Spiedel, the wrestling coach at Penn State.

I immediately sent Charlie a message inviting him to come out to dinner aboard our ship that evening. He declined, stating he had a previous commitment, but asked me to come ashore, that he would show me around.

I met him the next afternoon, and he took me on a tour of the island in his jeep. The flag officers (admirals, generals, etc.) had their own thatched hut bar and lounge with two bartenders on duty under Charlie's jurisdiction. He asked one of them if he had any new pictures of natives.

After being told there were no duplicates, Commander Speidel asserted that if there were any, he would get to keep it. About halfway through the stack, Charlie exclaimed, "Here's one. Gaz, this one is yours."

It was a young native woman, nude to the waist.

"When I was a little boy and saw my mother in similar attire I asked her what those things were. "My tonsils," she replied.

So I sent the picture home to Deenie and told her to show it to my mother and point out what beautiful tonsils this young woman had.

BECOMING A FATHER

While we were in Pearl Harbor I received mail from Deenie with the happy news. Her family doctor in Rutherford had confirmed that she was pregnant.

We had decided while we were together in Newport that we wanted to have a child and that it was imperative that, after the war, I return to Penn State and get my degree. If she were to become pregnant, therefore, she would go to State College and rent an apartment near my parents.

State College was still a small town with a population of about 7,000 and an equal number of Penn State students when college was in session. Mother and Dad lived in a first floor Heatherbloom apartment facing Nittany Avenue, about three blocks from downtown and the Penn State Campus.

Deenie was able to get an apartment directly across the hall from my parents. That was a mixture of good – my parents watched out for her, and bad – because Deenie felt a little intimidated at first because she did not know them very well. That issue became resolved, and it worked out well.

Bill Graffius, a friend a couple years younger than I, had a medical deferment, was married and lived in the Heatherbloom with his wife, Eleanor, also pregnant and due to give birth about the same time as Deenie.

Deenie and Eleanor became very close friends and spent most of their days together. Later, Bill told me several times about the stares he received when he escorted two very pregnant around town.

After leaving Hawaii there was no possible way to make or receive phone calls. The only communication we had was U.S. Mail and sometimes it took several weeks for mail to reach us.

Our dear sweet Marianne Wickersham Green was born November 7, 1944 in the Centre County Hospital in Bellefonte, Pennsylvania. I received the news in mail delivered to the *Manatee* on November 29 and two days later I received additional mail that included a telegram my father had sent to me.

Our ship's doctor, Charlie Straub, called Deenie's letter to me the best description of a birth, by the mother, that he had ever read. She included every detail, from the first labor pains until Marianne made her debut.

TRAGEDY IN ULITHI ATOLL

Ulithi (also known as Urushi, or Mackenzie Island) is a coral atoll, in the western Pacific Ocean, now in the Federated States of Micronesia. Its islets have a total land area of 1.75 sq miles. Its huge lagoon is the world's fourth largest (209 sq. miles).

Before its recapture by the U.S., it was the site of a Japanese seaplane base, but was abandoned by the Japanese before American troops landed. Prior to occupation by U.S. forces on September 20, 1944, there were numerous U.S. air raids to soften up the area, so there was no ground opposition.

The area became a massive U.S. Naval base for the rest of the war, which included the battles of Okinawa, Iwo Jima, Lingayen Gulf and the landings planned for the Japanese mainland.

With its huge deep atoll, large enough to contain a thousand ships, it provided an ALMOST perfect staging area. It was thought to be ALMOST anti-submarine proof with its underwater coral wall almost completely surrounding the bay and protected by huge nets at the entrance. It was ALMOST, but not totally.

Sinking of the Mississinewa

On the morning of November 20, 1944 a Japanese one-man submarine on a suicide mission succeeded in sneaking through the entrance nets and at 5:45 AM rammed and exploded against the *USS MISSISSINEWA* (AO-59), our sister ship. It had just been serviced and had 440,000 gallons of aviation gasoline and a full load of fuel oil on board.

There, but for the Grace of God go I.

Just two days before, we had been berthed at that same spot. We were exiting Ulithi Atoll to go back to the fueling area when we passed the *Mississinewa* about to enter. As always we signaled. The three officers and 60 men who died in the attack were our friends. We had been at Newport with them and on the firing line for several months. Nearby ships rescued the survivors.

Discovery of the wreckage: After searching from March 27 to April 6, 2001, the ship was located, 57 years after the sinking in 130 feet of water.

THE TYPHOON

Compared to today, weather forecasting was primitive in 1944.

On December 17 we had a rendezvous with a fast carrier force desperately in need of fuel. We began at 11:00 under atrocious weather conditions that got progressively worse as the day went on.

Task Force 38 included seven fleet and six light carriers, eight battleships, 15 cruisers, and about 50 destroyers. The carriers had just completed three days of heavy raids against Japanese airfields, suppressing enemy aircraft during the American amphibious operations in the Philippines.

It was not unusual for us to fuel three ships at one time. On this day we began with the carrier *USS Hancock* on our port side, plus the destroyers *Swenson* and *Maddox* starboard and astern. It was the worst day we ever had fueling at sea.

We suffered heavy damage to our fueling rigs and lost sections of hose. Despite this, the records show that we delivered 8,000 barrels of oil and 60,000 gallons of aviation gas to the *Hancock* and successfully fueled the *Swenson* and *Maddox* before all fueling operations were stopped.

I had the 2000 to 2400 (8 PM to midnight) watch that night, and I remember our captain, who had been going to sea for 40 years, saying repeatedly that our task force commander (Admiral Halsey) did not know what he was doing. Captain Smyth said, "He is taking us right into the eye of the storm."

At about midnight Admiral Halsey gave the order for all ships to turn on running lights and operate independently. No one forecast the severity of this storm, nor could anyone have predicted the severe damage it would cause to the fleet. This storm inflicted more damage on the Navy than any storm since the hurricane at Apia, Samoa in 1889.

146 planes on various ships were lost or damaged beyond economical repair, or were swept overboard. Most tragic, was the human loss when three destroyers who could not be fueled, *USS Hull*, *USS Spence*, and *USS Monaghan*, capsized and sank.

While 90 officers and men were rescued, 790 dedicated sailors died.

MY MOST HARROWING EXPERIENCE

I don't know how many Navy ships earned a battle star for service in the South China Sea during World War II, but the *USS Manatee* was one.

In early January of 1945, while the fleet continued to bombard Japanese placements in the Philippines and on Formosa, a group of oilers were detached from the main body to accompany the Fast Carrier Force to the South China Sea.

This was a strategic divisionary tactic to keep the Japanese off balance. The landings at Lingayen Gulf to recapture Luzon were about to begin. Sending our fleet to attack Japanese shipping and shore installations on the mainland of China was designed to make the Japs think the invasion would be there.

We were part of a small group of oilers and support vessels ordered to make a surprise trip through the Surigao Straits and the Sulu Sea on a moonless night to rendezvous with the fleet off the China coast... This turned out to be the most harrowing experience of my entire Navy career.

First, we had to travel with blackouts in effect at all times, which meant NO exposed lights anywhere on the ship. Also, our task group, totaling perhaps twenty heterogeneous ships, traveled in extremely close formation and executed changing zigzag plans designed to confuse the enemy.

Part of our journey was through very narrow stretches of water bordered by land occupied by the Japanese on both sides. We could see gunfire from shore aimed at our escort vessels, which responded by shooting flares high in the sky to expose the Japanese installations and then rejoining our formation.

It was a miracle we did not have a major disaster. Good navigational charts were not available so the danger of running aground was ever present. On one zigzag maneuver an escort carrier off my port quarter (left rear) turned right when we, with all other ships, were turning left as instructed. To avoid a collision we had to turn hard right.

Why was this so harrowing for me?

Because I was officer of the deck and, at age 24, responsible for the safety of my ship and the 300 men aboard when it happened.

CLOSING IN ON JAPAN

Iwo Jima, 1945

It was during the Iwo Jima and Okinawa campaigns that our logistic support group reached its final stage of development.

More oilers reported from the Atlantic Fleet and large number of ammunition, dry cargo and fresh provision ships and aircraft carriers also joined the group. The light cruiser Detroit was added as flagship to further protect and facilitate the handling of these ships.

In addition to petroleum products, the oilers now supplied mail, aircraft belly tanks, depth charges, freight, motion pictures, transportation service and a large number of personnel replacements. Transfer of this super-cargo during the fueling operations became common and it was seldom that a ship asked for and received just fuel.

The support group had become a floating supply base, enabling the fleet commander to maintain indefinitely his strikes against the enemy.

In early July we began a new procedure whereby a group of fast oilers only, including the *Manatee*, would lend support to the Fast Carrier Force by moving quickly during hours of darkness to within two hundred miles of the Japanese coast, rendezvous with the task force, then retreat to a safer area during daylight.

We were scheduled to return to California for routine maintenance, but then the first atomic bomb was dropped on Hiroshima. Immediately, our orders were canceled. We returned to the fueling line and. following the dropping of the second bomb on Nagasaki. Japan surrendered on August 14, 1945.

On September 2 the formal surrender ceremony took place on the deck of the *USS Missouri* in the Tokyo Harbor. We were with the fleet less than 200 miles away and watched as wave after wave of carrier-based planes, 450 in total, flew over as the ceremony concluded.

This impressive demonstration underscored the power that had brought Japan and the United States to this time and place.

We rejoiced, returned to Ulithi and waited until September 25 for the orders that would send us to the San Pedro Navy Yard. OH HAPPY DAY!

Japanese surrender on USS Missouri, 1945

THE WAR IS OVER (WELL ALMOST)

Yes, the war was finally over and the jubilant crew of the *USS Manatee* left the Ulithi Atoll without being part of a convoy or task group for the first time since we had arrived in Pearl Harbor nearly a year and a half before.

The only problem was DID ALL THE JAPANESE MILITARY KNOW IT WAS OVER?

Our orders leaving Ulithi were to use the same precautions as had been in effect before the final peace treaty had been signed. That included full duty watches 24 hours a day and darkened ship, with no running lights or exposed light of any kind, from before sunset until after daybreak.

The US Navy was certain that there were Japanese submarines still lurking in the waters of the Pacific and we were traveling without any escort protection. Additionally, there was always the concern that floating mines may have become dislodged and floated out to sea.

In other words, the war really did not end for us until we were within a few hundred miles of Long Beach, California, home of the San Pedro Naval Base. By that time it became real for us: the Navy had announced its "separation" plan which was the point system that determined the eligibility of each officer and enlisted man to be released from active duty.

We had a remarkably stable group of officers on the *Manatee*. Of the seventeen officers on board when we returned, fifteen had been with the ship from the day it was commissioned in April 1944.

The most important statistic was that ten of us were already eligible to go home as soon as we arrived in Long Beach.

The *Manatee* was scheduled to be in dry-dock for about four weeks. With ten of us eligible, had we chosen to go home immediately the other seven would not have been able to have more than one week's leave. Therefore all ten of us agreed to stay with the ship so all the other officers could have three weeks leave before returning to sea again with the *Manatee*.

When we docked at San Pedro we received a stirring dockside welcome – the kind you see in the movies. THRILLED! WE WERE HOME!

HOLLYWOOD WELCOMES US

The first thing I wanted to do when I could get off the ship was call home, talk to Deenie and my parents and hear a gurgle or two from Marianne, who was almost a year old. It was joyful, delightful and wonderful.

I remember the food I craved was: fresh milk and ice cream. Our ship schedules were very relaxed. We had enough deck officers so that we only had the officer of the deck duty every fourth or fifth day.

That meant we could be gone from the ship on liberty overnight without having it count against accumulated leave.

This was important because, upon separation, we would be paid for any leave not taken and I had accumulated something like 45 or 50 days.

At sea the only entertainment we had was movies. I vowed if I ever got close to the motion picture capital of the world, Hollywood, a visit there would become top priority.

I had a good entrée. My former shipmate, Emmett Davis, had visited there when he was on his way to communications school in Annapolis and stayed at the home of Otto Preminger, a top director at 20th Century Fox.

With an invitation in hand to a Masquers Club reception and dinner, Doc Straub, a fellow Penn State alumnus and I took off for Tinseltown. Upon arrival I placed

Otto Preminger

a call to the studio for Otto Preminger. I told his secretary I had just returned from the Pacific and was trying to locate Lieut. Davis. Preminger came on the phone immediately, did not know where Davis was but invited us to be his guest the next morning at the studio.

At the Masquers Club that night we had our picture taken with our host, Charles Coburn, a cigar-smoking, monocled, character actor who left Broadway for Hollywood in 1937 and appeared in 72 movies after the age of 60. We also met the headliner of the evening, Jose Iturbi, Spanish pianist who had just starred in the 1943 Musical "As Thousands Cheer."

Also, I met an Army colonel I had played soccer against at West Point. He said that, because of our long unbeaten record, the chance to beat us was more important to them than trying to beat their traditional rival, the U.S. Naval Academy.

CORNELL WILDE AND LINDA DARNELL

Otto Preminger had a car waiting for us at the 20th Century Fox gate with instructions to take us to the set where he was directing "Centennial Summer," a costume period piece set in 1877 Philadelphia.

The cast included Cornell Wilde, Linda Darnell, Jeanne Crain, Walter Brennan, Constance Bennett and Lillian Gish. We met all who were there. Preminger asked Cornell Wilde and Linda Darnell, not in the scene they were shooting, to be our guides, to show us around the studio. They were very gracious to us.

Otto Preminger's head script girl took us to lunch at the studio commissary. She had reserved a table next to Victor Mature, June Haver and Peggy Cummins, the British actress who had just been imported to play the lead in "Forever Amber."

However, when Otto Preminger was chosen later to direct "Forever Amber." He picked Linda Darnell to play the part.

That afternoon they were changing scenes on the Preminger stage, so we took a sightseeing tour of the giant outdoor sets—farm yards, country estates, blitzed London, the watery streets of Venice, acres and acres of man-made replicas of every description.

Before we said our reluctant good bye we watched a rehearsal for "Kitten on the Keys," starring Maureen O'Hara, Dick Haymes, and Harry James Orchestra. (Unfortunately Harry James's wife, Betty Grable, the No. 1 World War II Pinup Girl, was not there for us to ogle.)

We concluded our Hollywood visit by going into a nightclub on Sunset Strip and catching the comedy routine of Ben Blue and Slapsie Maxie Rosenbloom, a former fighter who turned thespian. He still holds the all time record of 106 fights while World Light Heavyweight Boxing Champion.

The picture of Dr. Charles W. Straub, Class of 1926, and Gazzy Green, Class of 1941, with Actor Charles Coburn standing between them appeared in the *Penn State Alumni News*. Both the Doc and I had returned to our families in Central Pennsylvania before the story appeared in April, 1946.

CHAPTER FOUR

FAMILY HOMECOMING

On November 1, 1945 I bade farewell to my ship the *USS MANATEE* that had been home to me for 18 months and to my friends. In the evening I boarded my first commercial plane for an eight-hour overnight flight from Los Angeles to Pittsburgh, with stops in Albuquerque and Chicago.

In Pittsburgh I transferred to the Pennsylvania Railroad for a two hour trip to Altoona, where my family had come to meet me. When I arrived, there standing on the platform were my Mother and Dad, plus my beautiful wife, Deenie, holding this gorgeous baby girl Marianne, five days short of her first birthday.

What a HAPPY, HAPPY DAY!

Marianne sat on my lap for the 40-mile trip to State College, facing me, staring at my face and playing with my nose. She was just learning to walk, so when we arrived home she was ready, with a little prodding, to show me. She was so cute. She would take about three or four steps, then sit down, look up and say, "OOPS".

We had never had alcohol in our home while I was growing up, except for the one time Bill brought home a bottle of wine at Christmas when he was out of school and working. I remember my father taking a healthy swig and then feigning dislike by saying, "That's awful."

And Baby Makes Three. Joyful homecoming in November 1945 to meet Marianne Wickersham Green five days before her first birthday.

But Dad's surprise for me when I arrived home was that he had gone out and bought some beer and put it in our refrigerator to get cold.

When I started in college, Dad said to me, "I am not going to tell you not to drink because I know you will. I am going to ASK you not to drink anything except beer. And I did not." I honored him, and he rewarded me.

Deenie, Marianne and I had our own home. It was a one-bedroom apartment with living room, bedroom, kitchen-breakfast area, and a bath. It was cozy and convenient, across the hall from my parents, and a three block walk to downtown State College.

It was the first day for a very grateful family beginning a new life together.

ST. ALBANS NAVAL HOSPITAL

In high school I lettered in three sports – soccer, basketball and tennis. Of the three, I always considered tennis to be the safest, until many years later, when I fell and broke my elbow playing tennis in Florida, and then when I stumbled and broke my hip after we moved to Sun City.

Until that time the only broken bone I ever had was my nose-from playing basketball. The resultant deviated septum has plagued me all my life. The air intake through one nostril is fine, but through the other is very limited.

My good friend Doc Straub suggested that a sub mucous resection, a minor surgery, could correct this defect. He thought perhaps I could get it done at the Navy's expense before I went on inactive duty. With the cooperation of Captain Smyth they wrote my orders, upon leaving the *Manatee*, to report to the U.S. Navy Hospital at St. Albans, Long Island, for examination.

My five days travel time permitted me first to go to State College, on to Deenie's home in Rutherford, New Jersey, then to St. Albans. When the doctors there examined me, they decided my problem was not serious enough to merit surgery.

My orders were re-written to send me to the nearest separation center in Manhattan. The next day I was placed on inactive duty, FREE to return to civilian life, FREE to take Deenie and Marianne home to State College.

When I left college in June 1941, I needed about 30 credits to graduate. During the last few months aboard ship I took two correspondence courses, which were completed when I passed the written exams at Penn State.

These credits were added to my math course from Boston University. Then, I was delighted to learn that I was entitled to credits from Midshipman School at Notre Dame as being equivalent to advanced ROTC. Now, beginning February 1, I would be able to finish in one semester.

I took five required courses totaling 15 credits, got four A's and one B, made the Dean's List, and had the highest average of any senior male business administration student that semester. You would think I got religion. I had.

I had learned to study and now had Family Responsibilities.

LESSON IN HUMILITY

My good friend Ridge Riley, for whom I had worked when he was Director of Sports Information at Penn State, had been named Assistant Alumni Secretary and would soon become Executive Director.

Deenie and I had saved a little money, and I would attend school on the GI Bill so financially we were fine. But I had always worked while going to school, and I wanted to get back into the swing of things again.

Ridge and I had corresponded through the war so I went to talk to him about working for him again. When I approached him he was very friendly and cordial, but he questioned me for about an hour and then said, "I'm not sure what we might have available. Let me think about it, and you come back tomorrow morning at eight o'clock."

I reported on time, and he was waiting for me. He took me over to a desk facing a wall and had me start folding and stuffing envelopes. He showed me where to get more when I was finished. He told me to take an hour for lunch and come back at one o'clock. Nobody spoke to me until five o'clock when Ridge asked me if I wanted to come in again the next day.

Day 2. Same as before. Nobody spoke to me other than to say good morning. I went to lunch by myself, but when I returned, Ridge came over and said he wanted to talk to me.

We walked over to his desk and, with a big smile on his face, he said, with an outstretched hand, "WELCOME BACK." He then explained what he had been doing.

"I grew up in Annapolis," he said, "And I knew so many Navy Officers who became just plain LAZY. I just wanted to make sure that had not happened to you.

"Now, here is what I want you to do," he continued. "I am going become Executive Director of the Alumni Association in July.

"I want you to take over responsibility for Editing the *Penn State Alumni News* for the next four months so I can travel and spend my time visiting and organizing District Alumni Clubs."

JENNY LIND BED

Deenie slept in a beautiful solid maple Jenny Lind bed growing up as a child in Rutherford, New Jersey. When I returned home to State College from the Navy, I learned that her Jenny Lind bed was in our bedroom and that was what we would be sleeping on for the next several months.

It was a lovely bed. There were no such things as king- or queen-sized beds in those days. While the Jenny Lind was not a full-sized double bed, I had been told it was a three-quarter size. It was comfortable. We were young, very much in love, and it was fine.

It was the only bed we had until we moved into the Veterans Housing Project in Altoona after I started to work for Procter & Gamble. It was at that time the solid mahogany bedroom suite Deenie had purchased was delivered. Marianne graduated from her crib to the Jenny Lind bed.

I can't recall much, if any, discussion about the Jenny Lind bed until about three years later after we had moved from Altoona to Philadelphia to our new home in Camp Hill. It was then we decided it would be nice if Marianne and Adene could have twin Jenny Lind beds.

We visited every furniture store in Central Pennsylvania looking for a three quarter size Jenny Lind bed but to no avail. Finally we learned we could special order one from Sears Roebuck in Chicago.

Our whole family was excited anticipating the delivery. Finally the three quarter size Jenny Lind bed arrived. We had it delivered to the second floor bedroom that Marianne and Adene would share.

We uncrated it. The solid maple wood was almost a perfect match with the Jenny Lind bed Deenie had slept in growing up in New Jersey, We were delighted and all excited as we assembled the new bed, set it up in place and stood back to admire the two matching beds now in place.

Imagine our shock when we discovered the new bed was much wider than the original bed we had slept in all those months.

Deenie's original Jenny Lind bed was a twin-sized (SINGLE) bed. No wonder it had been so cozy.

MY LAST SEMESTER

I would consider February to June, 1946 to be the four most productive months of my life up until then.

Not only did I complete my schooling, I was a responsible husband, a father and did a credible job working for Ridge. This was important because I was about to start my business career, and the new Penn State Placement Director, George Leach, had been hired while I was in the Navy.

Ridge took me to Leach's office to introduce us to each other and to give me a real boost to get me jump started. George took me under his wing immediately. This was the start of our relationship that became very close and then mutually productive for many years as I progressed in my career.

The first suggestion George made to me was that he would schedule a couple of interviews with recruiters just to give me some experience. He told me not to worry about anything—just be myself, and that he would find out after the interview what kind of impression I had made.

After counseling me, he said he would select only those companies that offered the best opportunities for me. I was not sure what I wanted but I knew it was in the areas of sales, sales promotion or advertising.

Then, George called me one day and said Procter & Gamble was coming that afternoon and wanted to talk with the "five best applicants we have". He wanted me to meet a Mr. Jim Rogers, whom he described as a top-notch P&G Sales Manager.

Rogers was impressive, a big aggressive former football player. I knew he was interested in me, but his questions were disarming. Do you belong to a fraternity? Answer, yes. Are you president of your fraternity? Answer. No. Why not? Answer, I am a town boy; I don't live in the house. If you did, would you be president? Answer, I am not sure I would be president, but I would certainly be one of the officers.

Sixty-Four Thousand Dollar Question: If we interview 40 men, and we can hire only one, why should you be that one? Answer: Because I have been successful in everything I have ever done and see no reason why I should not be successful in Procter & Gamble. RESULT: I WAS HIRED!

STUDENT VETERAN'S SOCIAL LIFE

In the spring of 1946, I was in the vanguard of veterans returning to college. The massive influx did not come until the fall of 1946 and in 1947.

We veterans were still almost novelties on campus. In my fraternity, Phi Gamma Delta, for example, there were only about four of us who had returned, and we were treated with great respect.

It did not take me long to realize how much I had changed from an 18 or 19-year old kid to a 26 year old man. The beer parties, the student hi-jinks that had been so much fun were no longer relevant.

I followed in my father's footsteps and became a Mason, but my time in that organization while in State College was too short to be really meaningful. I also joined the American Legion and Veterans of Foreign Wars but, basically they were just bars, and I spent very little time there.

Instead, I renewed my friendship with one of my best friends from before the war, Jim (Wiff) Long, who returned from the Navy just before I did.

Wiff had been an engineering officer and had married a girl from New England he had met when he was studying at MIT. She was a Spanish senorita, a black haired, dark skinned part-Cuban beauty named Perlita, but known by her nickname "Dart", acquired from dating boys at Dartmouth.

We had much in common with Wiff and Dart. We all drank beer and loved to play bridge. They had two boys, Billy and Keith. We had our Marianne. They had a new starter home. We had a cozy apartment. We spent many wonderful evenings together. Wiff, a trained metallurgist, had gone to work for the Titan Metal Company in Bellefonte. I was eager to start with P&G.

I had to begin by July 1 to qualify for a year-end Procter & Gamble bonus. That presented a problem. I would have to skip my graduation ceremony if Deenie and I wanted to visit her family before I started my job. I was afraid to tell my mother. She had said many times, "I just want to live to see you graduate."

Mother's response when I told her, "Oh, you just go to Rutherford. I don't care about going to the graduation. I just want you to graduate!"

CHAPTER FIVE

ABOUT TO BECOME A SALESMAN

My instructions were to meet Joe Keeley at 6:00 Sunday evening at the Penn Alto Hotel for dinner. A room reservation had been made for me until Friday.

Altoona was 40 miles west and, with a population of about 80,000, the nearest big city to State College. When we were growing up, it is where my parents took us at Christmas to Gable's Department Store to see the trains.

Altoona was a one-industry town, home of the maintenance shops of the Pennsylvania Railroad, located in the center of the main business district. The time was 1946, before we had an Environmental Protection Agency.

After I had been a salesman there for a year, my big boss, Jim Rogers, the man who hired me, came up from Philadelphia to work with me. He said, "Gaz, if you can't sell soap here you will not be able to sell it anywhere. ALTOONA HAS GOT TO BE THE DIRTIEST CITY IN THE WORLD."

Not only did the railroad run through the middle of the city, downtown Altoona lies in a valley. All of the train engines were coal burning and exhaled huge clouds of smoke. It was usually necessary for automobile drivers to use headlights until the smog burnt off around noon.

Procter & Gamble was famous for the thoroughness of its training programs. My first lesson, that Sunday evening, was the importance of planning, so that when we called on our first grocer at 8:00 Monday morning we would have a clear outline of our objectives and how to accomplish them.

As we approached our first store, my trainer, Joe Keeley, said we would review our objectives, that he would make the presentation to the grocer, and then after we returned to the car, we would review the call. I started to learn the paper work, wrote the order, and listed it on the daily report.

We repeated this for every call the first day. The intensive training continued that evening as we reviewed everything we had done and devoted two hours to planning our calls for the second day.

WELCOME, GAZ, TO THE P&G TRAINING PROGRAM.

MY FIRST SALES CALL

As we started the second day of my sales training, my trainer, Joe, told me we would alternate calls this morning. He would take the first, I, the second, etc. That way we could critique each other's presentations.

We made about six calls before lunch, allowing plenty of time for discussion. Joe was very helpful. He was an experienced salesman who had returned from military service and was being groomed for promotion. He did very well, eventually, becoming a very successful Boston District Manager.

I really liked this method of training. It was designed to help the novice gain confidence which leads to success. After lunch Joe took the first call. We analyzed his presentation, then reviewed my objectives for the next grocer.

As I got out of the car, Joe just sat there. "Aren't you coming in, I asked?"

"No," Joe answered. "You take this one by yourself."

I gulped, and must admit I had some queasiness in my stomach as I approached the store. Our call book sheets contained information about every grocer and, even though Joe had never been in this store, he handpicked one where the grocer was sure to be friendly.

What the call book did not say, however, was that this owner had only one arm. That, in itself was a shock to me. But while I was making my presentation to him he was butchering meat with a cleaver. So, here I am, nervous as can be, trying to sell soap to a one-arm man wielding a meat cleaver.

Is it any wonder I have an indelible memory of my first sales presentation by myself?

But the system worked. Joe and I spent almost every waking moment together for the rest of the week. We continued to alternate calls until Friday morning, when I took them all. Joe observed, made suggestions, but did everything to bolster my confidence.

The plan: I would be by myself the second week and then Paul Glennon, my Supervisor, would come from Philadelphia and be with me for three days.

DEENIE IS PREGNANT

Max Rettig became my Supervisor in September 1947. This started a lifelong friendship for our two families. Max was a real "man's man." He was from Connecticut, played quarterback at Purdue after Cheshire Academy and then was awarded two silver stars and three purple hearts in WWII.

Max served as a captain in the same infantry division in Germany as Dutch Janney, a major who, as New York District Manager for P&G then recruited Max to come to work for the Company after the war.

Max confided in me in Altoona that the company wanted to move me to Philadelphia but recognized that Deenie was pregnant, so they would delay the move until after the baby was born and things had gotten settled.

Deenie's mother had said she would come and stay with me and help me take care of Marianne, almost three years old, when Deenie went into the hospital. She timed her trip perfectly, arriving one day before Deenie went into the hospital to have the baby.

Our Marianne Wickersham Green was named for Deenie's mother, whose maiden name was Mary Ann Sutton before she married Luther Wickersham.

Deenie and I were so sure the second would be a boy and would be named for me, that we never even considered another girl's name.

My mother's maiden name was Mabel Adelaide Kreamer before she married my grandfather, William Stevenson. We had decided that we would never saddle a child with the name Mabel. There were too many popular ditties like "Mabel, Mabel Set the Table."

When Deenie's mother and I came home from the hospital after the new baby was born, the two of us sat in rocking chairs on the tiny front porch of our barrack and talked about names. I loved Deenie's mother. She was every inch a lady.

She told me about visiting her sister Edith in Salt Lake City, meeting a friend, Adene Southwick and always loving the name Adene. We had it!

ADENE STEVENSON GREEN b. September 18, 1947 in Altoona, PA.

MOVING TO PHILADELPHIA

When Max Retting was promoted to Unit Manager in Harrisburg he was renting a row house at 5337 Chester Avenue, out past the University of Pennsylvania campus in West Philadelphia.

Max and Martha had two girls Dianne and Debbie, almost the same ages as ours. They occupied the first and second floors and rented out the third floor. While Max paid $85.00 to lease the property and got $35.00 rent from the apartment, it still was tricky because he had to provide the utilities.

Max got permission from his landlord to let us take over his lease and told me he thought we could get more rent for the apartment. That later proved to true; we had no trouble getting $50.00 when we rented it again.

My new sales territory started in the Main Line suburbs of Philadelphia, Ardmore, Haverford, Bryn Mawr, and included all of Montgomery County out past historic Valley Forge to Norristown and Pottstown. It took me about 30 minutes to get from my home to the nearest part of the territory

Bud Wilson, my new Unit Manager, was about 10 years older than I and had also been a Navy Officer. He had been a salesman in this same territory before the war, was experienced, and knowledgeable, and enjoyed renewing friendships with grocers he had known for years.

Our big new product was TIDE, which in a very short time became the largest selling soap category product of all time. I was maturing, and learning, and soon was given the opportunity to train new salesmen.

We rented our third floor apartment to a wonderful couple, Joe and Barbie Mosher and their two little girls. Joe, a Brown University graduate was in the four-year Architecture program at the University of Pennsylvania.

A young MD, John Meehan, just starting his practice, and his bride, Dottie, rented the row house next door. We couples blended and formed very close ties. Deenie got pregnant; I got promoted, but did not have to move.

LIFE WAS GOOD!

GRAHAM IS BORN

My new title was Office Head Salesman. I reported directly to Jim Rogers, the District Manager and was available for any assignment he might want me to undertake.

Primarily, my responsibilities were filling in for salesmen who were sick or injured, interviewing applicants, and training new salesmen. I myself was learning the responsibilities to move up and become a Unit Manager.

Jim Rogers had a son. Bud Wilson, Paul Glennon and Dick Haag, the other Unit Managers each had a son. Then Gazexer Graham Green III was born on December 8, 1948 and I had my son. Max and Martha Rettig had their two girls, were expecting a third child, but the baby had not yet arrived.

At the next Unit Managers meeting all of the aforementioned were wondering what Macho Max would say to me when he came in. It was a typical Max Rettig remark.

Instead of congratulations, he said, "What's the matter Green. Did you lose the touch? Anybody can have a boy. It takes a real man to knock the xxxx off of them before they come out."

We now were a family of five. Everything was fine except we were having difficulty making ends meet. Even though I had progressed in my career, and had been promoted once, my salary was still less than $300.00 per month, and we had depleted all of our savings.

Max knew I was getting discouraged. He told me to hang on; it was just a matter of time until I would become a Unit Manager.

And he was right.

Early in 1949 Bud Wilson was promoted and transferred to Cincinnati. Max came back to Philadelphia as Bud's replacement and I went to Harrisburg to succeed Max.

I COULD NOT HAVE BEEN HAPPIER!

TRADING FAMILIES

Kurt Rettig was born soon after Graham. Max had his son, and we again had similar families: GIRLs, Dianne & Marianne; GIRLs, Debbie & Adene; and BOYs, Graham & Kurt. Their mothers, Deenie and Martha, had become very close friends, nursed their babies together and our families bonded.

Since I was going to Harrisburg, and Max to Philadelphia, to work, and we had similar families, we could save money by Max moving in with my family, sleeping in an extra bedroom, and I would do the same with Martha and his kids. We decided that breakfast only we would have "at home".

Both Deenie and Martha agreed to the plan. Our boss, Jim Rogers thought it was a brilliant idea. He saw how much money it would save the Company in hotel bills until we relocated our families. So, Monday through Thursday, for a couple of months, we just exchanged families.

Max was looking to buy a home on the Main Line outside Philadelphia and finally found just the house he wanted in Wayne. Meanwhile, my Dad, who did not have very much money, told me he could borrow money on a life insurance policy and loan me the money for a down payment on a house to help us get started.

Dad went house hunting with me. I valued his judgment and advice. We found a three-bedroom home in a new development, at 6 Village Road Highland Village, Camp Hill, one of the nicest suburbs of Harrisburg on the west shore of the Susquehanna River. With $2,000 down and a Veterans Administration Loan. I could meet the purchase price of $12,500.

The house was perfect for us. It was the largest house in this section of about 30 homes. The initial owner, who lived there one year, had added a patio and completed all the landscaping. We were in a neighborhood of young couples with lots of children. We had a wonderful yard for the kids to play in.

Up at the corner, a half block away, the United Lutheran Church of America had built a mission church with Rev. Arthur Neal, a young, aggressive minister just out of Gettysburg Theological Seminary, in charge.

Rev. Neal visited us and literally grabbed Deenie and me by the scruff of our necks and got us involved in his church. It was a mutually wonderful move.

I HAVE TEN SALESMEN

In my first responsibility as a Sales Manager, I had ten salesmen headquartered in Lancaster, Lebanon, York, Harrisburg, Carlisle, Chambersburg, Altoona, State College, Williamsport and Sunbury.

They ranged from brand new to very experienced. I could always remember when the oldest, Russ Thomas in York, started with the company—February, 1920—because it was one month before I was born.

Some of the others I knew quite well: Sam Stringer in State College had become a good friend. Before I left Altoona I recommended Joe Weber, a neighbor, and he was hired. Likewise Bill Budinger in Williamsport whom I had known at Penn State. I had given the initial sales training to Jim Shimp in Sunbury and Don Whipple in Lebanon.

The biggest problem I had was following Max Rettig. It was like the football coach who succeeded Vince Lombardi. The salesmen idolized Max and I was not Max! I took over a unit ranked second out of fifteen in March and managed to manage it all the way down to fourteenth by December.

Then, as we started the New Year, I decided I had to be myself. The company always gave us strong promotions for January to get us off to a good start. I set as the goal for our unit to sell and ship 80,000 cases in January, double what our average had been per month for the previous year. This included my target of 10 new 1,000 case Carload Accounts.

Then I assigned all salesmen their personal objectives, showed them how I felt they could sell the initial carloads and told them not to take any order from any potential account who did not buy the carload on the first attempt. "Call me, " I said, "I will then come and help you get the carload order.

Just before we got off the train in Harrisburg when we returned from the District Sales meeting in Philadelphia, Joe Weber said to me, "Gaz, I think we're going to have a big month in January."

I replied, "Joe, I know we are going to have a big month. If we don't, there are going to be some new faces around here, and mine is not going to be one of them."

That message got around fast. We missed our goal by 2,000 cases. The one salesman who did not follow my instructions chose a new career path.

RECRUITING AND TRAINING

In fiscal year 2005 Procter & Gamble generated 30 billion dollars in profit. Compare this with the company I started with in 1946 when total worldwide sales, not profits, total SALES were $350,000,000.

One of the reasons I was so attracted to P&G was that all promotions came from within the Company. Everyone started at the bottom of his department and worked his way up. Jim Rogers, who had hired me told me the greatest contribution I could make to the Company was to recruit and train.

I hired and trained a couple of real hotshots when I was in Harrisburg, both out of Dickinson College in Carlisle. In my mother's family, Dickinson was THE college. It was a small Methodist school, and two of her brothers went there. Uncle Chalk graduated first and then Uncle George, State Senator in Pennsylvania for 26 years, who also received his law degree there.

The two hotshots I hired were Hank Lehr and Harry Diffenderfer. Both worked for me as salesmen and later as Unit Managers. Lehr remained with the Company, retiring after many years as District Manager in Baltimore.

I always enjoyed having sales people around me who were creative. One of my favorite memories was when we introduced JOY, the liquid dishwasher detergent. Diffenderfer had grown up in Duncannon, a little town 18 miles north of Harrisburg where the Juniata River flows into the Susquehanna.

Diffenderfer had made the arrangements, and we were all set to have the Volunteer Fire Department in Duncannon put Joy into their high speed nozzles and cover the Juniata River with suds.

Our plan was to have TV Cameras, Life Magazine and Associated Press Photographers line the banks of the Susquehanna River and exclaim, "JOY COMES TO HAR-RISBURG!"

Just before we were going to execute the plan I thought maybe I should call my boss and see if he could have any objection to it. ALL HELL BROKE LOOSE, and I learned the importance of getting approval in a big corporation.

GIANT SALES OF GIANT TIDE

When Hank Lehr was Unit Manager, he lived in his hometown of York. Harry Diffenderfer had the same position and lived in Wilkes Barre. Gordon Smitley, also a very creative guy, headquartered out of State College.

Our Company had put a special merchandising allowance on Giant Tide for six weeks. I loved to sell Giant packages because it took so few sales for the volume really to add up.

I mentioned to each of these three that when I was a kid it had been customary for the circus advance man to give two free tickets to every store that would put a poster in the window.

Lehr picked up on the idea immediately. The York Interstate Fair was the seventh largest annual fair in the United States. We talked about offering to promote the York Fair throughout 40 counties of Pennsylvania and Maryland, the two states from which they drew their following.

Lehr scheduled a meeting with the Board of the York Fair to make his presentation. He told them, "We will get promotional material promoting your fair in 90% of the grocery stores. The only place a woman goes more often than the grocery store is the bathroom. We would get the material up for you there if we could. We will do the next best thing."

"All we need from you are the free tickets to give to grocers for putting up your materials which state Tide Promotes
the York Interstate Fair," Hank told the Board Members. They
loved the idea. Our Tide brand people also loved the idea
and produced special materials for us.

We offered two free York Fair tickets to every grocer and
every supermarket manager for every ten cases of Giant Tide
they put on display along with the Fair promotional material.
Our goal: 50- to 100-case displays in big stores.

IN ONE MONTH WE SOLD THE EQUIVALENT OF
NINE MONTH'S NORMAL VOLUME OF GIANT TIDE.

Diffenderfer's father-in law owned a drive-in-theater and
said ticket sales only paid for the movie rental. He said HIS
PROFIT CAME FROM THE CONCESSION STAND. Free
movie tickets became the follow-up.

OUR FIRST TV

When I became unit manager my monthly salary was
increased to $350.00 per month. We also participated in the
Procter & Gamble profit-sharing plan, the second oldest in
corporate America. We could not get any of this until we
retired or left the company after ten years in the plan.

The big incentive for the sales department was the yearly
bonus, which was calculated on the basis of the district's ac-
complishments for the calendar year against sales quota. It
was paid in February and, because we could earn up to three
months salary in bonus, was greatly anticipated.

In the spring of 1949 television was still in its infancy.
There were practically no TV Stations outside major cities,
but WGAL-TV had gone on the air in 1948 in Lancaster, forty
miles from Harrisburg.

So, with our bonus we bought our first TV, a beautiful
10-inch (yes, that's right 10-inch) console model. Actually,
7-inch was the most popular size, but we splurged and
bought the larger model. We had a giant rotating antenna
on our roof to give us a clear picture.

I remember we were warned not to sit too close to the
screen or it would ruin our eyes. The recommended formula

was to sit back one foot for each inch of the TV tube size. If that were true today, I would be sitting at the end of my driveway watching Penn State football games on the 60 inch screen Graham helped my buy after Mutti (Deenie) died.

We had the ONLY TV set so all the little children in the neighborhood came in to watch cartoons. That meant Deenie had a daily diet of taking boots off and putting boots on for a bunch of kids, many pre-school age.

Tuesday night at 8:00 everything stopped so we could watch Milton Berle and the Texaco Comedy Hour. Professional wrestling also was big. There was not yet any national network TV.

Television was so new that the only station we could get concluded its telecast at ten o'clock.

It was such a novelty that sometimes we would just sit and look at the test pattern after the programs ended. And I swear that is the truth.

THE NEW HARRISBURG DISTRICT

Procter & Gamble was growing by leaps and bounds. In about 1951 the Philadelphia District, which had four Unit Managers and forty salesmen, was split into two Districts, each with three Unit Managers and about 24 salesmen. This was designed to achieve better trade coverage.

Jim Rogers, who had been my District Manager from the outset, was moved to Cincinnati to head a new division responsible for all specialty sales, including to United States Military establishments worldwide.

Max Rettig was named District Manager for the revised Philadelphia District and Jack Morgan, another man about the same age as Max and I, was appointed Manager of the new Harrisburg District.

While I liked Jack Morgan immediately, it was only natural that I would be disappointed to lose Jim Rogers, who was a giant of a man, both personally and physically.

Jim grew up in the steel making town of Steubenville, Ohio. He won a scholarship to Miami of Ohio where he played tackle on the football team quarterbacked by Paul Brown, the football legend who later coached at Ohio State and founded the Cleveland Browns who are named after him.

Jim was also president of Sigma Chi during the year, 1930, that his fraternity celebrated the 75th anniversary of its founding at Miami.

Rogers told me that, back when he was in college, Paul Brown was probably the most miserable SOB he had ever known. He said that as QB the only reason he stayed alive was that he was so small nobody would hit him.

Jim Rogers was a great leader and teacher. I had so much respect for him that I would do almost anything to please him. I knew he liked me, so I was shocked one day after we had been with a salesman, when he said, "Gaz, do you realize that salesman does not like you?

"I wouldn't either if you treated me the way you treat him," he continued. "You are picking at him. Don't ever pick at someone.

"When you need to give a man Hell, give him Hell so that he knows it."

JACK MORGAN—ALL-AMERICAN BOY

Jack Morgan was the nearest thing to the All-American boy I have ever known. He grew up in a Masonic orphanage in California. In high school he was all-Southern California end in football, state half-mile champion in track, and valedictorian of his graduating class.

He won a National Honors Scholarship to Harvard where he was all-New England end on one of Dick Harlow's great football teams that played a very competitive schedule. Academically, at the end of his junior year he was able to transfer into the Harvard Graduate School of Business.

Jack, as with so many of us, had his educational career interrupted by WWII. He was commissioned an Ensign and assigned to the Navy Supply Corps in Washington. After the war, he returned to the "B" school, as the Harvard Business School was known, and completed work for his MBA.

P&G Recruiters had found Jack and, since he was from Southern California, recommended him to the Los Angeles District Manager where he was hired to begin his career. With his background and ability he progressed rapidly.

Jack had met his wife, Ginny, daughter of a Boston lawyer, while he was at Harvard. They had two children, Steve and Nancy, a little younger than our three. Ginny was feisty, but levelheaded and fun.

We played bridge at each other's home almost every Saturday night, putting kids in their pajamas before we went out so they could go to sleep, and then we would pack them back in the car to go home at the end of the evening.

I was becoming impatient, and I am sure Jack suffered more than one headache trying to keep me satisfied until "My Opportunity" would come.

Finally we received word that Neil McElroy, President, and T. J. Wood, VP Sales, were coming to Harrisburg to have breakfast and work with me.

I had just enough time to get some huge super market displays of our products so I could show them stores, carefully selected at random.

It worked, and shortly after I was given a special assignment in Cincinnati.

P&G SPECIAL ASSIGNMENT

My assignment in Cincinnati was as special assistant to Dutch Janney, the Southeastern Division Manager. Everybody knew I was in training to become District Manager, but that was never announced in advance.

When I left Harrisburg I had to give up my Company car, so we had to go out and buy one. I had not owned a personal car since before I went into the Navy when I drove my 1929 Oldsmobile for which I paid $100.00. We found a paneled Ford Station Wagon a couple years old and were happy.

Upon arrival in Cincinnati I was given my schedule for the next five weeks. I would be at headquarters the first week, meeting various executives, being interrogated, attending brand marketing meetings, and being challenged.

I was given a list of four specific subjects to concentrate on. For example, determine the best arrangement for a super market soap department, the procedure to secure it, and how to replicate it.

T. J. Wood, VP Sales, gave me HIS personal challenge: He said I would be working with 20 to 30 of the best Sales Managers in Procter & Gamble and that if I did not learn at least SOMETHING NEW FROM EACH ONE OF THEM IT WAS MY FAULT. I was to report to him at the end of my trip.

WOW! What an assignment. Even to this day, more than 50 years later, every time I hear or read something new, I say to myself, "This has been a good day. I learned something new."

I was stimulated and had no problem until the last few days. Then I would constantly say to myself, "What have I learned from this person that is NEW?" Then I would dig in, think and ask, until I finally had my answer.

I was scheduled through Harrisburg, so I could have a weekend at home at the end of three weeks. It was the first time I had been away for more than two or three nights since I had been in the Navy.

Deenie and the children were there to meet me at the Harrisburg Airport. I remember Marianne saying, "Oh Daddy, I'm so happy I could cry."

The tears were running right down her cheeks.

PROMOTED TO DISTRICT MANAGER

In the summer of 1953 Procter & Gamble made an important announcement:

Max Rettig went on special assignment in Cincinnati to prepare to become sales manager of all bulk Fats and Oils; Jack Morgan became Philadelphia District Manager; Gaz Green was named Harrisburg District Manager.

It could not have been more perfect for us. The American Water Works Company, for whom Deenie's father worked as a sanitary engineer, had moved its headquarters from New York to Philadelphia. Her parents had purchased a lovely new home in Wynnewood on the Main Line.

Deenie was born in Harrisburg and had three aunts and three cousins living in the area; My Uncle Chalk and Aunt Nell also lived there and Uncle George, a Senior Member of the Pennsylvania State Senate, had his office just across the street from mine which faced the State Capitol.

My parents still lived in State College and we were going to continue to live about half way between our two families. This time I was again eligible for a Company car and had gotten a substantial salary increase. We could plan our lives on a more permanent basis and begin to look for a larger home.

One of my major responsibilities was college recruiting, which I enjoyed thoroughly. Within my district I had several of the finest colleges and universities in the United States including, Penn State, Bucknell, Lehigh, Lafayette, Dickinson, Franklin & Marshall and Gettysburg,

George Leach, the placement director who had recommended me to P&G, suggested that I attend a seminar sponsored by his counterparts at the above-mentioned schools. He then invited me to a lengthy after-hours bull session where I could get to know his friends on an informal basis.

This paid off handsomely for me. I had an inside track with many of them from that time on. Richard Flowers from Franklin & Marshall even arranged for me to speak to his entire student body on "Planning Your Career." I encouraged students to spend their summers working in the field they expected to enter upon graduation.

It was great for recruiting and excellent PR for P&G.

BENEFITING FROM A BAD ECONOMY

I have always been a positive person. Jim Rogers and Paul Glennon both had told me about their experiences of selling soap during The Great Depression of the 1930's.

Dutch Janney, my Division Manager, called me to say that he and the tough, crusty Vice President of Sales, T. J. Wood, would make a two-day trip to some of his Districts to talk with the field Sales Managers about business, which was horrible, the most difficult I had ever experienced.

He said they would fly in and have lunch with me and my Unit Managers, next Tuesday. The first action I took was to call a strategy session. I sent my Office Head Salesman, Clark Church, a Phi Beta Kappa from Dartmouth, to the Capitol Library to get economic data for coal mining, steel production, railroad maintenance activity, agriculture, etc.

Then I told each Unit Manager to be prepared to talk about how adverse economic conditions can help his business. Mr. Wood's first question played right into our hands. "Church," he said. "I understand you worked in Scranton. My brother lived there and hated it. What is so bad about it."

Clark Church, "I don't know, Sir, my wife and I loved Scranton. We made many friends there."

Then he asked each Unit Manager about his business. Harry Diffenderfer: "Well, as you know, Mr. Wood, there is a lot of unemployment in the coal mines. That helps us in two ways. When men are out of work they wear clean clothes and wives use more soap; retailers have trouble paying their bills and owe money to our competitors but not us, because we sell C.O.D."

Gordon Smitley: "I agree with what Harry just said. I have Johnstown and Altoona with the depressed steel mills and car shops. This helps our business because our competitors get discouraged and give up and we don't."

Hank Lehr; "I don't have the advantage of these bad economic conditions. But in spite of that we are doing well and will have a good year."

Janney told me later that we had scored a real hit. Everyone else gave them excuses. Wood raised Holy Hell in Pittsburgh that evening.

QUICK THINKLY

I was back at Penn State recruiting potential sales prospects for Procter & Gamble.

George Leach, the placement director had recommended me to P&G before I had my first interview, and over the years we had become very good friends.

While I was interviewing, George popped his head into the room and asked me if I had ever met Dr. Ossian McKenzie, the new Dean of the Business College, After determining I would be staying in town overnight he said, "Let me call him and see if we can get together at the end of the day and have a drink." He then reported to me a little later that the Dean had invited us to his home at 5:15.

When we arrived we learned he had also invited his new Assistant Dean, so the four of us had a couple of leisurely drinks to get acquainted.

After a while the Dean asked me, "Gaz, what kind of a man are you looking for?" "The straight A student?" "The Athlete?"

I responded immediately, that rather than any specific type like that, we are looking for a man who can QUICK THINKLY.

Then, I paused, and thought—that just did not SOUND right.

I looked at all three of the others and then concluded---
They have had as much to drink as I have.
Maybe they would just think they heard it wrong...

JOE DIMAGGIO'S CONSECUTIVE HITTING RECORD

On another recruiting visit to the campus at Penn State I bumped into an old girlfriend, Sally Tregellas Close just after I had finished having lunch at the Corner Room, an old and famous hangout. Sally and I had worked in the Alumni Office and were actually just really good friends. I refer to her as an old "girlfriend" because we actually did have a couple of memorable dates.

Sally was skinny as a rail, but I knew she had a rare talent that I could win a wager on every time she was in a group that did not know her. She could chug-a-lug a glass of beer faster than any man I have ever known.

The Saturday night beer party was a weekly event in the basement social room at almost every fraternity and every party had at least one show-off who was an easy foil for a bet. I don't know how Sally did it. She just leaned back, opened her mouth, poured it right "down the hatch" without even appearing to take a swallow.

Sally and I were both in Washington in the summer of 1941. This was the year that Joe DiMaggio was out to break the major leaguer consecutive hitting record. I followed DiMaggio's efforts closely and realized that if he kept his streak going I could see him when the New York Yankees played the Washington Senators at Griffith Stadium.

Sally was a baseball fan so we bought tickets well in advance, had box seats for June 29 to see the afternoon DOUBLE HEADER when Joe DiMaggio TIED and BROKE the existing record. As I recall he had six hits in eight times at bat! What is so remarkable about his record that finally ended at 56 consecutive games is that it was established in 1941 and no one has come within 12 games of it since that time. It may never be broken.

Sometime after World War II Sally married Bill Close from State College and went back to work at Penn State as Private Secretary to the President of the University, Dr. Milton Eisenhower, whose older brother Ike was President of the United States.

When we had our surprise reunion at the Corner Room, Sally said to me, "I am going back to the office now. I will check Dr. Eisenhower's schedule. Call me. I would like you two to meet each other."

DR. MILTON EISENHOWER

I called Sally Tregellas as she had instructed. She said, "I have a thirty minute appointment for you with Dr. Eisenhower from 3:30 to 4:00."

After Sally had given me the kind of introduction you could not buy, Dr. Eisenhower and I sat down to visit. He, too, like Dean McKenzie, was interested in what kind of men we were looking for in Procter & Gamble.

This was a subject I was delighted to discuss. Among the questions directed at me during my first P&G interview were, "Do you belong to a fraternity?" "Are you President of your Fraternity?" "Why not?"

After I had progressed into management I learned why.

My interviewer, my boss for six years, and the role model for my career, Jim Rogers had been President of his college fraternity and felt that when a man is elected leader of a group of his peers with whom he has lived for three or four years, he MUST have demonstrated leadership ability.

Why were fraternity presidents and other campus leaders not signing up for sales opportunities with

Milton S. Eisenhower

America's leading companies? When I asked young student leaders what they would like to do the most common answer was Personnel Work.

Why? My conclusion it was fear of failure.

My answer, if you have sales aptitude and proper training you can have a wonderful career in sales.

The best definition I have ever heard for selling is "getting another person to see your point of view."

INTEREST IN POLITICS

P&G had an excellent way of evaluating personnel. If you had eight salesmen, but could only keep one, which one would it be? If you could keep two, who would they be? The District Manager did the same for all salesmen and Unit Managers within their category.

Combine that with making a decision at the end of three years on everyone, "Will I be happy having this person working for me for the rest of his and my careers?"

I really worked at building a strong sales organization, and it paid many dividends. Procter & Gamble had very high standards. I found that if I set my goals higher than theirs, I would work harder and have much less stress.

One day Roy Wilkinson, Penn State lobbyist with the Pennsylvania State government, dropped by my office to see me. Roy was a very fine attorney from Bellefonte (where Marianne was born). I had known him and his younger brother for years.

I have already mentioned that I had met Dr. Milton Eisenhower, Penn State President, through his secretary, Sally Tregellas. I was not aware, prior to my visit from Roy, that US President Dwight W. Eisenhower was not happy with the Pennsylvania delegation in Congress. Roy was asked to start a grass roots organization dedicated to recruiting stronger candidates for the House.

This fit exactly with my interests. All my life I had been a strong Republican, and Pennsylvania had just elected a Democratic governor. Ike's ranch near Gettysburg was in my Congressional District. I welcomed the challenge to help and accepted Roy's invitation to be part of the core group. Dutch Janney said it was OK as long as it did not interfere with my work.

We had an organizational meeting with Dr. Arthur Flemming, who later became Secretary of HEW under Eisenhower, as our special guest. He was to be point man for the project and outlined our objectives.

I couldn't have been happier. Janney was easy to work for. He left me alone. I was relaxed. My job was going well. We were living in our dream house. I had a wonderful family, church and politics as outside interests. But, one thing you can be sure of – CHANGE IS INEVITABLE.

FOOD DIVISION CREATED

We had an annual worldwide management meeting in Cincinnati. Rarely were we called there for any other reason. We knew something important was going to happen when we District Managers were asked to come to corporate headquarters in the spring of 1954.

Procter & Gamble was known basically as a soap company. But they had been selling Crisco shortening since 1913 and, in becoming the largest supplier of fats and oils to the commercial baking industry, had built the most sophisticated research labs in the world.

With little fanfare P&G had developed a line of cake mixes that was far superior to anything on the market. In addition, one of the products developed in their labs that revolutionized the industry was an emulsifier that prevented the oil in peanut butter from separating.

To capitalize on unusual opportunities for growth, a whole new Food Products Division had been created. It would have a separate sales force, and the current national sales organization would be split. Initially, only a couple of areas were affected, but this was a MAJOR CHANGE.

Max Rettig had invited me to stay over after the meeting and spend the night (Friday) at their home with

Crisco—Better than butter for cooking

Martha and the family. Dutch Janney, his old friend and MY immediate boss, had been named Sales VP for the new Division, and this would fuel a lively discussion.

On the way home Max pulled over to the curb, stopped the car and said, "There is something I need to talk with you about." He proceeded to tell me that I was to be offered the position of Sales Manager in New York. They knew how happy I was and wanted to know if I would be willing to move.

I was SHOCKED. We had an almost ideal situation, had been in our Dream House less than a year and here we are talking about uprooting. Finally, I asked Max, "What would you do?"

He said, "I would take it. You will have the most important sales area in the Company. Everybody will know what you are doing."

I don't think a slept a wink that night.

ONE HUNDRED 20-YEAR OLD PINE TREES

They had cut down 38 twenty-year old Pine Trees when they built the home we purchased in New Cumberland. But they left more than one hundred of them still standing on the beautiful hillside acre we owned.

This was our dream house. The man who built it hand-rubbed the mortar between every brown mountain stone used in the three bedroom one-story ranch home and a similar two-room playhouse he built for his daughters. Matching stone pillars marked the entrance to the circular driveway.

Our home was eight blocks from where Deenie's mother, four sisters and one brother grew up. Her grandfather, a blacksmith, died at an early age but her grandmother held the family together. Deenie had fond memories of visiting "Grandmother's" home when she was a child.

After not being able to sleep all night when Max told me about the pending New York decision, I flew home to Harrisburg and broke the news to Deenie. Neither one of us slept Saturday night either.

I will never forget that Sunday morning, the two of us walking arm in arm up the hill through the pine trees behind our home asking what should we do? We talked about our children. Where did we want them to grow up?

We talked about our own lives. Deenie had grown up in suburban NY, had worked in the city and always talked about how exciting it was. I, on the other hand, loved being close to Penn State and could have lived in Pennsylvania for the rest of my life.

We could not discuss this with our parents. First, it might upset them, and second, it was not yet official and if the word leaked out that I had violated Max's confidence he and I both could be in trouble.

So we made the decision by ourselves, but definitely together. When we came to the conclusion that we were too young to turn down such an opportunity, no matter how difficult it might be in the months ahead until we got moved and settled, we decided we would go.

I called Max, who was pleased with our decision. Martha gave Deenie re-assurance. Exhausted but relieved, we slept well that night.

THE WAITING PERIOD

The next few months were frustrating. It is always a time of readjustment when you get a new boss. But, when you get a boss for whom you have no respect, it becomes very difficult. I won't tell his name because I don't expect to be saying anything complimentary about him.

Several young men, eventually including both Hank Lehr and Harry Diffenderfer, were on special assignment in training to become District Managers in the rapidly expanding new Foods Division.

Every one of these men came to Harrisburg for one day of their training and I would usually try to spend a half day with each. Several said they had seen my name on The Chart as District Manager designate for New York. I cautioned them that I could not talk about it.

The new National Soap Sales Manager was Jack Hanley, a fellow Penn State Alumnus whom I had known when we were in school before the War. The thought of continuing to work under "my boss" and Hanley, who had an immense ego, confirmed that my decision to go to New York was correct.

Unintentionally I got myself in hot water with Hanley a few years later. Bob Shetterly had become VP Foods Division and Hanley VP Soap. One day at lunch in New York, Shetterly asked me if I had known Hanley at Penn State. I said, "Yes, but not well. I said that when I was playing soccer I would see him around the locker room. He was cross country team assistant manager."

Shetterly exclaimed, "Assistant manager of the cross country team. How low can you get?" I knew I was in trouble. Shetterly went back to Cincinnati and told this story in the Executive Dining Room,

The next time I saw Hanley he said, "What the Hell did you tell Shetterly about my being manager of the cross country team? I played football."

Well, that surely was news to me.

This period may have been a lesson in patience for me. I knew that my new boss had been caught cheating in a friendly poker game in Cincinnati and he was less than forthright with me. It certainly prepared me to be suspect of all politicians you believe are not telling you the truth.

SAYONARA HARRISBURG

Finally, Chauncey Warren, the new Manager for the Eastern Food Products Division, came to Harrisburg. Chauncey was a graduate of Colgate, a contemporary and close friend of Dutch Janney and Jim Rogers, and had been promoted from District Manager in New York.

I had been with Chauncey socially several times, and of course had heard much about him from both Rogers and Janney. Also, Max Retting had worked with him in New York and told me quite a bit.

Of course, I knew why he was coming, and he knew I knew.

His opening remark was, "Gaz, I have something very important to talk with you about. We want you to go to New York and head up our sales operation there. This has been kept very secret. Only two parties knew about it—the Republicans and the Democrats."

He told me what my new salary would be. I had been forewarned by Max that it probably would no more than cover my increase in cost of living, so I was not disappointed. Max was right.

Twice I had received very generous P&G stock options while I was in Harrisburg. I was already vested in them and had ten years in which to exercise my options. These would assure our children of getting fine educations.

Bill Boggs was named my replacement. Bill had been a bulk products salesman and I was happy to see the company recognize his ability. They had transferred him over to the Soap Sales Division for added experience before moving him into management.

A big advantage for me was that Bill was coming from New York and was able to give me insight into the personnel I would be acquiring, particularly the Unit Managers.

I was to spend the month of September orienting Bill in the Harrisburg District and then report to my new job in New York October 1.

I was READY AND RARING TO GO!

FRIDAY NIGHT MEMORIES

In Harrisburg I was usually away from home two or three nights each week. I always planned to arrive home on Friday in time for dinner, and then during the evening Deenie and I would catch up on our week

As Secretary of the Board of Trustees of the Lutheran Church, I was the highest ranking lay person in the church. That was really no big deal, but our minister Rev. Arthur Neal was a strong leader and we willing followers.

I am not sure whether this was true of all churches in the American Lutheran movement, but we had Communion four times a year. The church had a pre-Communion service at 7:00 PM the Friday night before Communion Sunday, and our minister insisted that every Board member attend this service to set a good example for the congregation.

Having arrived home just in time for dinner, after a three hour drive, on this particular Friday evening, probably the last thing in the world I wanted to do was go to church. However I did, sat down and became relaxed. In fact I became SO relaxed that I fell sound asleep.

In the middle of the sermon I received a jolt in the ribs from a man I did not know. "I'm sorry sir," he said. "I hated to do that, but you were beginning to SNORE."

Another Friday night produced wonderful memories. Again, I had been away, and after dinner Deenie and I sat at the kitchen table, had a couple of beers, caught each other up about what was happening. We began to talk about how fast Marianne, Lois and Graham were growing.

This led into a discussion about whether we should have another child. Our first three were born within a four year period. The more we talked the more convinced we were that, Yes, we should have another child.

That discussion turned out to be one of the most important we ever had. It was on a Friday night about the middle of February in 1953 and it produced the happiest possible result. Nine months later, on November 19, our baby, Lois Winifred Green, arrived.

Violinist Lois Reiter now is a wife, teacher, mother, and an absolute joy!

DISHONEST SALESMEN

Oh what a learning experience it was for me when I became a Sales Manager. One evening I received a phone call from a grocer in Carlisle requesting that I come to his store the next day. He said he had some information about my salesman that he wanted me to have.

The salesman in that area was a very impressive young man, an army veteran graduate of Gettysburg College, married with children. The grocer confided in me that this salesman was "kiting checks."

I didn't even know what "kiting checks" meant until the grocer explained it to me. I don't think you can do it now with electronic check clearing, but back then you could write a check on a bank in one town and cash it in another and it could take three to seven days for it to clear.

Check kiting was to write a new check and deposit the proceeds to cover a previously written check for which there were insufficient funds to cover. True, the salesman was doing this and he was terminated immediately.

A second salesman, a friend from Penn State I had recommended, ended up working for me. Jim Rogers called and said something looked fishy on this man's reports and that I should investigate.

I drove to Williamsport, learned from his wife that he was working in Lock Haven, my birthplace, 26 miles away. I knew the location of the major stores. At 1:00 PM I found his car parked in front of a restaurant. Not there.

Next door was a pool hall. Subconsciously I knew I did not want to find him. Finally I opened the door and spotted him back at a pool table. After observing, I approached the table. He turned white when he saw me.

"Let me see your daily report for today," I said when we sat down in his car.

He handed me a blank report. A cash audit revealed he was short about $2,000.00. His mother bailed him out. He was terminated.

Happy ending! Three years later this former salesman and college friend was waiting for me at a big Penn State football game. He wanted to tell me how well he was doing. He had a good job with DuPont and no longer handled any money.

CHAPTER SIX

MALE MENOPAUSE

When we made the decision to accept the New York position, I had no idea how much affect the move would have on the lives of our family members and on my own life. This is one of the reasons I decided to write this book.

I loved my mother dearly, but she became such a victim of the depression that she was totally averse to taking any risk. If I had listened to her I would never have played any sport. She was always afraid I was going to get hurt.

Mother also, unconsciously I am sure, reduced my self-confidence as I was growing, rather than bolstering it. When two of my childhood playmates Donald and Philip White would come to my house to play, it was OK for them to act normal, but when going to their house, mother always cautioned me, "You watch how you act and what you say. Dr. White is on the faculty."

Dr. White and Mrs. White were always nice to me, except that if Don or Phil and I got into an argument their mother would always stick up for them.

If the same thing happened at my house, my mother ALSO stuck up for them.

I hope I kept my vow that I would never do that to any of my children.

As I reflect on my life, there is almost nothing I would change. If we had not moved to New York, Marianne would not have met Oscar; Adene probably would not have met Richard, even though Aunt Mary had gone to Vassar; Graham would not have met Carole; Lois would not have learned to say "y'all" in time to raise a Texas family fathered by Dr. Charles Reiter.

The male menopause, my change of life, began literally with the move to New York.

Every time Frank Sinatra sings, "New York, New York. If You Can Make It There, You Can Make It Any Where," I know how important our New York experience was to all of us.

I hope to share this with you through this book.

ARRIVAL IN NEW YORK

I arrived in New York October 1, 2004, ready to start the next exciting phase in my career. The Procter & Gamble Sales Office was at the corner of 3rd Avenue and 44th St, one block from Grand Central Station. I stayed at the Hotel Lexington at 48th St, five blocks away.

Returning to Manhattan brought back wonderful memories. First, my Dad taking me to Yankee Stadium in 1932 to see Babe Ruth, Lou Gehrig and all those great Yankees play the Boston Red Sox. Then at age 17 my trip to NY with George Zins when we spent six hours in a burlesque show.

My first two months were spent recruiting, interviewing and hiring to be ready for a December 1 startup of our new sales department. I would have three Unit Managers and 24 salesmen. Recruiting salesmen was top priority.

Two of my three Unit Managers, Harry Hoffman and Jay Goerk, were young Colgate graduates who had only been P&G salesmen for about a year, but had good previous experience. Jay had worked for Standard Oil of New Jersey and Harry had been an FBI agent under J. Edgar Hoover.

The third Unit Manager, Jim Rendall, had been shot down over Germany and interred in a concentration camp for about two years. He was solid and very dependable. I also had an Office Head Salesman, Bob Evans, who was very bright, so I felt really good about this nucleus.

The Office Manager in NY was a veteran, Holmes Miller, who knew the Company so well that he was able to give me invaluable help. He took me shopping for furniture and said, "Gaz, we have no budget limit for you, so we are going to get you the best furniture we can find." And he did.

For my office we bought a beautiful solid mahogany desk, a huge swivel chair with wine-colored leather and four matching chairs. Holmes gave me other interesting advice. He said that Chauncey Warren, his former boss, liked to lean chairs back and would get hair grease stains on the wall.

We selected a style chair that was impossible to lean back on. Chauncey was forever frustrated when he came into my office and could not lean back on the chairs. But we never told him what we had done.

DESI & LUCY

The move to New York changed our lives forever. and broadened the opportunity for growth for me personally, and for our whole family. It was EXCITING!

While I was living in Manhattan by myself I had many evenings free and could walk to the theater district in ten minutes. I learned that it was easy to get a single ticket at the box office for many popular shows.

I remember getting a seat in the fourth row for Victor Borge for his one-man show. I also had an excellent orchestra seat to see Jayne Mansfield in "Will Success Spoil Rock Hunter," the only Broadway show she did before she was killed in an automobile accident.

The most exciting event in my first two months, though, was having dinner with Desi Arnaz and Lucille Ball at the height of their popularity with their TV show, "I Love Lucy." They had made a movie, "The Long, Long Trailer" and the last stop on their national promotional tour was New York.

The P&G Toilet Goods Division was one of their TV sponsors. My good friend, Paul Flory, Division Sales Manager, had one extra ticket and invited me to be his guest at the Plaza Hotel private party. There were 24 total guests seated at six tables, four to a table plus one extra chair.

Desi and Lucy put on a little skit, then each rotated sitting for about 15 minutes at each table with waiters serving drinks and hors d'oeuvres. Lucy ended up at our table. Desi pulled up his chair and joined us.

Paul, his wife Caroline and I must have talked with Desi and Lucy for an hour or more. They were down-to-earth and delightful.

Desi was nothing like the dumb Cuban he played on the show. Lucy told us privately that he was the brain behind Desilu Studios and their whole operation, which included the production of other TV shows and movies.

Many years later when we started to go to the Chautauqua Institute programs we discovered that Jamestown, NY was Lucy's hometown. I visited her museum several times and relived the memory of that dinner.

BUILDING OUR BUSINESS

Our core product was Crisco, but we grew rapidly with the introduction of new products like Big Top and Jif Peanut Butter, Fluffo Shortening and the sensational Duncan Hines Cake Mixes which quickly outsold the previous industry leaders, Betty Crocker, Pillsbury and all others combined.

Procter & Gamble had designed a "state of the art" peanut butter plant for Bill Young, owner of the W.T. Young Foods Company in Lexington KY.

Young had built a very successful business by selling his Big Top peanut butter in promotional glassware to grocery chains throughout the United States.

In 1955 P&G bought W. T. Young. This provided our Foods Division with its first new product. We introduced Big Top in a 6-oz sherbet glass, a 9-oz. goblet and a standard 12-oz jar. The concept was for a household to collect a set of matching sherbet and goblet glasses through repeated purchases of Big Top in those containers.

Offering periodic promotional opportunities had worked very successfully for Young. When the P&G sales organization secured widespread distribution and merchandising support, sales were sensational at the beginning and for several months.

Then, almost without warning, the saturation point arrived. Sales slowed. Big Top sherbets and goblets on the shelf in stores began to collect dust and sales stopped. At this point son G. Graham Green III showed the sense of humor he was developing by referring to our product as BIG FLOP instead of Big Top.

Jif came to the rescue by becoming the first peanut butter introduced as a new product using the emulsifier P&G had developed that prevented peanut oil from separating and rising to the top of the jar.

Jif joined the Procter & Gamble tradition of having the No. 1 brand when it overtook Skippy and Peter Pan and became the leading-selling peanut butter throughout the United States.

P&G PUBLIC RELATIONS

Procter & Gamble was such an interesting company. If I were a historian I would love to write an in-depth account of what a fine company it was. I have often said that if I had never worked for another company I would have assumed all big companies were like P&G, and I would have been totally wrong.

P&G began in 1837. When I joined the Company in 1946 I believe R. R. Dupree was the first president who had not been part of the founder's families. He was succeeded by Neil McElroy who later became Secretary of Defense under President Eisenhower.

Neil McElroy

I have always been interested in public relations, and Procter & Gamble's approach to this back in the 1950's was very interesting. While most major companies were striving to be in the news, Procter's PR firm, Hill & Knowlton was challenged to keep the company's name out of the headlines.

The word "lobbyist" was not a familiar term. But P&G was well represented in Washington by Bryce Harlow who was well connected and highly respected.

When President Eisenhower decided to put major emphasis on education, Neil McElroy was named Chairman of the blue ribbon committee.

I've always thought Bryce Harlow was responsible for this appointment, which later led to McElroy becoming an international figure as Eisenhower's Secretary of Defense during the Cold War.

PRESCOTT BUSH'S NY APARTMENT

Jervis Janney, Chauncey Warren and Gazexer Green were three men who needed nicknames. Janney's was Dutch. Warren had none. I thought he could use his middle name. "What, and have people call me Archibald?"

One of my new responsibilities was the National Headquarters of A&P, the largest grocery chain in the United States. Janney had been District Manager in NY immediately after WWII. When he was promoted to Division Manager, Warren succeeded him, and then I came into the picture.

Janney, who played varsity football at Princeton, came from a socially prominent Baltimore family. His wife, Betty, was related to Connecticut U.S. Senator Prescott Bush and his Presidential offspring, son George Herbert Walker Bush and grandson, George Walker Bush, both of whom became transplanted Texans.

I can't remember whether Dutch told me they were the black sheep of the family because they went to Yale or whether he was the black sheep because he went to Princeton, It was one or the other.

In the spring of 1955 Dutch brought Betty to New York for a few days while I was still a "bachelor." They were staying in Prescott Bush's NY apartment. Chauncey also was in town. Dutch decided it would be a good opportunity for me to get to know their old friend Joe Mylott, head buyer at A&P.

What better way to do it than to have a few drinks, reminisce and share some war stories. After about an hour of swapping tales, Betty Janney got everybody in a good mood by talking about overhearing a long distance phone conversation Dutch was having one evening with Joe Mylott.

A&P had just decided the elephant pictured on our Jif Peanut Butter label bore too close a resemblance to the elephant on the trading stamps one of their major competitors issued to customers.

Betty said she was proud of her husband having risen through the ranks to become a Vice President of Procter and Gamble.

And here he was talking to another adult about what animal they would be able to use on a peanut butter jar.

DRINKING AT LUNCH

One of the promises I made to myself when I went to NY was that I would not get in the habit of drinking alcohol at lunch.

P&G did not go in for lavish entertainment so I rarely took a customer to lunch. Since nearly everybody commuted into the city from different areas, as Long Island, New Jersey, Westchester and Connecticut, inviting a client for dinner had to be for some very special occasion.

One of the veteran buyers at A&P National Headquarters, Bill Schneider, was one of the nicest guys you would want to deal with – when you had an appointment with him in the morning. I could not understand his change in personality when I had to see him one afternoon. Until…

Bill suggested we get together for lunch some day, and I said fine. The area around Grand Central Station had many good restaurants to choose from. I asked him where he would like to go and he mentioned one I did not know, but said that was fine with me.

It became obvious this was one of his favorite haunts when the bartender sent a drink over to Bill as soon as we sat down. The Maitre D' then asked what I would like. It was a very interesting lunch. Bill had been with A&P a long time and shared some of its history and his experiences with me.

Founded in 1859 by George Huntington Hartford, The Great Atlantic and Pacific Tea Company became the world's largest grocery chain, growing to more than 15,000 stores in the 1930's. It was a private company owned by John and George Hartford, who had no children, and wanted to groom their nephew, Huntington Hartford, to run the business.

Bill was assigned the task of training Huntington, a Harvard graduate, who had no interest in the business. He was a playboy. Bill told me he could not even get Huntington to get up in the morning to come into the office.

After inheriting the A&P money Huntington bought Hog Island in Nassau, changed the name and became the developer of Paradise Island in the Bahamas. That was much more interesting than selling groceries.

They just kept bringing Bill drinks—six before he went back to work!

AFTER ALL MY KINDNESS

The A&P Tea Company from about 1930 until the 1960's was the biggest retail grocery company in the United States.

Their headquarters were in the Graybar Building next to Grand Central Station in New York. You would not have believed their buying setup if you had not seen it yourself.

More than once I sat in their waiting room wondering how much the combined salaries would total of the supplier executives waiting to see one of the buyers. The system was archaic.

They had one long counter with as many as three buyers interviewing salesmen at one time. If anyone spoke loudly you could hear him all around the room. There were no secrets. There was no privacy.

I will never forget the time that Ernie Lass, one of the buyers, who was normally very cooperative with me, gave me such a hard time it was embarrassing to me.

The next time I saw him I said, "Ernie, one time I took care of our children when my wife was away. Marianne, my oldest daughter had been a big help to me, but in the evening I scolded her for something."

She started to cry and said, "After all my kindnesses this is the way you treat me."

I told Ernie that was the way I felt when he acted so mean to me.

It worked!

He apologized and I never had a problem with him again.

GRAND CENTRAL STATION

The description "as busy as Grand Central Station" is part of the American lexicon. It is an expression we have heard all our lives that conjures up a picture of hustling crowds coming and going, always in a hurry.

It was the busiest railroad station in the United States and the hub for commuters to Manhattan from wealthy suburbs of Westchester County and Connecticut. Though we had a Pleasantville address, I commuted from Tarrytown because of better train schedules.

Jackie Robinson, the Hall of Fame baseball player who broke the major league color barrier was still starring for the Brooklyn Dodgers when I arrived in 1954. I was fortunate to be able to see him play.

After he retired he became a Vice President of Chock full o'Nuts, a coffee company whose offices were near mine. The train Robinson came on from his home arrived at just about the time mine did and I saw him often. He was affable, approachable and always had had a big smile.

A&P Headquarters, on the 24th floor of the Graybar Building facing Lexington Avenue, had a direct entrance from Grand Central. My office was one block away.

One morning after I finished my meeting with Walter Sullivan, Peanut Butter and Cake Mix Buyer, I looked out his window facing west. Looking down on Vanderbilt Avenue, I saw a crowd of photographers in front of the Vanderbilt Hotel and a police escort in front of a caravan being formed. I realized what it was and made a hasty exit to the elevator.

I walked through Grand Central and up to the Vanderbilt Avenue exit. Just as I got to the curb the police escort and the first limousine stopped right in front of me, perhaps ten feet away.

The windows of limousine were clear glass. There, sitting in the back seat, were two of the most famous men in the world Nikita Khrushchev, First Secretary of the Russian Communist Party from 1953—1964 and Andrei Gromyko, Foreign Minister from 1957 to 1985.

Unfortunately, I did not speak Russian and could not understand them.

WINDMILL FARM

Deenie and I looked at homes from New Jersey, through lower Westchester County to Greenwich, Connecticut. After living in Harrisburg, everything was so expensive that we were getting discouraged.

Then we discovered a really neat, new area near Armonk, north of White Plains, built around a former estate called "Windmill Farm." It featured a lovely small lake and clubhouse for the residents. We found a four bedroom split-level floor plan that we loved. Also, it was one we felt we could afford.

The only problem was that we had not found anybody who thought our "dream house" in New Cumberland, PA, was their dream house. Procter & Gamble had not yet developed any plan to help transferees sell their homes.

Finally, after going to Windmill Farm several times, I had dinner with the developer. He offered to buy our home if it were not sold when our Windmill Farm house was ready for occupancy, about four months later.

Papers were signed and we thought we were all set – until about one week before we were scheduled to move. The developer backed out on the deal.

It was one of the biggest disappointments either Deenie or I had ever experienced. But when it was all over we realized a lesson hard to understand at first, but true: GOD HAD ANOTHER PLAN FOR US!

After our extreme disappointment, we rented a furnished house for the summer in Bronxville so our family could be together. Then God showed us the first part of his plan; He found a home for us to rent in Pocantico Hills.

A year and a half later Ken and Katherine Bassett, parents of Marianne's best friend Beth, invited us to become their new next-door neighbors. To facilitate this they offered to sell us the most beautiful acre of wooded land in Westchester County, perfect for us to build our home on.

We bought the plans for our Windmill Farm house, asked the people occupying it to tell us what changes they would make after living in it for 18 months, incorporated their changes, and built a better house for less money, in what turned out to be the most interesting neighborhood in the world.

GOD WAS RIGHT! HE HAD A BETTER PLAN IN MIND FOR US.

HOW I MET HARRY TRUMAN

We had been in an all-day meeting of district managers in New York. Actually it was the first of a scheduled two-day meeting at the Berkshire Hotel at the corner of Madison Avenue and 52nd Street.

There were about seven of us and at the end of the day we had reservations at Mama Leone's Italian Restaurant for dinner. On the way we planned to stop at Toots Shor's watering hole (bar) made famous by Yogi Berra of the New York Yankees who once said, "No wonder nobody ever comes here anymore. The place is too damned crowded."

Walking across town on 52nd Street it was commonplace to see limousines stop at the curb and discharge passengers. We were in no hurry, just strolling along, talking. I saw two women alight from a limo and walk across the sidewalk to the entrance of a restaurant.

The chauffeur was helping a gentleman out of the back seat of the limo and after he handed him his cane, I recognized who it was.

Turning to one of my companions I said, "That is President Truman. Let's go over and say hello."

This was after Truman had been President, but before John F. Kennedy *Harry S. Truman* had been assassinated, so there was no Secret Service protection around him.

Mr. Truman had just stood erect when I extended my hand to him and said, "Mr. President, I am Gaz Green. I would like you to meet some of my friends."

He answered, "How do you do. Mr. Green."

The others in our group had stopped walking so I introduced all of them to President Truman. Ernie Addy, Harry Diffenderfer, Jim Hooker, Don Chaney, Jack Sand and Chauncey Warren. Truman was very gracious.

I glanced over in the doorway of the restaurant and there were his wife, Bess, and daughter, Margaret glaring at him.

They were waiting for The President so they could go in to eat.

DUNCAN HINES CAKES

Another memorable event from my New York Procter & Gamble experience was the unveiling of the new line of Duncan Hines Deluxe cake mixes that were about to be introduced into test market in the Syracuse district. Six Food District Managers were involved in the introduction because of the need to get approval at A&P, First National, Grand Union, ACME and Food Fair chain store headquarters.

That meant some of my old cronies, Ernie Addy, Harry Diffenderfer, Jim Hooker and Hal Chaney would be coming into New York the night before the meeting. I agreed to stay at the hotel with them so we could be together in the evening.

We had a late supper, then decided to go out and have some fun. We did not get started until about ten o'clock. By the time we had hit our third or fourth club we all had probably had too much to drink. We knew our meeting was scheduled to start early in the morning, but the reality did not set in until we received our wake-up calls after about four hours sleep.

From our hotel we took a cab at 8:00 AM to the headquarters of the Compton Advertising Agency. Greeting us at the door were Bart Cummings, president of Compton, and Mark Upson, vice president of the P&G Foods Division.

We were whisked immediately to an upstairs conference room and were barely seated before we heard a drum roll, the doors flew open and with a flourish they rolled in a cart holding six freshly baked Duncan Hines Deluxe Cakes: WHITE, YELLOW, DEVIL'S FOOD, SPICE, FUDGE MARBLE and BURNT SUGAR!

We were expected to OOH and AH about the cakes with each bite we took

It is funny how you don't have exactly the same fervor for sweet pastries when you have just finished breakfast and are slightly hung over.

The remark that TOOK THE CAKE, literally, for me was when Mark Upson said, "Here, Gaz, you have not had any of the BURNT SUGAR cake yet."

No, I did not regurgitate. I liked my job too much.

BEN HOGAN, SAMMY SNEAD

In the 1950's a golf tournament that attracted 16 of the top professional golfers in the world was held in New Rochelle, NY, which was about 30 minutes from where we lived in Pocantico Hills.

This PGA tournament was sponsored by Goodall-Palm Beach Men's Clothing until discontinued after being acquired by Burlington Mills. This unique tournament was for 90 holes in four days, calling for 18 holes on Thursday, 36 on Friday, and 18 on Saturday and Sunday.

I decided to take a day of vacation that Friday, so Graham and I could go watch the morning round. It was perfect. We figured correctly that the crowd would be small in the early morning and then grow the rest of the day.

Sam Snead & Ben Hogan after the 1954 Masters

We arrived before play had begun and immediately went over to where Ben Hogan was practicing. I particularly wanted to see Hogan because he had been the professional at the Hershey Country Club where my Uncle Chalk was a member and claimed Hogan was the greatest golfer in the world.

This was the first professional golf tournament I had ever attended. I was amazed to see how closely you could follow the players. Graham and I walked down the middle of the fairway about five feet behind Sammy Snead and Dr. Cary Middlecoff, an MD turned professional golfer, who had his arm wrapped around Snead's neck telling him a joke. Suddenly they both burst into laughter.

Another of the top golfers we saw that day was "Terrible Tommy" Bolt, who was famous for his temper and his proclivity for throwing or breaking golf clubs when he hit a bad shot.

Professional golf then was nothing like it is today. I remember that just a couple of years before, the Harrisburg Open, an Annual Tour event, raised the $15,000 total prize money by getting 150 sponsors @ $100.00 each.

It was great for spectators. I doubt we paid more than $1.00 for our all-day tickets and we were right with the golfers.

Our description: UP CLOSE AND PERSONAL WITH THE PROS.

GRAHAM'S LOST TRUNK

Our new home was on Old Sleepy Hollow Road, Pleasantville, NY. This was interesting because it was the original road that connected Pleasantville to Tarrytown, which was where the Headless Horseman rode in Washington Irving's classic "The Legend of Sleepy Hollow."

While Irving's tale was fictional, he identified certain genuine landmarks in the story, based on his visits to the Tarrytown area as a boy.

Dee and Lois took violin lessons in Pleasantville from Boris Koutzen, a Russian violinist who had retired from a career with the Philadelphia Symphony and taught in a studio in his home. Koutzen also conducted the Chappaqua Chamber Orchestra and the Vassar College Orchestra.

Other than that, and an occasional meal in Pleasantville, most of our activities were in Tarrytown, where I commuted via the New York Central. Marianne and Dee, after finishing eighth grade at the Pocantico Hills School, went on to graduate from Sleepy Hollow High School in Tarrytown.

But, our mailing address was Old Sleepy Hollow Road, Pleasantville.

When Graham was about ten or eleven he sent his trunk home from summer camp via Railway Express. In those days, shippers were so dependable it was not necessary to insure items being shipped.

Graham had been home one week, then two weeks, and there was no sign of the trunk. I had been calling Railway Express in Pleasantville with no result. Finally, after three weeks, on a whim, I called Tarrytown Railway Express, and sure enough, it was there.

Graham and I went to Tarrytown to retrieve the trunk. The address label was as clear as it could be: TO: G. G. GREEN, OLD SLEEPY HOLLOW ROAD, TARRYTOWN, NY.

When I asked Graham why he had sent the trunk to Tarrytown, he said, "Daddy, I could not spell Pleasantville."

Lucky Tarrytown was not Poughkeepsie. We might never have found it.

JANE AND PETER CARLYLE

Jane Carlyle was a singer/actress who, like many theatrical people in New York, had other skills and worked as an office temporary when she was between shows. She came to work for me shortly after our family moved to Pocantico Hills.

Jane was a single mom with a cute little boy, Peter, who was about 11 years old. They lived down in Greenwich Village, which was a difficult area to raise a child, but Jane did a wonderful job with Peter. I got to know him because he often came to our office after school and waited until his mother's work was finished to go home with her.

Our Dee and Graham were just 15 months apart, and Peter was a year older than Dee. We invited Jane and Peter to come have Thanksgiving with us. It was the start of a wonderful friendship. Our kids loved Peter, and it was mutual. Jane said many times it gave Peter the family relationship he was missing.

Jane was a tall, good looking blond (or redhead, depending on her mood) who had been the "golden voice" of Minneapolis and had come to New York to further her career.

We had many enjoyable and memorable evenings together. When Jane and Peter came up for the weekend, we would invite friends, usually Les and Marie Scott and John (who sang in our church choir) and Dottie Baverstock and all get around the piano and sing. Mutti played the piano and Jane provided her fabulous soprano voice.

One song, which would guarantee much laughter, was a duet that Jane and I worked very hard together to master, "Indian Love Call."

This was one of the many songs that had been made popular by Jeanette MacDonald and Nelson Eddy, America's Singing Sweethearts in the 1930's.

Every time I tried to hit the high notes of "I'm in love with you, ooh, ooh, ooh," listeners would break up laughing. We never did get through the song.

WALDORF ASTORIA DINNERS

There were several national organizations supported by Procter & Gamble that met in New York every year such as National Manufacturers Association, Grocery Manufacturer's Association, Brand Names Foundation, etc.

Top executives from Cincinnati would usually attend and then go home before the final dinner. That was where Harry Faught, Paul Flory and I came in. We were the managers of the three major divisions of the company in NY, so they would give us the tickets and we would represent the company.

Every dinner had either a prominent speaker, name entertainment, or both. Drinks, lavish food, everything was free.

It was fun for a while, and then it became more of a chore. Work all day, go to dinner, catch a late train, not get home until midnight and have to go to work the next day.

I remember one night I had a couple of drinks before I got there, sat down at the table and picked up the program  to see what the entertainment would be. PAT BOONE, I said to myself loud enough that I startled the stranger sitting next to me.

Handing my program to him, I said, "Would you please autograph this from Pat Boone to my children?" And I gave him their names.

"Hey," he exclaimed. "That's a heck of a good idea. Would you do one for me to my children?"

"Of, course," I replied, and two sets of children were lucky enough to receive autographs, even though bogus, from Pat Boone, one of the most popular singers of the day.

Peter Carlyle was understudy for a child actor in a play starring Henry Fonda. He sent a program to Marianne, Dee, Graham and Lois autographed by Fonda.

Or, perhaps it was an artful imitation.

EXPLAINING FACTS OF LIFE TO GRAHAM AND PETER

Over the next few years Peter really became part of our family. He once lived with us for several months while his mother, Jane, crisscrossed the country in the touring company of a Broadway musical. Peter commuted with me to his regular school in New York and came over to the office after so we could go home together.

We had moved into our new split-level home on Old Sleep Hollow Road, and it was a perfect setup. Graham's room, with twin bunk beds, was on the lowest level, which included a large family room, the utility room and laundry, private bath and a two-car garage.

Our friend Les Scott had taken Graham and Peter fishing in a private lake on the Rockefeller Estate. By the time they returned home just before dark they were worn out and ready for bed.

Mutti went down to the utility room to iron some laundry. This is a discussion she overheard from the two boys in Graham's room:

Graham, "Pete, do you ever swear?"

Peter, "Uh huh, once in a while."

Graham, "What do you say?"

Peter, "Promise you won't get mad?"

Graham, "I promise."

Peter, "Like sometimes a boy gets me down on the ground and makes me mad I say, Oh s-h-i-t, shit."

There was dead silence and then Graham said, "You mean s-h-e-t, shet."

Peter, "No, no. It's s-h-i-t, shit, shit.

Graham finally agreed, "Yeah, you're right."

The real challenge, for me, came when Mutti and Jane decided I needed to talk to the boys about the facts of life. The three of us were alone in the car driving to Maine.

After the boys had listened attentively and silently to everything I knew about the birds and the bees I asked them if they had any questions. "Yes," said Peter. "You said I should get a jock strap. How would I know what size to buy?"

I went with Peter to buy his first athletic supporter. I don't think he took it off the rest of the summer. It was his mark of manhood.

OPENING NIGHTS

Twice while living in New York we were invited to an "Opening Night," once to the premier performance of a Broadway musical, the other time to the gala reopening of the Museum of Modern Art.

Don Ameche and Elaine Stritch starred in a lavish musical production in which our friend Jane Carlyle had a minor role. Jane was an important member of the cast as the understudy, or backup, to the lead. I remember her telling us that first time she played the lead role opposite Ameche he squeezed her arm every time he thought she was taking attention away from him.

On opening night the usher escorted us to our seats in the fifth row of the orchestra section. About five minutes later Peggy Cass, a well-known TV talk show personality, and her husband sat down next to us.

We were having a wonderful conversation with them

until the usher came back, asked to see their ticket stubs and moved them back several rows. Were we ever smug? Until the same usher came back, examined our tickets and sent us up to the balcony. End of feeling superior!!!! But, it was still very exciting.

The Museum of Modern Art was founded by the first Mrs. John D. Rockefeller, Jr., and upon her death Nelson became chairman of the board.

Peggy Cass

The Museum had been badly damaged by a fire and was closed for several months. Our neighbor and good friend, Bernie Jones, was superintendent in charge of the renovation. We were Bernie's guests opening night.

We really hobnobbed with the ritzy crowd that night. Nelson had not yet become governor but was also Board Chairman of Rockefeller Center and very prominent socially. Many members of the Rockefeller family were there. In particular, I remember Rodman pointing out to me that his younger brother, Michael, was there dressed in a tux and tennis shoes.

"That's just like him," said Rod.

LOOK SAD ENOUGH LONG ENOUGH

Lois, being five years younger than our other kids often seemed to get left out. For that reason, we tried very hard to include her, or do something special. When she about nine or ten we decided we would have a special "Lois' Day" in

New York watching the Ringling Brothers, Barnum & Bailey Circus in Madison Square Garden give their its performance of the new season.

Deenie brought Lois in on the train to meet me at my office, which by then was in the Crowell Collier Building at the corner of 51st and Fifth Avenue across from Rockefeller Center and from St. Patrick's Cathedral. Mutti took her to Best & Company to buy a new pair of shoes.

Then Lois wanted to see Renoir's "In the Meadow" at the Metropolitan Museum of Art. Mutti's father had died that year. Even though we were not Catholic she took Lois inside St. Patrick's Cathedral so she could light a candle in honor of Baba, as all the children called him. Lois' cat "Nosey" had disappeared and been gone from home for about two weeks, so Lois also lit a candle for her. Nosey showed up after Lois lit the candle?

Following dinner in a nice restaurant, we headed to the Garden for the circus. Anytime we went to an amusement park or did something special like this we gave each of our children an allowance.

For the circus we gave Lois $5.00 with the standard admonition: spend it any way you want but don't come back for more. Lois did not get past the sideshow before her money was all gone. When we found our section and were seated the vendors began hawking a Red Bulb Flashlight that every child should have. Lois looked at us painfully, but we shook our heads, "No."

After the first act they turned out the lights. The PA blared, "OK all you children now twirl your red flashlights to show your appreciation." Red lights were everywhere. When the white lights came back on, there sat Lois between us with her head looking down at the floor. Mutti and I could not stand it. We both tried to get a vendor at the same time.

Successful, we handed the red flashlight to Lois. She smiled and said, "I knew if I looked sad enough long enough, you would get it for me."

CAB CALLOWAY

Hi-De-Ho

I first heard Cab Calloway and his band at Hecla Park, near Bellefonte, when I was about 15 or 16 years old.

Cab Calloway—the legendary "Hi De Ho" man—was an energetic showman, gifted singer, talented actor and trendsetting fashion plate. A truly "larger than life" figure in American pop culture, immortalized in cartoons and caricatures.

He was a headliner at the Cotton Club in Harlem in the 1920's and played the role of Sportin' Life in the original Broadway production of George Gershwin's Porgy & Bess. He also led one of the greatest bands of the Swing Era.

Cab Calloway (Photo: William Gottleib)

It would never have entered my head that many years later he and I would have children in the same homeroom and attend a parents meeting together.

Nor would I have ever dreamed that we would celebrate the first election of Nelson Rockefeller as Governor at the victory party in the playhouse on the Rockefeller Estate.

It was at the victory party that Cab's wife, ZUELMA and I became kindred spirits by comparing "unusual" names when she learned my first name was GAZEXER. CAB, whose birth name was CABELL also contributed to the cause by naming their daughter CABELLA.

One of the things I respected Cab most for was his support of his children. He came to all his children's performances at the Pocantico Hills School. And, when his daughter Chris was a student at Sleepy Hollow High School in Tarrytown, and she had a lead in the school play "Our Town," Cab and Zuelma were in the audience.

Twice he donated his services free to the schools, paid his musicians scale, and played for high school dances at Sleepy Hollow. I am delighted that our daughters Marianne and Dee were able to see and hear this legend perform in person.

MAJOR LEAGUE BASEBALL

When we lived in Pennsylvania, Marianne, Dee and Graham all had school savings accounts at a local bank. The amount each had was something between $25.00 and $50.00. We withdrew what they had so we could open new accounts for them in New York.

Lo and behold, a bank in Tarrytown advertised "Two Free Tickets for a NY Giants vs. Philadelphia Phillies baseball game at the Polo Grounds." That was perfect for us. It could have been a scene out of "Cheaper by the Dozen" when I took the three children to open their accounts and collect their free tickets to see their first major league baseball game.

In those days you could buy good reserved seats to the Giants and Dodgers games at a reasonable price. I asked my Sunday School Class of 7th and 8th grade boys if they wanted to go to a game and received an enthusiastic "Yes."

I phoned the Giants' group sales director, told him I wanted to bring a Sunday School Class and found him to be very cooperative. He got us 12 reserved seats about 15 rows behind the visiting team dugout for a Giants-Dodger Saturday afternoon game. We had nine boys and three dads.

Gill Hodges

As soon as we arrived at our seats some of the boys went down to the Dodger dugout to get autographs. I told those who stayed to hand me their programs, and I would give them whatever autograph they wanted.

Everything was OK until one of the boys pointed out that I had spelled Duke Snider's name wrong. I had signed it Duke Snyder.

A very polite little German boy, Manfred Brunken, asked me, "Mr. Green, which one is Gil Hodges?"

I replied, "He's right down there, Number Fourteen."

"Thank you, sir," Manfred replied.

Then, turning toward the field, he shouted, "COME ON, MISTER HODGES!"

OTHER SPORTS MEMORIES

While I was still a 'bachelor' in New York, Harry Faught and I attended a big event in Madison Square Garden as guests of the New York Daily News, the sponsor.

This was an inter-city boxing match that featured the Golden Gloves Champions from Chicago vs. the Champions from New York. This annual event had been going on for several years and was the springboard for many amateur fighters to go to the Olympics or to begin their professional careers.

On the card that night was a 19-year old 175 lb. light heavyweight from Louisville, Cassius Clay, fighting for the Chicago team. He lived up to the tremendous buildup he had been given. He won handily that night and went on to win the Olympic Light Heavyweight Gold Medal.

As he matured and added some weight he fought as a heavyweight and now is considered by many to have been the greatest heavyweight champion of all time, fighting under the name of Mohammed Ali. Several years later we watched him train and defend his World Heavyweight title in Houston.

Graham and I had the good fortune to watch Mickey Mantle and Roger Maris when they were both trying to break Babe Ruth's record of 60 home runs in a season.

Cassius Clay aka Muhammad Ali

But the game Graham and I would never forget was the National Football League championship game between the New York Giants and Vince Lombardi's Green Bay Packers. Bart Starr was quarterback for Green Bay and the Giants featured running back Frank Gifford.

One of the Green Bay coaches was a friend of Jim Reid, who worked for me. Jim and his brother-in-law went with us, and we sat in the section reserved for the families of the coaches and players. The weather was horrible. It was +27 degrees when the game started and dropped to nine above.

156

A 30 MPH wind blew across the frozen field directly into our faces.

After the game, half frozen, we had to walk several blocks to our car only to find that the poor man parked in front of us could not find his keys.

At least we could get into our car, turn on the heater and get comfortable.

CLIFF SHILLINGLAW

One of our neighbors on Old Sleepy Hollow Road was Dr. Clifford Shillinglaw, an Iowa farm boy, the first of his family to go to college. Upon graduation from Iowa State University with a degree in AgBioChem, he was awarded a four-year scholarship to graduate school sponsored by the soft drink industry.

After receiving his PhD he felt he owed something to the industry and accepted a position with the Coca-Cola Company. Coke at that time was a one-product company. All of that was about to change, and Cliff made a tremendous contribution to the growth of the company.

When I first knew Cliff, he was vice president of Research & Development for Coca-Cola International. He was also president of the Board of Trustees of Union Church of Pocantico Hills when I first joined the board. He was also father of Ann Shillinglaw, best friend of our daughter Dee.

Tragedy came to the Shillinglaw family when Ann came home from school one afternoon and found her mother dead from carbon monoxide fumes in their garage. It was deemed an intentional suicide but Ann felt she was responsible, for not having looked hard enough for her mother when she got home. Cliff became very close to our family because he credited Mutti with having provided Ann with the loving support no one else could give her.

Paul Austin, President of Coca-Cola International was named President of the Coca-Cola Company in Atlanta. His first move was to take Cliff with him to Georgia as VP of R&D for the parent Company. Cliff maintained an office in New York and visited his old neighborhood regularly.

On one of those visits I mentioned to him that I had read an article in Super Market News that the Coca-Cola Company planned to buy the Duncan Foods Company in Houston. I asked him if they planned to bring any new people into the company.

About a week later I received a letter from Cliff saying that he had talked with Charles Duncan, President of Duncan Foods Co. about me, that Charles was very interested in meeting me and that I should send him my resume.

Another new chapter in my life was about to begin.

SAYING GOODBYE TO P&G

When I made my decision to leave Procter & Gamble and start my new career at the Cola Company I wanted to leave on the best possible terms.

One of my prized recruits to P&G, Harry Diffenderfer, had left the company to become national sales manager of H. J. Heinz. He immediately began offering opportunities to top young sales management prospects from P&G.

After three or four left to join him at Heinz, top P&G and Heinz executives consulted. Diffenderfer had to stop recruiting and was ostracized by P&G.

Part of what happened when I resigned became almost comical. I called my division manager Jack Sand and read my very politely written letter to him. Sand's response was, "You can't do this. You can't resign." Finally, he said, "Let me talk to Marquess (National Sales Manager). I'll get back to you."

Five minutes later Sand called and said, "Marquess wants you to come to Cincinnati so we can talk to you." After I told Sand I would not come, he said I had to. "No, Jack, I do not have to. It would just be a waste of the company's money. My decision is final."

Sand called again. "Will you meet Marquess at LaGuardia Airport if he flies in this afternoon in the company plane?" "Sure," I said. "I will be happy to."

P&G bragged that there was no nepotism in the Company, and there was very little. But everyone knew that Jack Marquess's uncle was an executive in the company.

Marquess was a "know it all." It was not hard to dislike him. He was from Atlanta, home of the Coca-Cola Company. I did not want to give him an opportunity to say one word to anyone in Coca-Cola before I started, so I refused to tell him where I was going or to what company.

My last day I called the Sales VP, Dutch Janney, who had been my boss, either directly or indirectly, for almost my entire career, and told him my plans. He congratulated me and wished me well. I knew he was sincere.

I said, "I want to leave the company with the feeling that if I bump into you, or any one else with P&G, at an airport, or anywhere, either of us can say to the other, let's go have a drink." THAT WAS THE WORD THAT WENT OUT – AND IT ALWAYS REMAINED THAT WAY.

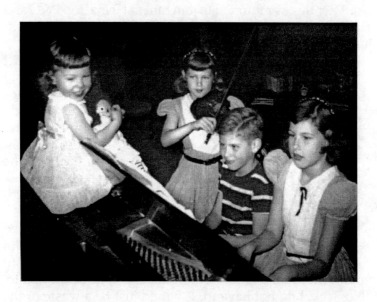

CHAPTER SEVEN

INTRODUCTION TO THE ROCKEFELLERS

Is it luck, fate or just good fortune that dictates major changes in your life?

After we signed the two-year lease, beginning in September 1965, on Betsy Gibson's home on Stillman Lane in Pocantico Hills we drove over to the Union Church (the only church in the village) to meet the minister, Rev. Hansen. We told him we wanted to become active in the church.

At Rev. Hansen's suggestion we both agreed to teach Sunday school classes. I would have the 7th and 8th grade boys while Deenie accepted responsibility for 6th grade boys and girls.

A beautiful new addition to the church was under construction but would not be completed for several months. Until the addition was finished our facilities were very cramped. My class met in the boiler room.

The first member of the Rockefeller family I met was young Larry who was in 7th grade, the same age as our Marianne. Larry lived and went to school in New York during the week, but came with his parents to their home on the estate almost every weekend.

We were one of the few families whose children went to church every Sunday, so I guess we stood out. The first Sunday we attended we sat in the third row on the right hand side of the church, not knowing that the Rockefellers, by tradition, always sat on the left side, beginning at the front.

Thus, in short order we met Larry's parents Laurance and Mary French Rockefeller, Nelson and Mary Todhunter Clark Rockefeller, and David and Peggy Rockefeller. They were all very friendly, and we would stand outside the church after the service and just visit.

Then one Sunday, Nelson introduced us to his oldest son Rodman, who had just come back from Germany after serving in the Army. Rodman volunteered that he would like to teach Sunday school. He took over the 6th grade class, and Deenie became Superintendent of the Junior Department.

That was the beginning of a long close relationship between Rod and his wife Barbara and Deenie and me.

THE ROCKEFELLER FAMILY

The impact of the Rockefeller family was everywhere. They owned 10,000 acres of prime real estate in Westchester County. 3,000 acres were fenced in and included Kykuit, the home of John D. Jr., a private 18 hole golf course, and homes for Nelson, Laurance and Winthrop. A bridal path under the highway connected the separate estates of John D. III and David.

Kykuit (Historic Hudson Valley)

The estate also featured a million dollar playhouse with indoor and outdoor tennis courts and swimming pools, bowling alleys, game rooms and a ballroom for dancing and social events. They had over 200 full-time employees and a security force of 38, larger than the combined police departments of Tarrytown and North Tarrytown, the nearest cities.

They also had one large garage for their assorted automobiles, including a Rolls Royce and Bentley and their own horse stables, groomsmen, and more than one hundred miles of bridal trails.

The Rockefeller family paid 70% of the taxes in the Pocantico Hills School District and maintained a private lake with a sand beach behind the school for swimming. Then they donated the land and built a community outdoor recreation area with an Olympic-size swimming pool and two tennis courts.

Almost all the homes in the village were owned by the Rockefellers and occupied by their employees. There were a couple of exceptions: Ted Gommi was President of Schenley Import Company, and Welman Schrader was Editor of the Aviation Section of *Encyclopedia Britannica* and other periodicals.

Les Sleinkofer was Superintendent of the Estate and Les Scott, the Assistant Superintendent. They handled all the Rockefeller social entertaining and kept their kids out of trouble.

Les and Marie Scott became our best friends and introduced us to Clif and Bunny White, with whom we later shared four grandchildren.

JOHN D. ROCKEFELLER, JR.

After we had been in Pocantico Hills about two years, Laurance Rockefeller called me over to meet his father John Davison Rockefeller, Jr., standing in front of the church. He introduced me by telling his father that I had been teaching Larry in Sunday school and by saying how active both Deenie and I had become in the church.

John D. Rockefeller, Jr. (UPI)

John D. Rockefeller, Jr. was a philanthropist who gave more than $537 million to educational, religious, cultural, medical, and other charitable projects. The son of John D. Rockefeller, founder of the Standard Oil Company, and Laura Spelman Rockefeller, he was born in Cleveland, Ohio, on January 29, 1874, and died in Tucson, Arizona, on May 11, 1960. He received a BA degree from Brown University and was a member of Phi Beta Kappa.

On October 9, 1901, he married Abby Greene Aldrich, whose father was U.S. Senator Nelson W. Aldrich of Rhode Island. Six children were born to the couple: a daughter, Abby, and five sons, John D. III, Nelson A., Laurance S., Winthrop and David Rockefeller.

His wife Abby died in 1948. In 1951 he married Mrs. Martha Baird Allen, a former concert pianist and widow of Arthur M. Allen, a classmate at Brown and a close friend.

John D. Rockefeller, Jr. believed that his inherited fortune should be used for the public good. His net worth in 1928 is estimated to have been the equivalent of $6.5 billion in 1988 dollars.

Rockefeller devoted his life to philanthropic and civic activities, to further international, interfaith and interracial concepts. Among his gifts were large sums to educational organizations, religious causes, hospitals, scientific projects, conservation and parklands, and historic preservation. He was responsible for the restoration of Colonial Williamsburg in Virginia, and he donated the land along the East River in Manhattan for the site of the United Nations headquarters.

My favorite memory of "Mr. Junior" was the beautiful smile on his face, as he sat in the front row of our church and watched while an infant child was baptized.

LAURANCE S. ROCKEFELLER

While I was also on a first name business with Nelson and David, I probably knew Laurance better than any of other famous brothers, including John D. III and Winthrop.

The Rockefellers had a policy that one of the brothers would represent the family on the Board of Trustees at Union

Church. When I was asked to serve on the board, Laurance was already a member, and we worked together. Later, when I was nominated for president he supported me.

In my first year as president I faced an unenviable problem. Church attendance was pitiful. We could not get any of the young people to go. My own kids were rebelling. Rev. Hanson was just plain boring. We were a non-denominational church so we could hire anyone we wanted.

Laurance S. Rockefeller

Some of the veteran Trustees and Deacons came to me and asked me to do something. Finally, I agreed to talk with Rev. Hanson, knowing that as a minister in good standing he could easily be assigned to a Methodist Church. There would be no difficulty about a reassignment.

My meeting with Rev. Hanson went well. He offered to resign, and I assured him we could work everything out amicably. I felt good about it.

Then all Hell broke loose. Les Sleinkofer, Superintendent of the Estate received a phone call from Governor Nelson Rockefeller telling him to resign from the Board of Trustees, and for Assistant Superintendent Les Scott to resign from the Board of Deacons and "not get involved in this mess at the church."

I called for a special meeting of the Board of Trustees, and Laurance, representing the family, came up from New York. We had no choice but to bring out in public what we had tried to handle in a private way.

At the end of the meeting Laurance came over to me and said, "Gaz, we as a family had no idea the people in the congregation felt this way. We will support you."

Stay tuned! There is more to this story. WHY WAS GOV. ROCKEFELLER SO UPSET?

LAURANCE ROCKEFELLER'S LEGACY

Each of the five brothers carved out a niche for himself. After Laurance graduated from Princeton he went to Harvard Law School until he decided he did not want to become a lawyer. He became a venture capitalist and environmentalist.

He was the money behind Capt. Eddie Rickenbacker; a World War I Fighter Pilot in starting Eastern Airlines in the 1930's and was its largest stockholder. After WWII, Eastern became this country's most profitable airline.

He provided the financial support to J. S. McDonnell, Jr. in 1939 to start McDonnell Aircraft Co. Laurance bought his first shares in the company before it had produced a plane, investing $10,000. Less than ten years later he was one of the largest stockholders in this company which became a leading supplier of military aircraft.

Laurance invested in hundreds of start-ups, initially in aviation and electronics and later in computers (Intel and Apple) and biotechnology. His gifts of land, literally from the redwood forests to the Virgin Islands amounted to hundreds of thousands of acres.

While his venture capital helped establish many companies, his lasting legacy will be as a conservationist and for building national parks. He advised every president from Eisenhower to George H. W. Bush who, in presenting him the Congressional Gold Medal, described Laurance Rockefeller as a Hidden National Treasure.

PICTURE THIS SETTING: It is an October Friday night in the social room of the Union Church. About 30 men and women from the church are present to hear Mrs. Laurance Rockefeller talk about a trip their family had just taken to the 49th and 50th states. Laurance is running the slide projector.

After they leave Alaska and arrive in Hawaii, Mary is describing a large tract of land on Maui with a spectacular ocean view. In a quiet voice she told us that Laurance is thinking about building a resort there. Then she said, "Larry, why don't you come up here and tell the people about your ideas?"

He did, and all I could think was what a scoop this would be if a news reporter were sitting in the audience!

NELSON ROCKEFELLER

Two years younger than Laurance and an extrovert, Nelson had an exciting personality and charisma that everyone recognized upon meeting him. One of the busiest men in the world, he always took time to stop and listen. With women, he was particularly charming.

When he decided to run in 1958 for his first term as Governor of New York State, his son Rodman asked Marie Scott and me to be co-chairs for a Citizens for Rockefeller movement for our part of Westchester County.

When I learned that the *Tarrytown Daily News*, one of six county daily newspapers under a single owner, would solidly back Nelson, I pulled out my old portable typewriter to write a series of articles on the theme, THOSE WHO KNOW HIM BEST SUPPORT NELSON ROCKEFELLER.

I interviewed people who had known Nelson intimately, some since his childhood. I found his Scoutmaster, his Sunday school teacher, the groomsman who taught him to ride, as well as civic and local educators and business leaders. I guess I wrote about 12 to 15 articles.

I commuted from Tarrytown to New York every day, driving past the *Daily News* office on my way to the station. At about 7:15 AM I would slide my article through the mail slot in their front door. At about 6:00 or 6:30 PM on my way home I would pick up a copy of the newspaper. and there, without fail, was my article, exactly as I had submitted it, on the front page.

Gaz Green with Nelson Rockerfeller and Marie Scott, which appeared in the Tarrytown Daily News *the day Nelson was elected governor of New York for the first time.*

For my last article before the election, I summarized the series. To my surprise, all six newspapers in the group ran it throughout Westchester County as their editorial endorsing Rockefeller for Governor.

The picture of Marie and me, taken with Nelson just after he and we had voted appeared the next day on the front page of the *Tarrytown Daily News*.

We felt like celebrities rubbing elbows with Dewitt and Lila Acheson Wallace, *Reader's Digest* founders, at the victory party at the Playhouse.

Nelson won a landslide victory over Averell Harriman, the incumbent, and went on to become the only four-term governor in the history of New York. He then was chosen to fill out the unexpired term as Vice President when Gerald Ford succeeded President Nixon, who had resigned in disgrace.

NELSON & REV. HANSON

We were shocked when Nelson Rockefeller phoned Les Sleinkofer and told the Superintendent of the estate to resign from the Board of Trustees immediately and to tell his assistant, Les Scott, also, to resign from the Board of Deacons.

This was absolutely contrary to the way the Rockefellers operated. Their relationship with Union Church had always been very supportive, but not dominating or dictating policy. For the Governor of the state to order two of his family's key employees in such a way was unthinkable.

Why did he take this drastic action? Only after a period of time did we learn the real reason.

What we did not know was that Nelson had developed an intimate relationship with Happy Murphy, an attractive woman twenty years younger than himself, and planned to divorce Mary Tod Rockefeller, mother of his five grown children, Rodman, Anne, Steven, and the twins, Mary and Michael.

How did Rev. Hanson fit into the picture? He was Nelson's friend, confidant and advisor. And I feel sure that when Nelson was told by Rev. Hanson his job was in jeopardy, he said, "Don't worry. I will take care of it."

But it did not work out that way. After Laurance told me the family would back us, Rev. Hanson resigned, and it became a closed matter.

Announcement was made that Nelson and Mary Tod had started divorce proceedings. The timing could not have been worse. Their son, Michael, who a year earlier had been graduated from Harvard cum laude, was reported missing from an archeological expedition in New Guinea. After weeks of intense searching, hope was abandoned, and we attended a private memorial service for Michael in the sanctuary of Union Church. It was so sad to see the family in their grief, split by the divorce.

Mary Todhunter Clark Rockefeller, the mother, came in first and sat on one side of the aisle with her surviving sons Rodman and Steven. Then Nelson, the father, entered and sat on the other side of the aisle with daughters Anne and the surviving twin, Mary.

MARGARETTA "HAPPY" FITLER MURPHY

The first time I ever saw Happy Murphy was when she and her two little boys sat behind our family in church one Sunday. I had no idea who she was, but when the service ended I turned to compliment her on how well behaved the boys were during church.

With that the two boys darted across the aisle, put their arms around the governor's legs and exclaimed, "Uncle Nelson." I just assumed she was a friend of the family. Wow, was I wrong!

When the scandal finally hit the newspapers we learned that Happy's husband was a medical doctor employed by the Rockefeller Medical Center.

I remarked earlier about how charming Nelson was with women. My wife, Dee, and Marie Scott had often said, "He can put his shoes under my bed anytime." That ended when they learned he was already putting his shoes under Happy's bed.

Nelson had always wanted to be President. He missed the opportunity in 1960 when Richard Nixon lost to John Kennedy. Rockefeller felt he could have won that election, so he set his sights on 1964.

All was going well for the Rockefeller campaign until he decided to make changes in his personal life. In 1961, he and his wife had separated, and in 1963 they divorced. Less than a year later he married 36-year old Happy Murphy, who had already gotten her divorce. Soon support eroded as people started to think, "Do we really want a man running the country who leaves his wife after 31 years of marriage so he can marry a younger woman, one who had surrendered custody of her four children?"

The state of New Hampshire is small in both size and population, but when the Presidential primaries start, it has the attention of the entire nation. Rockefeller was a graduate of Dartmouth College in Hanover, New Hampshire, and he was hoping that a big win would put him on the covers of the leading news magazines and make him the favorite.

But it became an uphill fight when the publisher of a leading newspaper in the state labeled Nelson Rockefeller, "A Wife Swapper."

Happy Rockefeller

NELSON & HAPPY WEDDING

No, I was not invited to their wedding, but without trying I became involved in the firestorm that followed.

After Rev. Hanson resigned, Rodman Rockefeller and I were members of the search committee named to find the new Minister for Union Church. Rod and I drove to Liberty, NY, a vacation resort in the Catskill Mountains, to observe Rev. Marshall Smith, a Presbyterian minister, who had been highly recommended.

Rev. Smith accepted our invitation to speak in Pocantico Hills, after which the congregation voted unanimously to invite him to be our minister. He was a skilled orator and experienced thespian who could bring new excitement to our pulpit.

Marshall Smith had been in the church only a few months before he called and said he needed to talk with me. He told me that he was about to be censured by the National Board of the Presbyterian Church for marrying two divorced people, Nelson Rockefeller and Happy Murphy, without securing that board's approval prior to the wedding.

He explained to a combined meeting of our Boards of Trustees and Deacons that he had not sought permission from the Presbyterian Church to protect the privacy of the Governor. He knew he would be censured but that would amount to just a slap on the wrist, and it would not affect his standing.

It was agreed that any media inquiries regarding Rev. Smith would be directed to me as president of the Board of Trustees. I would merely state that he had not violated any laws of Union Church by performing the wedding ceremony of two of our members. There was no mention of divorce in our bylaws.

It was front page news for a couple of days, then blew over and became a non-event.

THE 1964 PRESIDENTIAL CAMPAIGN

Little by little we learned more about Nelson's trysts with Happy.

While he and Mary Tod were married he had a little Japanese style cabin built up on a hill behind the Union Church, accessible only through a locked gate on a private road. If anyone got past that point the cabin was protected by a moat and a drawbridge. This assured him total privacy with Happy.

As much as he was able to hide his infidelities from the public during his five-year affair with Happy, it was his marriage to her that literally cost him his dream of becoming President of the United States in 1964.

He recovered from his setback in New Hampshire, campaigned vigorously across the country, and two weeks before the last Republican primary, in California, Rockefeller held a comfortable 13-point lead over his opponent, Arizona Senator Barry Goldwater.

Confident that he could win the final prize, Nelson pulled out all the stops in a relentless (and extremely costly) negative campaign aimed at portraying Goldwater as a dangerous politician. "Who do you want in the room with the H-bomb button?" asked a Rockefeller pamphlet mailed to over two million voters across the state. Goldwater followers retaliated with their own smear campaign, engaging in disruptive tactics that included bomb threats made to the Rockefeller headquarters.

Rockefeller was still leading the polls when, three days before the election, Happy gave birth to a baby boy, Nelson Jr. As Rockefeller interrupted his campaign to fly to New York, Goldwater went into high gear, filling the airwaves with ads that touted his impeccable family background and questioned his opponent's morality.

On June 2, California voters chose Goldwater over Rockefeller by a narrow margin of less than 3 percent, ensuring the Arizona senator's nomination at the Republican convention to be held in July.

Rockefeller would have to wait another four years to pursue his dream.

CLIF WHITE AND GOLDWATER

The 1964 Republication National Convention was held at the Cow Palace in San Francisco.

F. Clifton White, father of Carol White Green, also grandfather of my grandchildren Tabitha Green Barr, G.Graham Green IV, Meghann Green and Garrett Green, and co-great grandfather with me of G. Graham (Quint) Green V and Cleopatra Barr, was the real hero of this convention.

We have written before how Clif engineered a grass roots campaign for Goldwater, which had never been done before. It caught the Rockefeller forces by surprise and the coup d'état came at the convention.

Clif set up a communications command post in a trailer outside the Cow Palace. He had direct telephone connections to each state delegation, and a red hotline so he could reach all delegations at the same time for critical communications.

The atmosphere at the Republican convention was heated as Nelson stepped up to the podium to address the belligerent crowd: Rockefeller would not give up the nomination without a fight.

"During this year I have crisscrossed this nation, fighting ... to keep the Republican party the party of all the people ... and warning of the extremist threat, its danger to the party, and danger to the nation," he said, taking his time as the crowd cheered "We want Barry!"

"These extremists feed on fear, hate and terror, [they have] no program for America and the Republican Party. It is essential that this convention repudiate here and now any doctrinaire, militant minority whether Communist, Ku Klux Klan or Birchers."

It was, according to many, Nelson Rockefeller's finest moment—but it did little to stop the conservative wave that was transforming the GOP. Nor was it heard by very many people at 1:00 AM in the Eastern Time Zone.

Goldwater sealed his own doom two days later when, after getting the nomination, he named someone other than Clif White to be his campaign manager for the Presidential race. He suffered a resounding defeat.

JOHN D. ROCKEFELLER III & IV

John D. III

As John D. Rockefeller, Jr.'s oldest son, John D. III was reared to assume the lead role in his generation's philanthropic endeavors. A world tour following graduation in 1929 from Princeton concluded with his working for the Institute of Pacific Relations conference in Japan.

He then joined his father's office in New York City and immersed himself in the operations of the many institutions associated with the family.

He became a board member of the Rockefeller Foundation, the General Education Fund, the Institute of Medical Research (now Rockefeller University), Colonial Williamsburg, and the China Medical Board, among others.

John D. III also headed causes of his own. He founded the Population Council, spearheaded the development of Lincoln Center, revitalized the Japan Society and organized and maintained a lifelong interest in the Asia Society. He died in 1978 in an automobile accident at the age of 71.

John D. IV

Perhaps because of his father's intense interest in Asia, Jay Rockefeller studied at the International Christian University of Japan in Tokyo for 3 years following his graduation from Harvard. I first met him when he spoke at Union Church on "Student" Sunday while he was at I. C. U.

After serving two terms as Governor of West Virginia he was elected to the U. S. Senate where he still serves. His wife was the daughter of Senator Chuck Percy of Illinois.

While his uncles Nelson and Winthrop, who served as Governors of New York and Arkansas, were noted for their outgoing, gracious personalities, I am afraid I always found Jay to be aloof and lacking the warmth so noticeable in most of the other family members.

WINTHROP ROCKEFELLER

I only met Winthrop, the fourth son, once, at the memorial Service at Riverside Church in New York following the death of John D. Rockefeller, Jr. But I felt like I knew him well from reading so much about him.

Winthrop attended Yale for three years but did not graduate. In early 1941 he enlisted in the U. S. Infantry and fought in WWII, advancing from private to Colonel, earning a Bronze Star with Clusters and a Purple Heart for bravery in action aboard the *USS Henrico* in a kamikaze attack during the Battle of Okinawa.

His life between the end of WWII and his death in 1973 could be divided into two periods. First, from 1946 until 1951: a playboy and heavy drinker which was the antithesis of the Rockefeller Family reputation, and second: his exemplary life in Arkansas for 20 years beginning in 1953.

He fell in love with his newly adopted state, guiding it to a complete economic renaissance and leading efforts to build medical clinics in the poorest counties. He served two terms as governor. His son, Winthrop Paul, served for ten years as lieutenant governor until his death of cancer at age 57 on July 16, 2006...

Winthrop maintained a home on the Pocantico Hills Estate while he lived in Arkansas. One summer he offered his home to his old army doctor buddy, Graham Hawke and his wife, for vacation. Les and Marie Scott became friends with the Hawkes and invited us to share an evening with them.

Prior to moving from Harrisburg to New York, I would read in the gossip columns about Winthrop, or "Winnie" having married a chorus girl. Barbara "Bobo" Sears in 1948.

The Hawkes had been best friends with Winnie and Bobo and never dreamed Bobo had any ulterior motive in marrying him—until the day Winthrop Paul was born. Then she knew she had Winthrop by the nose.

She wanted MONEY, lots of it. She made his life miserable. He had no alternative but to give her a divorce and a reported $5,000,000 in 1951.

THE GOSSIP COLUMNISTS HAD THEIR ULTIMATE STORY!

DAVID ROCKEFELLER

Another of my favorites was David, the youngest of the "Five Brothers," who, after earning his PhD at the University of Chicago, began his career in Banking and International Finance. His path led him through various posts at Chase

Manhattan Bank to the presidency and eventually board chairman.

When I first moved to New York, and before we moved to Pocantico Hills, I opened an account with a large bank in White Plains. I had been granted a very valuable stock option which I could not exercise unless I borrowed money using the stock as collateral.

My bank in White Plains said they could not loan me the money, quoting some government regulation. I knew that my friends in Cincinnati were borrowing from their banks so I asked my friend Les Scott if he thought it appropriate for me to get David's advice after church. Les said absolutely. It was a business matter. I was not asking him for a personal favor...

The following Sunday I explained my situation to David, and he said to call the Rockefeller City branch across the street from my office, and tell the VP in charge that David had said to call. David then said, if he can't take care of you, let me know. I am sure we can do it downtown at the main office.

In your lifetime you will never see a brighter red carpet than was awaiting me at Chase Bank. I was treated like a Fortune 500 corporate executive from that day on.

Our son, Graham, and David and Peggy's son, Dickie, had become friends. Graham would often go home with Dickie after church on Sunday and then one of us would pick him up later in the afternoon. I remember Graham reporting that when he saw David reading the N. Y. Times, Graham asked him if he followed the stock market. The answer was YES.

Another time, on a week day, I received a call from Mutti asking me to pick up Graham at the Rockefellers on my way home. David had also just arrived home. He and Peggy met me at the front door and he said, "Gaz, tomorrow is our 25th Wedding Anniversary and they have just erected a tent on the grounds for the occasion. I have not seen it yet. Come look at it with us."

MARC CHAGALL

In the front of Union Church a rose window honors Mr. Junior's wife, Abby Aldrich Rockefeller. This was the last work by the great French painter, Henri Matisse. This leaded glass window was created in his Nice, France, studio and was enroute to the United States by ship to be installed in the Union Church of Pocantico Hills when Matisse died in 1954.

David Rockefeller called me at home one Saturday morning in 1961, the year after Mr. Junior's death, and said, "Gaz, Mr. & Mrs. Marc Chagall are at our home today. We are talking to Mr. Chagall about doing a memorial window at the church in honor of Father. We are going over to look at the church now and thought you and Deenie would like to meet us there."

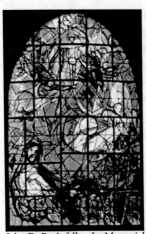

John D. Rockefeller, Jr. Memorial Window by Marc Chagall

David and I toured the church with Mr. Chagall while our wives visited with Mrs. Chagall. Born in Russia, Chagall had lived for many years in France. David spoke French fluently, but the conversation was in a language I could not speak. Fortunately, David was my interpreter.

Mrs. Chagall had remarked that her husband, at age 73, already had enough work to keep him busy for the remainder of his life. The Rockefeller family, therefore, was delighted when he agreed to accept their proposal to create a window based on Luke's Parable of the Good Samaritan. The theme was recommended by Dr. Robert McCracken, Senior Minister of the Riverside Church in New York, as the most powerful symbol of Mr. Junior's life.

Marc Chagall returned to Pocantico Hills on May 14, 1963 for the dedication of "The Good Samaritan Window," a fitting tribute to the life of John D. Rockefeller, Jr. David and I escorted him into the church.

Joe Kidd, a prominent artist and illustrator who was a member of the church, made a charcoal drawing that captured the expression on the face of Mr. Chagall as he looked up and saw his masterpiece in place for the first time. Chagall autographed the drawing. A limited 20 copies were made. We have one in our home which we still display with pride these many years later.

Chagall was later commissioned to create the eight smaller windows in the church, the first of which was dedicated to Michael Rockefeller, Nelson's 22 year-old son who was lost in an archeological expedition in New Guinea in 1961. Union Church is now famous for possessing this spectacular art.

DARTMOUTH VS PRINCETON

I have always been a big sports fan, especially of football and baseball, and have been a subscriber to Sports Illustrated for many years.

In 1958, after Nelson had been elected Governor of New York, I was sitting at the dining room table of our home on Old Sleepy Hollow Road on a gorgeous fall Saturday November morning. I was reading in *Sports Illustrated* about the Ivy League Championship game between Dartmouth and Princeton that was to be played that day.

The phone rang. It was Rodman Rockefeller calling to tell us that his father, a Dartmouth alumnus, and his mother had gone to Venezuela to rest following the election campaign and would not be able to use their tickets for the game that afternoon in Princeton. Would Deenie and I like to come?

Is the Pope Catholic?

We decided to drive separate cars so Rod and Barbara would be free to spend the evening with some of their friends.

Little did we realize until we got there that we would sitting between Rod and Barbara, Dartmouth fans, and Princeton alumnus Laurance and his wife Mary. Both teams were undefeated. Palmer stadium was a great venue, the weather was perfect, and the game lived up to its billing. The Dartmouth Indians, led by all-American halfback Jake Crouthamel, won the game and the Ivy League Title.

After the game Laurance and Mary invited us to go back to his club at Princeton for tea. When we sat down Laurance suggested I sit with Mary and he with Deenie so we could all become better acquainted.

Laurance had gotten a cup of tea for each of them with the tea bag floating on top of the hot water. Not only was there no string attached to the tea bag, there were no spoons. Unknown to me, Deenie faced a dilemma. How was she going to get the tea bag out? Finally, Laurance nonchalantly reached in with thumb and forefinger.

When in Rome do as the Romans do. When at Princeton, do as the Princeton Tigers do.

ROCKEFELLER BRIEFS

♦ Beulah Nelson, the Rockefeller seamstress describing
  Mr. Junior modeling a new union suit for her so she
  could tailor one to fit and then make a dozen more exactly the same.

♦ Laurance and Mary's son Larry had been in my Sunday school class until he went away to prep school. In
  response to my question about how Larry was doing,
  his mother said, "He is much better now. He got caught
  smoking in his room and was restricted for a month.
  That is over now, so he is fine."

♦ Loaning money to a Rockefeller. Rodman sat with us in
  church one Sunday. Just before the offering plate arrived
  Rod leaned over and asked me if I could loan him $5.00.

♦ A 14 year-old Rockefeller granddaughter (name with-
  held to protect her identity) coming to a church Hallow-
  een party dressed as a beggar walking around through
  the crowd saying chanting, "Alms for the poor."

♦ The outpouring of affection for Joe Plick, the groomsman who taught three generations of Rockefeller children to ride. There must have been 40 family members
  at his memorial service. They even arranged for Mr.
  Junior's soloist from Riverside Church to sing because
  Joe liked the music at for Mr. Junior's service so much.

♦ Lucy Rockefeller's garden wedding reception on the
  estate when Johnny Baverstock and I arranged to have
  a special waiter keep our champagne glasses full at all
  times.

♦ Playing soccer on Saturday mornings with Larry Rockefeller and other boys from my 7th & 8th grade Sunday
  school class.

♦ Having Larry and those same kids try to outsmart me
  when I first started teaching Sunday school and was
  trying, unsuccessfully at first, to maintain discipline. I
  finally won that battle and thereafter enjoyed the experience.

KENNEDY ASSASSINATION

Of all my recollections from the ten years we lived in Pocantico Hills and had the rare privilege of developing relationships with several members of one of the most respected families in the world, the most indelible memory I have came from being in church with Governor Nelson A. Rockefeller the Sunday morning after President John F. Kennedy was assassinated.

The date was November 24, 1963.

Our nation, if not the entire world was in shock. Two days before, the unthinkable had happened. Our young and vigorous President had been shot and killed.

Nothing seemed real.

This Sunday was a day of mourning. Churches everywhere were jammed to overflowing. Union Church of Pocantico Hills seated about 130 and normal attendance was 50 to 60.

The Rockefellers usually had from five or six to perhaps twenty family members attend on any given Sunday. On this particular day all family members who were in residence at their Pocantico Hills homes were there. I had never seen so many at one time at a regular Sunday service. They filled almost the entire left side of the church.

Nelson was one of the last of the family to arrive. He sat on the end seat across the aisle one row in front of me. Less than four feet away I could not think of anything else, except what must be going through his mind. Here was the Governor of arguably the most important state and himself a serious candidate to become President of the United States.

It was a sad, sad day—destined to become almost unbelievable less than an hour after church when we returned home, and, along with millions of other people throughout the United States, watched our television sets.

We sat in disbelief as we witnessed the live shooting of the accused assassin Lee Harvey Oswald by a deranged Dallas night club owner Jack Ruby.

NELSON FOR PRESIDENT 1960

After Nelson Rockefeller won the landslide victory over Averell Harriman for Governor of New York State in 1968, it became obvious that his ultimate goal was not confined to New York State.

I remember his son Rodman telling me, that after having served in appointed positions in government, his father felt the only way he could ever have real clout was to be elected.

I also remember when working on his campaign with Rodman's wife, Barbara, I showed her parents an article about Nelson's immense popularity. Their response, "That will sure help him on a national basis."

It was not until I was working on my memoirs, however, that I discovered *The Rockefeller Files*, a book by the late historian Gary Allen, published by CPA Book Publishers, P. O. Box 596, Boring, Oregon 97009.

Allen offers a theory that Nelson had made a deal with Nixon not to run against him in 1960. In return Nixon would appoint Henry Kissinger and Alexander Haig, both Rockefeller loyalists, to key positions in his administration.

The conspiracy theory was that Kissinger and Haig then engineered the Watergate break-in and subsequent revelations that led to the forced resignation of Nixon as President of the United States.

I knew that Kissinger had been Nelson's foreign affairs advisor for several years. After Kissinger retired, he and his wife moved into a home on the Rockefeller Estate in Pocantico Hills. I had never heard, though, that Haag also was a close Rockefeller associate.

Anyone who wants to read more about the power of the House of Rockefeller in government, banking and international affairs can look up on Google *The Rockefeller Files* by Gary Allen.

CHAPTER EIGHT

EXCITING NEW CAREER

In January, 1965 I reported to the Duncan Foods Company offices in Houston to begin my new career with the Coca-Cola Company.

The Duncan Foods Company was a regional coffee company whose main product was Maryland Club, distributed in Texas, Oklahoma and Louisiana. The President was Charles W. Duncan, Jr., who, still in his thirties, had rescued the family business from financial disaster. He then merged the Butter Nut Coffee Company in Omaha, Nebraska into Duncan Foods. This merger had caught the attention of the Coca-Cola Company, which was intending to expand its beverage product line. Coke had already purchased the Minute Maid Company who owned Tenco, an instant coffee plant in Linden N. J.

Actually, what really made Duncan Foods Company attractive to Coca-Cola was the chance to acquire two outstanding young executives, Charles Duncan and 40 year-old Don Keogh, Butter Nut marketing VP. This wisdom was proved correct when, later in their careers both Duncan and Keogh served as presidents of the Coca-Cola Company.

Keogh was another Iowa farm boy. He went to Creighton University in Omaha and worked at WOW, a powerful radio station while in college. When television was in its infancy, he and Johnny Carson worked together at WOW-TV. Keogh produced Carson's first TV program, an afternoon children's show.

The Butter Nut Coffee Co. was bought by Clark and Gilbert Swanson, the famous Swanson Brothers who had introduced TV Dinners and sold their company to Campbell's Soup Company. My wife Pat's deceased husband, Bob Cords, worked for the Swansons in marketing the TV dinners, and they brought him along to Butter Nut and then to Duncan Foods.

The first weekend I was in Houston, Gilbert Swanson's son, Gibby, wed the daughter of a Duncan Foods salesman. The day before the wedding I was invited to go along with

Gilbert to see the almost completed Astrodome for the first time from Judge Roy Hofheinz's private suite.

That should have been enough excitement, but I learned it was just the first of many great and interesting experiences.

HOUSTON ADVERTISING FORUM

The principal reason I chose to join the Coca-Cola Company was the opportunity I was being given to become a complete marketing manager.

In Procter & Gamble, those who started in the advertising department received cross training in sales. The same opportunity was not available to those who entered through the sales department.

Don Keogh and Charles Duncan had devised a plan where I would have no sales responsibility initially but would serve in a newly created position, Director of Marketing Services. My responsibilities included advertising, sales promotion, market research and packaging with a manager already in place for each department. Later on I was given the additional responsibility for new product development and the consumer taste-testing program.

At the end of my second week the Houston Ad Club sponsored its annual forum at the Shamrock Hilton Hotel. This was just after Braniff Air introduced colorful airplanes. One of the five outstanding presentations at the forum was by Mary Wells of Jack Tinker & Partners in New York who conceived and implemented the idea copied by nearly every other airline.

Before the dinner that evening Deenie and I, along with Bob and Ruth Cords and six or eight other people, were invited to a private cocktail party hosted by John Lear, Marketing Director for the Astrodome in the large suite Judge Hofheinz maintained at the Shamrock for entertaining,

The special guests were Harding Lawrence, president of Braniff, and Mary Wells, the celebrated advertising genius. We spent an hour visiting.

After the dinner, we stood with them as we waited for valet parking to bring our cars. First to arrive was a fire engine red Ford Mustang to be driven by Harding Lawrence. He held the door for Mary Wells before they disappeared into the night.

I was forced to quip, "THE MORAL OF THAT STORY IS DON'T TINKER WITH ONE OF JACK'S PARTNERS."

Within months our host, John Lear, was named Vice President of Braniff, and Harding Lawrence had filed for divorce from his wife so he could marry Mary Wells.

SINGER ANITA BRYANT

Shortly after the Houston Ad Forum the Coca-Cola Company agreed to be a sponsor of the Houston Astros baseball post-game broadcasts. As Charles Duncan so aptly described the decision, "The Astros may not have a very good baseball team, but WE have the Astrodome–THE EIGHTH WONDER OF THE WORLD!"

Judge Hofheinz, the ultimate promoter, threw a lavish pre-season party for all the stations and sponsors of the Houston Astros Baseball Network. It included a preview of the nearly completed Astrodome, and a huge dinner with entertainment headed by Anita Bryant, one of the most honored and acclaimed popular singers of the day.

Anita Bryant was under contract to the Coca-Cola Company who provided her services to entertain for this event. Bob Cords and I sat and visited with Anita for about an hour as she got her first glimpse of the Astrodome.

At age 25, Anita Bryant was a well known American songbird and a kind of national icon treasured not just for her good looks and talent but for the use to which she put them. A former Miss Oklahoma, she had beautiful auburn hair, a rich clear voice and a flashing smile.

As a devout Southern Baptist and deeply patriotic, Anita was, like Billy Graham in that period, an approving presence for Presidents and their policies. She had entertained troops with Bob Hope during the Vietnam War, had been invited to the White House 14 times by Lyndon Johnson, and had sung the Battle Hymn of the Republic and God Bless America at both national political conventions.

She started a movement called "Save Our Children" which was the start of an organized opposition to gay rights that spread across the nation and the beginning of what came to be known as the religious right. Rev. Jerry Falwell came to help her. Their personal attacks on gays and lesbians were so vitriolic that both her marriage and her career collapsed.

Homosexuals and conservative Christians are now prominent on the national scene, but Anita Bryant has disappeared from sight.

We were fortunate to have met her when she was at the top of her game.

UNVEILING TINY TIM

About three months after I arrived in Houston, Don Keogh was sent to Japan on a special assignment by Paul Austin, Coca-Cola CEO. Since he would be away for three weeks he scheduled me to work with various salesmen and sales managers for both coffee brands. It was an eye-opening experience!

I have said many times that if I had spent my entire career with P&G, I would have thought every company was honest. If you could not, or would not, do it ethically, you did not last with the Company. What I found here was quite the opposite, particularly in the Butter Nut sales operation.

I had met the Butter Nut Sales Vice President, Tom Cleveland. He had been cordial, but a bit standoffish, as if to say, "Fellow, you've got to prove yourself to me before I accept you." His office was in Omaha, though he was scheduled to move to Houston in June.

My itinerary had me working in San Diego, Los Angeles and San Francisco, and then on to Kansas City and to Omaha where Tom had said he would meet my plane upon arrival so we could go have dinner together.

California was a total mess, but I had been told that before I saw it for myself. Just before he died suddenly of a heart attack, Clark Swanson had built a coffee plant in Commerce, California to expand Butter Nut to the West Coast. His brother-in-law "Bill" must have been a worthless VP since they had so little distribution, and Duncan and Keogh considered California a low priority for investment.

The Midwest was different. We had huge merchandising allowances that were to be paid one time only on any purchase. In Kansas City I found the district manager was paying these allowances three and four times on the same inventory. Upon questioning, he just said, "That is the way we do it."

When I had dinner with Tom Cleveland that night, he asked me how I had found things in Kansas City. When I told him, it became obvious that the district manager had already phoned him. Tom told me that he was the VP here and this was none of my business. He told me I was not to ask any of his men questions like that again. WOW! Did I have Tom's number? I had just unveiled Tiny Tim!

LUNCH WITH ARTHUR NIELSEN

Everybody is familiar with the term "Nielsen Ratings" which measure TV audiences for advertisers. Less well known was the service on which Arthur Nielsen started the A. C. Nielson Company, and was the bread and butter of his business for many years.

This was the measure of consumer purchases, by brand, in retail outlets. The Coca-Cola Company was Arthur Nielsen's

Arthur Charles Nielsen, Sr.

first client, and he had a soft spot in his heart for anyone who worked for Coke.

Part of my Don Keogh designed orientation program was to spend two days in Chicago divided equally between our advertising agency Tatham, Laird and Kudner and the A. C. Nielson Company. I already knew Art Tatham and Ken Laird, founders of what was also a major P&G agency. In fact, they had named the product Head and Shoulders.

Nielsen was a different situation. Statistics had been one of my favorite college courses so I was tremendously interested in Nielsen's sample selection, methodology and accuracy. I was told that Mr. Nielsen wanted to host me for lunch in his private dining room.

Every month I read *Tennis World*, the most popular magazine about the net game, and knew that Arthur Nielsen, Sr. and his son Arthur, Jr. had won two National Father & Son Championships.

I knew that Arthur had given $1,000,000 to the City of Kenilworth, Illinois, and also to his alma mater, the University of Wisconsin, to build tennis complexes. Both Father and son had captained the Wisconsin tennis team.

So, while we were having lunch I told Mr. Nielsen I was happy tennis did not have a handicap system like golf. (This was before the adoption of a numerical tennis rating.) I said I could talk a great game of tennis, as long the other person never got to see me play.

He said, "Young man, the next time you come up here I want you to bring your racquet. I have an indoor court at my home, and we will play there."

"No, No. I protested. I know your record and reputation in tennis. I could not afford to let you see me play. "But, thanks for the invitation."

FIRST TIME IN LAS VEGAS

I had never been to Las Vegas, so my first time made a lasting impression. I am not a gambler, but I sure love good entertainment, and Vegas has to be the Entertainment Capital of the World. Don Keogh loved Vegas, so I was grateful to him for introducing me to the Glitter Gulch.

The excuse to be there was the Western Grocers Association annual meeting. My old buddy Harry Faught who was P&G soap sales manager in New York for ten years with me, was also at the convention in his new role as Director of Trade Relations for Procter & Gamble.

When I introduced Harry to Keogh, and Don learned that neither Harry nor I had ever been to Vegas before he gave us a wonderful suggestion. We were staying out on the Strip, which was "New" Las Vegas. He told us that to experience the original Vegas we should take a cab down to the railroad station where all the early tourists arrived.

"Pretend you are getting off the train," he suggested, "and walk over to Glitter Gulch," where in 1965 they still had mostly nickel slot machines.

This was a good relaxing time for Harry and me to be together again. Our professional responsibilities were now completely different. P&G had bought Folgers Coffee and was about to challenge Maxwell House as the only true national brand.

Coca-Cola had its own plans for a national presence in the coffee business and I was to be an integral part of it. Also, Harry had been a close personal friend of Paul Austin when they lived and played golf together in Greenwich, Connecticut.

I have mentioned earlier how Harry Faught, Paul Flory and I worked so well together in New York when we were sales managers for the soap, toilet goods and foods divisions. We had our sales organizations calling on the same customers, and there could have been petty or serious problems. There were NONE, because we were determined we would solve them.

After Harry and I had absorbed the flavor of Old Las Vegas, Glitter Gulch, we decided to relax and have a beer together. We ordered one extra for Paul Flory, the other member of our trio, and drank a toast to him.

ASTROS TRAINING CAMP

Spring training was underway in Florida for the major league baseball teams, and the Grapefruit League was about to get under way.

Catching us completely by surprise, we were told that we would have a series of in-game commercials on the air starting the next day. Bob Cords and I had barely enough time to pack our bags and catch a plane. We arranged to have a creative writer from our agency meet us in Florida.

John Lear, Braniff Marketing VP, had made sure we had cards to his airline's private club at the Houston Airport. Bob and I went into the lounge to wait for the plane and discovered that Col. "Shorty" Powers, "Voice of the Astronauts" at the Space Center was also going to Melbourne, the

Gaz is judge of the Miss Astro contest. An eager Graham joins in the festivities, 1966.

closest airport for both Cape Canaveral and Cocoa Beach, home of the Astros.

Powers suggested we call him if we wanted to see the facilities at the Cape. We did and got a great "behind the scenes" tour.

The next morning we met with the Astros broadcast team, producer Bob Boyne and announcers Gene Elston and Lowell Paas to learn what they needed from us. We then started writing commercials. My job was to get legal approval by phone from Houston Attorney Sam Peak so they could be delivered live that day. I was still on the phone when the game started, Bob Cords and I shared a room in the Astros complex. The accommodations were modest, but they had a hospitality room for the press and special guests. Bob and I sat at the bar. I think Bob knew everybody. First, he brought over Mickey Herskowitz, the great sports writer for the Houston Post.

Next, Bob introduced me to Paul Richards, General Manager of the Astros who immediately invited us to join him and Arthur Daley, whose column "Sports of the Times" I had read regularly for years in the *New York Times*. When I started to talk about the fantastic Astrodome, Daley began to make notes. Writers from *Sports Illustrated* and major newspapers formed a circle.

The kid from State College, who wanted to be a sports reporter, finally had his chance to conduct a press conference with a major league executive.

He took full advantage of the opportunity.

ASTRODOME OPENS

The Astrodome opened as scheduled on April 9, 1965. When asked if it would be finished on time, Judge Roy Hofheinz's favorite reply was, "Yes, It's a night game."

The first event held was a game between the Houston Colts, newly renamed the Houston Astros vs. the New York Yankees with an all-star lineup which included Mickey Mantle and Roger Maris. A sellout crowd was on hand, including the President of the United States, Lyndon B. Johnson, sitting in Hofheinz Suite.

It was still daylight outside when the spectators entered the Astrodome, but dark when they emerged from the game after Mickey Mantle hit a home run in the ninth inning to give the victory to the Yankees.

Because the Astrodome was round, every section of the parking lot looked the same and people trying to find their cars became disoriented and frustrated.

The next day a *Houston Chronicle* writer wrote a humorous column about the dilemma. The one that took the cake was the wealthy Texan who stood in the parking lot and exclaimed, "Hell, ah can't even remember which one of ma cars I brought tonight."

The genius of Judge Hofheinz was evident everywhere. Every seat in the Astrodome was upholstered with arm rests; the restrooms were large and clean; the dugouts were twice the normal length so more

Judge Roy Hofheinz

spectators could say, "We sat behind the dugout."

Hofheinz invented the SKYBOX. He took the worst seats in the stadium and made them the most expensive by offering privacy, a bar, private rest room and, live TV of the game in progress. Every stadium built since 1965 has skyboxes in its design.

The Astrodome was built and owned by Harris County. Judge Roy Hofheinz, with a long term lease on the facility, built a fence around the huge parking lot surrounding the dome and charged admission, plus parking fee, to get inside. He took in over $1,000,000 the first year conducting tours alone.

BUYING HOUSTON HOME

We did not get serious about looking for a house in Houston until I had been there for about three months. Then Deenie came down for a weekend so we could search together. We looked at about five or six houses in one day and nothing we saw lit a fire for us.

We were probably spoiled from having lived eight years in the only home we had ever built, one whose design was just about perfect for our family.

Finally, on one Sunday in April, a real estate agent I was working with told me about an older home that had just come on the market. I looked and liked it immediately. It was the original home on a four-acre tract. Three law partners in a prestigious Houston firm had talked the owner into subdividing the tract into four one-acre sites and had built three gorgeous big homes

The home for sale was like an old New England home with a circular drive. It had about 4,000 square feet, living room, dining room, family room, huge kitchen with breakfast eating area opening to a brick patio through sliding glass doors. It also had a maid's house that could be used for guest quarters.

The owner was an Esso International Executive being transferred to Brussels, Belgium. He and his wife had been moved 21 times in 19 years, so they were used to being uprooted. People in IBM who had been transferred frequently referred to their company as, "I've Been Moved."

I was so enthusiastic about this home that after about an hour spent driving all around the neighborhood and realizing I could drive to my new office in five minutes, I went to the realtor's office and told her to draw up a contract. I called Deenie. She said if I felt that positive to go ahead. So, by 7:00 PM we had a signed contract, accepted by buyer and seller.

I was fine until I went to bed. Then I tossed and turned all night. I did not have buyer's remorse. I just wanted reassurance that mine was the right decision. I could not wait for sunrise so I could go back and look at the home and the area again.

After revisiting on a bright new day I was delighted and excited. When we finally met all our new neighbors we realized how VERY fortunate we were.

FAMILY ARRIVES

I went back to New York in June for daughter Dee's graduation from Sleepy Hollow High School in Tarrytown. The ceremony was held in the non-air conditioned high school gymnasium on a very hot humid night. I was relieved when it was suggested all men take off their jackets.

Deenie had done a good job of selling our home on Old Sleepy Hollow Road. So our family was finally ready for the move to Texas. Lois was at Camp Wa-klo at the base of Mount Monadnock, near Keene, New Hampshire.

The other five of us flew non-stop coach to Houston. As we approached the Houston airport a flight attendant came down the aisle saying, "Passenger G. G. Green, please identify yourself." When I did, he told me that a limo would meet the plane on the tarmac. We were to give him our baggage claims and wait until all the other passengers had left the plane.

The Greens arrive in Houston in July of 1965. Clockwise: Adene, Deenie, Gaz, Graham & Marianne. (Lois was at Camp Waklo in New Hampshire.)

On the ground the Eastern Airlines PR representative took us up to the first class ramp to take our picture arriving in Texas. Our baggage was already in the trunk of the Eastern Airlines executive limo when we took our seats for the trip to our motel.

After about two blocks the driver made a phone call, handed me the phone and told Deenie to pick up another phone in the second seat. The voices we heard were Bob Cords, Chuck Harding, Bob Hawkes and a couple of other men calling on my office squawk box welcoming us to Houston.

As we checked into the motel another limo driver stepped forward saying he was at my family's service for the rest of the day. In our rooms we found welcoming flowers, wine and cheese. A huge banner with pistol-packing cowboys was stretched across the swimming pool from one side of the motel to the other, "WELCOME G. G. GREEN FAMILY TO TEXAS."

We got into the second limo and drove to #2 Hedwig Court for the first time to see our new home. Later we learned that one of our neighbors on the court was hosting two tables of bridge. When they saw the limousine, it broke up the bridge game.

They could not believe the NEW NEIGHBORS were arriving in this style.

HARVARD BUSINESS SCHOOL

Three days after Deenie, Marianne, Adene and Graham arrived, I left for two weeks at Harvard Business School for a special course in marketing. This course introduced me to the Harvard Business School case study method. Our 60-person student group was perfect for discussions: about 1/3 from top advertising agencies, 1/3 from the media, and 1/3 from corporate.

We had, for example, the advertising manager for Buick; the publisher of Better Homes and Gardens; the Coca-Cola Brand Manager; representatives from NBC and CBS; all attendees with experience, fertile and mature minds.

The Harvard Business School professors were outstanding. I said after the program was over if I had had teachers like that in college I would have been a straight A student. I am sure my own maturity had much to do with it.

We lived in the regular business school dormitories, which were designed for maximum interaction and communication. Each "can" group consisted of three twin-bed rooms sharing one large bathroom. We went to school three hours per day, but preparation for class required at least six hours.

Be prepared or be embarrassed. We discussed a different case in every class. Every student had a large name plate on his desk. The professor typically would call on one student to describe the case, a second to give more detail about the problems, and a third to propose solutions.

Each professor was like an attorney leading a witness, except you could not be sure he was leading you in the right direction. I have never forgotten the case study on AVON where they hired many, many women whose families had suffered a tragedy or financial setback so they wanted or needed to earn extra income.

The turnover rate of employees was unbelievably high and our professor led the discussion so that the entire class was convinced this was THE problem that was having a terrible effect on their profits.

Finally, the professor let us out of his trap. AVON'S SUCCESS WAS A DIRECT RESULT OF EXTREMELY HIGH TURNOVER. Friends and neighbors bought because they felt sorry for these women.

OUR NEW NEIGHBORS

We could not have handpicked more wonderful neighbors than the three families already living in Hedwig Court, Piney Point Village, Houston 77024. The three husbands were partners in the Andrews Kurth law firm.

One of their other partners in this prestigious firm was Jim Baker, who later became Secretary of State for President George Herbert Walker Bush. Most important for the livelihood of our neighbors was that their law firm handled all of billionaire Howard Hughes's business and personal interests.

JIM DILWORTH was the primary courtroom litigator for the firm. He and Marie had three children Patty, Pam and Jimmy.

JIM DRURY was one of the few people who saw Hughes and was responsible for many of his major interests, including in the Bahamas. He and Frances had four children, Ann, Ellen, Sally and Bobby.

DICK GRAY was the lawyer who flew to Las Vegas the day after Hughes bought THE DESERT INN. Later he moved his family to the Sands Hotel and stayed there. He and Betsy had two children, Carolyn and Richard.

The three couples hosted a welcoming dinner for us shortly after we moved in. I remember telling them, "You three men are all lawyers. I am not, but my older brother is a lawyer in the Internal Revenue Service in Washington." They answered, almost in unison, "We will be friends."

On another occasion, I asked this group the question, "What will happen when Howard Hughes dies?" That time the response was, "Heaven forbid!" Then in serious discussion they agreed they would be secure for at two years because it would take at least that long to settle all of his affairs.

Our children became friends immediately. Graham, who for three years had been attending boy's schools, was now living with beautiful teenage girls about his same age, Patty Dilworth and Ann Drury, on each side of him.

Marianne and Dee had always brought their boyfriends to our homes. Boys normally don't bring their girlfriends home very often. Graham and Ann Drury fell in love. We loved Ann, and they spent as much time in our home as they did next door at the Drury's.

MARIANNE'S WEDDING

During the first semester of her senior year at Depauw University in Indiana, Marianne told her mother and me that she and her Swiss boyfriend, Oscar Hagmann, had discussed the possibility of getting married. Oscar was finishing medical school. They had decided the ideal time to be married, would be after his graduation, but before he started his residency.

Marianne felt, and we agreed, that the only way she could be sure it was the right thing for both of them, would be for her to leave school for one semester and go Switzerland. She did, and one day she called from Europe, told us they were engaged, and she was returning home.

Oscar then came from Switzerland and lived with us in our home for seven weeks prior to the wedding so we could really get to know each other. He had a wonderful, outgoing personality and was a fabulous entertainer in the Victor Borge tradition. Our friends and neighbors loved him.

Graham is best man at Marianne's wedding, 1966.

Two weeks before the wedding our doorbell rang. When Deenie opened the door, there stood Frances Drury, Marie Dilworth and Betsy Gray. They had come to offer to host the rehearsal dinner in place of Oscar's parents who could not be here for the wedding. Marianne had already accepted Betsy's kind offer to let her wear her wedding gown.

Oscar's cousin Irene Robertson and her mother "Aunt Mina" arrived in time for the rehearsal dinner at the Drury's, which was wonderful. When Oscar started to entertain it became memorable.

The wedding was in the First Congregational Church of Houston with our dear friend Dr. W. Leslie Pugh officiating. Graham was best man for Oscar, and Dee was Marianne's maid of honor. The reception was at the Forest Club, the tennis and swim club to which we belonged.

It is not a custom to decorate or hang tin cans from honeymoon cars in Oscar's home country, Switzerland. He loved it. He wanted everybody to know he was "JUST MARRIED." We had trouble convincing him he needed to remove the cans before they left for the beach at Galveston.

After their short honeymoon we said a teary farewell to the happy couple and to Marianne in particular, as she left to start her life in Switzerland.

ASTRODOME EVENTS

I was in "Hog Heaven" at the Astrodome. I had a reserved parking space just outside the door of the elevators to the press box level where, during every baseball game, I could eat a free dinner in the sponsors area, drink free beer (Schlitz), free soft drinks (Coca-Cola), and smoke a free cigar.

A. J. Foyt, three-time Indianapolis 500 winner.

In addition, I had two press passes, one for the Astrodome, and one for all National League games. Since Graham's full name was the same as mine we could, and did, go to many games together. Also, the Coca-Cola Company had a skybox plus eight choice box seats "behind the Astro's dugout."

"The Judge" as Hofheinz was referred to, brought all kinds of exciting events to the Astrodome that we were privileged to witness:

World Heavyweight Championship fights featuring Mohammad Ali. Bob Cords, Astro's second baseman Joe Morgan and I sat together to watch Ali in training. Morgan is now in the Baseball Hall of Fame.

The "Basketball Game of the Century" when the University of Houston, led by Elvin Hayes, ended UCLA's 2-year undefeated streak before 56,000 people in the first nationally televised college game. UCLA's star was Lew Alcinder (Kareem Abdul Jabbar).

The Houston Rodeos starring top entertainers and "Bloodless" Bull Fighting featuring top Mexican Matadors.

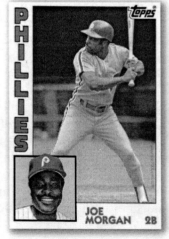

The celebration honoring Neil Armstrong, who on July 20, 1969, took a step out of the Apollo II lunar craft. This "giant leap for mankind" made Armstrong the first man to walk on the moon.

Famous Indianapolis Race Drivers competing indoors. My friend, Hugh Cohn, introduced me to A. J. Foyt and Mario Andretti.

And it allowed Actor John Forsyth (Charlie's Angels) and me to be judges in the Miss Astro contest.

Best of all though, was the opportunity I had, on several occasions, to sit in the radio booth with Gene Elston, Harry Kalas and Lowell Paas as they did the play-by-play broadcast of Astro games in progress.

FILMING UPSIDE DOWN COMMERCIAL

Anybody who has ever had anything to do with creating a commercial knows how difficult it is for even the very best advertising agencies in the world to come up with a commercial that is really different. Our agency, Tatham Laird and Kudner was one of the best.

Mike Farrell

Coffee is a commodity. It is very hard to find discernable differences between one brand and another. Folgers "Mountain Grown" and Maxwell House "Good to the Last Drop" were the two top national brands. It was hard to gain brand share against either of them.

MARYLAND CLUB IS TURNING COFFEE MAKING UPSIDE DOWN TO BRING YOU A BETTER COFFEE.

That message was delivered by Mike Farrell, who went on to fame as one of the stars of "M*A*S*H." The mnemonic device used to make the commercial memorable was to have the visual effect of a man hanging upside down in a woman's kitchen holding a cup of coffee. Mike Farrell was upside down.

Mike is best known for playing Captain B.J. Hunnicutt in the ever popular series "M*A*S*H." His eight years with the memorable show allowed the opportunity to both write and direct several episodes, earning him nominations for Director's Guild and Emmy Awards.

It took about a week to shoot a commercial like this. Bob Cords had gone out to Hollywood for the start of filming and on the first day called me to say we had a problem and should stop all work on collateral material. Hanging upside down Farrell's eyes become bloodshot. We had to paint glasses over his pictures for all support material.

I was there with Bob for the last two days of the filming. It turned out to be a GREAT commercial. Mike was a wonderful guy to work with. He even helped me up onto the trapeze bar he was using so I could experience what he was going through.

Mike came to Houston when we introduced the commercial to our sales organization. I had seen this done many times by Procter & Gamble and knew it was a proven way to get the sales organization motivated.

Oh yes. The other thing I remember about Mike Farrell was that he loved crossword puzzles and spent much of his time doing these when he was not needed in front of the camera. He was a real class guy!

TEXAS PRIDE

Texas Pride has fascinated me from the day I first set foot in Texas, and still does today. TEXAS PRIDE! It is like a "Can Do Spirit," or, stated another way, there is nothing we can't do!

Everything in Houston was exciting. The Space Center was putting Houston on the world map. The Astrodome opened. Jones Hall opened, and I was present opening night for both of these events.

The Standard Oil Company of New Jersey (ESSO), which eventually became EXXON, moved its headquarters from New York to Houston. Shell Oil Company did likewise. New home construction was booming, and urban sprawl extended the city limits.

Houston was the largest city in the United States without zoning. Developers built communities with deed restrictions to protect home owners from undesirable encroachment on their neighborhoods.

"The stars at night are big and bright…deep in the heart of Texas."

There is more truth than fiction in these words, especially if you are not a native. I remember after a parent's meeting one evening at Graham's Kincaid School we came outside and it was raining. Dee (Deenie had shortened her name to Dee when we moved to Texas) said excitedly to me, "It even rains bigger here in Texas." A man standing next to us said, "Another damn Yankee who has moved here."

TEXAS PRIDE. I remember attending a dinner at the Shamrock Hotel in March of 1966 with a group from the Coca-Cola Company. Announcement was made that Texas Western had just beaten the University of Kentucky to win the NCAA Basketball Championship. Everybody cheered.

Andy Anderson, sitting next to me, jumped to his feet, yelling, "Yeah, Texas did it again." I said to him, "Andy, do you realize that whole team is made up of black students from New York."

"THAT DOESN'T MATTER," he said. "TEXAS DID IT AGAIN!"

ELECT GRAHAM THE JOLLY GREEN GIANT

It was about 3:30 in the afternoon when my secretary, Liz Lindow, told me that Graham was on the phone and wanted to talk with me. When I picked up the phone he told me that he had just been nominated to be president of the student body at the Kinkaid School, and he needed help.

Graham was a decided underdog and was told he should have signs and his campaign ready to go first thing the next morning. I told him to come over to the office. We'd see what we could do.

All the people in our marketing department knew Graham and liked him. He had worked for the Coca-Cola Bottling Company during the summer, delivering and installing

vending machines, and then at night we
went to many of the Astros Baseball
games in the Astrodome together.

I called in Bob Cords, Chuck
Harding, George Sullivan and our
fine artist, Ben Thomas. Bob and
Chuck had good friends at the
Green Giant Company and
Graham was big, about 6-feet
3-inches tall, so collectively we
came up with the slogan "ELECT
GRAHAM—THE JOLLY GREEN
GIANT."

With the help of the Green
Giant Company all Graham and
his friends had to do was insert
"ELECT GRAHAM" on the top of
colorful green and white posters
promoting THE JOLLY GREEN
GIANT.

When the Kinkaid students arrived at school the next morning
they found a 20-foot green and
white banner designed by Ben
Thomas stretched across the
driveway entrance exclaiming:
"ELECT GRAHAM—THE JOLLY GREEN GIANT!"

Upon entering the school they found posters on all the
bulletin boards and something none could miss—signs
on every drinking fountain exclaiming "FREE WATER—
COURTESY OF GRAHAM—THE JOLLY GREEN GIANT."
Sound corny? Yes, but corn was one of Green Giant's best
selling products, and the kids loved the signs.

Graham was not expected to stand a chance. This was
only his second year at Kinkaid, and most of the kids in the
school had been together for several years. He ran a great
race, coming in a close second. We were proud of him.

GROUNDED WITH JOHN GLENN

The Coca-Cola Company was very good about letting me get back to New York to visit my family as often as possible since they would not be moving to Houston until school was out in June.

There was a nonstop flight from JFK to Houston that left New York at about 6:00 PM. We always flew first class in Coca-Cola, so this dinner flight with cocktails, wine and gourmet food was a very relaxing way to travel.

On one Sunday evening flight a couple with two young adult children came aboard just before they closed the door and proceeded back into the coach section. I recognized the parents immediately. It was the astronaut John Glenn, his wife Annie, and their children, David 20 and Carolyn 18.

I was (and still am) a great admirer of John & Annie Glenn. I remember watching a parade on TV as they were welcomed back to New Concord, Ohio, where they both had grown up, attended the public schools and Muskingum College. I am not embarrassed to say I had tears in my eyes watching this typical celebration of small town American heroes.

If our flight to Houston that night had been routine I probably would not have seen much of the John Glenn family. But this was before the new Houston Intercontinental Airport opened, and the old airport (now Hobby) was much more susceptible to forced closing by fog.

We circled Houston for about an hour that night with no improvement in the weather conditions. Finally the pilot announced that we would divert to New Orleans where we remained all night.

We all walked around the New Orleans airport where everything was closed or about to close and tried to find a place to rest comfortably. We were all tired, including the

Glenn family, and tried to rest anyway we could,. I was pleased that all other passengers respected their space (no pun intended). As much as I would have enjoyed talking to John and Annie Glenn, I too, respected their privacy and did not intrude.

If I had kept the original title for this book, "Shake The Hand That Shook The Hand O, or Almost Did," John, Annie, David and Carolyn Glenn would have been in the "almost shook the hand of" column.

TASTE TESTING PROGRAM

The Coca-Cola Company had no taste-testing program until in 1966, when they hired Norman Girardo, a Frenchman who was considered to be one of the foremost authorities in the world on taste testing methodology. I was assigned responsibility for the program in Houston.

Norman Girardo came from Atlanta to train me and get the program started. The methodology is made up of several different tests. The triangle taste test is used primarily for "difference testing." Each participant is presented three products, asked to taste all three and then choose the one that is different from the other two.

The triangle taste test is used to determine who can discriminate (i.e., consistently identify the one product that's different) and who cannot.

These discriminators are in turn used as members of small expert panels to assist research and development in formulating and reformulating products.

Triangle taste testing is also used in quality control to determine if a particular production run (or production from different factories) meets the quality-control standard (i.e., is not different from the product standard in a triangle taste test using discriminators).

It was in triangle testing that I discovered that I could not even tell the difference between regular coffee and decaffeinated coffee. I don't know how much money this has saved me. There is no need for me to buy premium beer or expensive wines.

Just call me dumb and lucky.

Years later when I was living in Sun City, Texas and president of Senior University Georgetown, I was pleased to be asked to introduce an oenophile to the audience. That was until I found he was an insufferable snob. So I told the audience how lucky I was that I could drink cheap wine and enjoy it.

When I looked up books about oenophiles on Amazon. com I could not find any. I found Ed McCarthy who wrote "Wine for Dummies." He said, "I'm not an expert oenophile. In fact I can't even spell it."

HE'S MY KIND OF GUY.

CORPORATE PACKAGING COMMITTEE

I was appointed to the Coca-Cola Company Packaging Committee and invited to take a one-week trip to visit five of the largest suppliers in the United States.

We were destined to be treated royally for five days, traveling in the company private plane, then being met by chauffeured limousines to take us to our hotels.

There were eight of us, including three Coca-Cola Company Vice Presidents, the Coke Brand Manager, a representative from Tenco, the instant coffee operation in Linden NJ, and myself.

Here was our schedule—

Monday: Toledo, Ohio—headquarters of Owens-Illinois.

Tuesday: Chicago—headquarters of Continental Can Company.

Wednesday: Chicago—headquarters of American Can Company.

Thursday: St. Louis—headquarters of Anheuser-Busch.

Friday: Richmond—headquarters of Reynolds Metal Company.

In every instance the CEO of the host company welcomed us at an evening informal dinner. In the morning we heard presentations by their marketing departments describing packaging innovations ready or in the pipeline.

After lunch we would get back on the Company plane and go to our next destination to be wined and dined again.

I remember we had steak every night until we got to Richmond, Virginia, where the Reynolds Metal Company

took us out to an historic spot on the Charles River and we
had beer and the most delicious Brunswick Stew I had ever
eaten in my life.

We all agreed it was a thoughtful and welcome change!

LEFTY O'DOUL'S WIDOW

After the creation of the Coca-Cola Foods Division, a
national sales meeting in Palm Springs, California was sched-

uled. Those of us who were making
presentations arrived two days early.

At breakfast on the second day, a
couple of guys reported having met
some "older ladies" from San Francisco
who invited them to their condo the
next evening. They whet my appetite by
informing me that one of them was Lefty
O'Doul's widow, Jean. I admired Lefty
O'Doul, so was eager to meet her.

I knew, for example, that O'Doul
had been a major leaguer for 11 seasons
and had two distinct careers over a
16-year span from 1919 to 1934, first as

Francis Joseph O'Doul

a left-handed pitcher for the Yankees and Red Sox until his
arm went dead.

O'Doul returned to the San Francisco Seals in the Pacific
Coast League and honed his skills as an outfielder for four
years. In 1928 he returned to the majors as an outfielder for
the N. Y. Giants, where over the next 7 years he scored high
in MVP balloting and was in the first all-star game in 1933.

He returned to the Seals in 1935 at age 38 as a player-
manager, continuing as manager through the 1957 season. He
signed and developed the three DiMaggio brothers, Vince,
Joe and Dominick.

During his playing career, and after it concluded, O'Doul
would become one of baseball's greatest ambassadors and
helped popularize the game in Japan. O'Doul headed several
tours to Japan with major league all-stars and became an
idol of fans across that country. He led the development of
professional baseball in Japan.

His widow Jean's account of Lefty's 1954 all-star trip to Japan fascinated me. Lefty had been Joe DiMaggio's best man when he married Marilyn Monroe. Marilyn accompanied the all-stars to Japan and literally stole the show from everybody. Leo Durocher's wife Laraine Day was along and was furious about Marilyn's adulation.

Marilyn filed for divorce nine months after her January 1954 marriage. It was sad the marriage did not last. After her 1962 death of an apparent suicide at age 36, Joe sobbed through her memorial service and sent roses to her gravesite three times a week for the next 20 years.

Marilyn Monroe

RAY SCOTT & JACK KEMP

Super Bowl I, pitting the champion of the upstart American Football League against the champion of the established National Football League was held in the Coliseum in Los Angeles on January 15, 1967. The game was the brainchild of Lamar Hunt, architect of the AFL and owner of the Kansas City Chiefs.

The first of these "Super" contests which, after 40 years, have become the most watched sporting event in the United States, between the Green Bay Packers and the Kansas City Chiefs drew a crowd of 61,946 fans and a television audience estimated at 60 million viewers.

The announcers for the telecast of this game were Ray Scott, long time "Voice of the Packers" and Jack Kemp, quarterback for the Buffalo Bills making his debut as a "color" commentator for the championship game.

Ray Scott's "day job" was host of a daily early morning news program on WCCO radio in Minneapolis. It just happened that Butter Nut Coffee was the sponsor of this news program, so when we were planning for a sales meeting in Minneapolis shortly after the Packers had won 35-10, we invited Ray Scott to come and be our dinner speaker.

Jack French Kemp, Jr.

Bob Cords, a long time Packer fan, and I were both excited and looked forward to meeting Ray Scott. I had no idea before I met Ray that he was from Johnstown, Pennsylvania, was a big Penn State fan and that we had many mutual friends.

Ray was there for our happy hour and was most gracious in greeting and talking with all of our salesmen. I particularly remember the story he told Bob and me privately about Jack Kemp. When you think of Kemp's political career, including a run for Vice President, it sounds almost unbelievable.

At the start of the telecast Ray Scott and Jack Kemp were standing outside the broadcast booth. The director gave them the signal that they were on the air, Scott, a veteran, welcomed Kemp, a novice, and asked him to say a few words. According to Scott, Kemp's lips moved but nothing came out.

JACK KEMP HAD A SEVERE CASE OF STAGE FRIGHT.

FINANCIAL PLANNING COURSE

When Paul Austin, a graduate of Harvard and of the Harvard Business School, became Coca-Cola President and CEO, he recognized an urgent need to upgrade the training of his management team.

He arranged with the "B" School, as Harvard, the pre-eminent graduate business school in the world was known, to develop special courses just for Coca-Cola and franchise Coca-Cola bottler management. K.V. Dey and I attended a program, "Financial Planning for the Non-Financial Executive" held at a Holiday Inn on Longboat Key, Sarasota, so that "B" School faculty and families could enjoy a beach vacation in Florida.

This was a smaller class, a total of 24. More than half represented independent Coca-Cola bottlers. Some, in fact, were third and fourth generation bottler owner family members. I had no idea of the animosity that existed between the company and the bottlers. I could not believe my ears at dinner the evening before our actual classes started.

The original Coca-Cola bottler contracts were into perpetuity and it was almost impossible for the "Company" to cancel a contract, no matter how bad the franchisee's performance was. Also, for many years it had been a one product, one size, and highly profitable business for the bottler.

Now, the Coca-Cola Company had expanded its product line to include Tab, Fresca, Sprite, and a variety of flavored sodas under the Fanta brand. Also, they offered Coca-Cola in many sizes and containers. Some bottlers were reluctant to make the financial investment for new equipment, or they flat out refused to add products to their line. The bottlers could not be forced.

In the national expansion of Sprite, Coke could not sell it in much of California because the Los Angeles bottler was already distributing Seven Up. The issue at dinner that night was Dr. Pepper, a Texas based product wanting to expand nationally through distribution by many Coke bottlers.

The thrust of our course was to understand how various legal accounting techniques produce different results. We organized into six, four-man teams competing to produce the best merger between two companies.

I am happy to report I was captain of one of the winning teams.

CHARTER FLIGHT TO VEGAS

Don Keogh was invited to make an important address to the Packaging Institute of America, which was holding a mid-winter conference at the Camelback Inn in Scottsdale, Arizona. Since packaging was one of my responsibilities, he wanted me to go along with him to the meeting.

After his schedule was confirmed, he accepted another invitation to be the after-dinner speaker two nights earlier in Phoenix. He said that by arriving early, we would have an extra day just to relax.

Keogh was a spellbinding orator and was much in demand as a speaker. He also drank heavily and had a reputation for being able to bounce back with no hangover after very little sleep.

Arizona had some crazy kind of liquor law at that time that did not set well with Keogh. After he had received the adulation and plaudits from his speech, he wanted to relax in a quiet lounge. Vic Hunter, West Coast VP of Tatham, Laird and Kudner, his wife Gloria Blondell, and I joined him.

Without warning, the waitress came over at midnight, told us the bar was closed, and started to take our drinks off the table, even though we had not finished drinking them. She told Keogh it was the law, but he was furious. She said we could not sit there with a drink after the bar was closed.

"OK, let's go to Las Vegas, "Keogh said to the other three of us. Vic, Gloria and I all tried to discourage him, with no luck. Finally, he looked at me and said, "Green, you can't get us to Vegas tonight."

Challenged, I went to a phone booth, got the number for a charter airplane service and within ten minutes had made arrangements with a pilot to meet us at the Phoenix Airport in one hour.

At 1:15 AM we took off in a six passenger single engine Cessna for the three hour flight. It was a beautiful moonlit night. We landed in Vegas a little after 4:00 AM and took a cab to the Desert Inn where Keogh was well known. He gave us each $100 to gamble. My assignment was to make sure the pilot had no alcohol to drink. Don Keogh said he would meet us at 7:00 for breakfast and disappeared.

RETURN FROM VEGAS

I am not a gambler, never have been, except playing bridge for one-tenth of a cent a point on the *USS LARAMIE* or two-bit limit poker on the *USS MANATEE*. I love Vegas for the entertainment and am actually glad I don't like to gamble. This has never been any temptation for me.

The pilot and I watched Vic and Gloria play blackjack for about an hour and then the four of us found a comfortable spot to sit, drink coffee and talk. I wanted to learn more about the exciting backgrounds of Vic Hunter and Gloria Blondell,

Vic Hunter served as advance man for Bob Hope when he entertained the troops around the world in WWII. Most commercials produced by Tatham, Laird & Kudner were produced in Hollywood, and Vic was a perfect talent scout for the agency.

Gloria Blondell was the younger sister of the more famous Joan, but had her own excellent career. History might say her most important role was in the 1938 film "Accidents Will Happen" in which she co-starred with Ronald Reagan, who went on to become President of the United States.

Gloria and her older sister, Joan, were daughters of a vaudeville comedian, and they were raised in the New York theater world. Joan

Gloria Blondell as Nurse Honeybee in "Riley's Operation," 1953.

Blondell got her start in the Ziegfield Follies and moved on to stardom in early Hollywood musicals, co-starring in movies with James Cagney and Dick Powell.

I remembered Gloria Blondell best for her role as Honeybee Gillis, William Bendix's next-door neighbor in the popular "The Life of Riley" TV Show from 1953 to 1958. A mutual friend, Bing Crosby, introduced Vic and Joan on a cross-country train trip from California to New York.

After Don Keogh rejoined us for breakfast, we were ready to start our return flight to Phoenix. Keogh made Gloria sit up front with the pilot with instructions to keep him awake and alert. Vic & Keogh sat in the middle seats, and I climbed in the back row where I could stretch out.

We took off and circled the air field several times gaining altitude necessary to start back over the Rocky Mountains to Phoenix.

I dozed off.

Suddenly the engine cut back. Through the quiet cabin I could hear the pilot exclaiming "MAY DAY, MAY DAY!" and requesting permission to make an emergency landing.

The Airport control tower gave our pilot instructions to land out at the end of the runway and emergency equipment would be there to meet us.

Believe me! That will get you awake in a hurry!

We landed without incident. Our pilot reported that he had oil spraying out of the engine onto his windshield and, even though there was no drop in the oil pressure, he had to make sure it was not something serious.

After a thorough check we were given the OK to take off again for our return flight to Phoenix. I promise you not one of us could sleep a wink after that experience.

More than two hours looking down on the jagged peaks of the Rocky Mountains in daylight became increasingly sobering as we realized the terrible risks we had taken the night before.

TEACHING MARKETING COURSE

Bob Barrus was the advertising manager of Ashland Chemical Company in Houston. We first met when Dee and I were waiting with Bob and Ruth Cords to fly to a national ad meeting at the Homestead in Hot Springs, VA.

I recognized a couple from First Congregational Church at the ticket counter. Bob said, "That's Bob and Roberta Barrus. They are going to the same convention we are." As soon as Bob Barrus had his tickets Bob Cords brought them over and introduced us to each other. That was the start of a warm and wonderful friendship that lasted until Bob died in 1998.

Bob Barrus and I attended three national advertising meetings together. We served together on the Board of Trustees of First Congregational Church. In fact, I succeeded him as president of this board.

Bob also was very active in the Houston Advertising Club, which wanted, in 1970, to sponsor a graduate level course in marketing at the University of Houston. On Bob's recommendation I was asked to teach the class with Lyle Metzdorf, a very creative Houston adman who had his own agency.

Gaz Green, 1967

The class was limited to 24 bright young advertising professionals representing agencies, the media, and various corporations. Virtually handpicked, they were an outstanding group. I remember one young man in particular who was promoted to general manager of the largest network TV station in Houston shortly after completing our class.

Teaching this group was a very rewarding experience. The thrust of the class was to introduce a new consumer product to the market. Lyle handled all the advertising strategy while I was responsible for introductory sales and marketing. When you teach you learn even more about your subject.

Two other bright young professionals were from the leading local Houston advertising agency, Goodwin, Danenbaum, Littman and Wingfield. Two years later I was recruited by John Paul Goodwin, founder and chairman of this agency to join his company as future president, so that he could retire.

I did, found I was like a "fish out of water," and moved on to a new life.

Next, I became a marketing consultant!

CONFIRMING TINY TIM

The marketing committee consisted of Don Keogh, VP Marketing Chairman; Tom Cleveland, Butternut Sales VP; Jim Parker, Maryland Club Sales VP; and me as director of marketing services. Keogh's secretary, Lucille Shaw was the secretary of the committee.

We met often, but not on any set schedule. We all traveled extensively so Keogh usually called for a committee meeting during the same week that we had some other event or meeting requiring our presence.

Most of our marketing committee meetings were routine. We might review budgets, forecasts, personnel, upcoming events, any number of subjects. I had a good working relationship with Keogh and Parker, but ever since the "Unveiling of Tiny Tim," I had been very leery of Tom Cleveland.

It was interesting to me that Don Keogh, Jim Parker and I always kept our office doors open. Tom Cleveland, on the other hand, kept his door closed all the time, and the only way you could see him was through his secretary.

On this particular day, Lucille Shaw called each of us in the morning and said, "Mr. Keogh would like to have a short meeting of the marketing committee at 11:00." As soon as the meeting started, Keogh said, "Lucille, read that letter that Tom Cleveland sent me."

She began to read a letter Cleveland had written to Keogh critical of me. He had not discussed the situation with me, nor had he copied me on the letter. When she finished reading, Keogh said, "OK, Tom, what's this all about?"

I am sure Cleveland was completely surprised that Keogh had put him on the spot like this. He stammered and made a very weak charge that I had told the ad agency in Chicago something that he claimed was his responsibility. After ten minutes Keogh adjourned the meeting and told us to work it out.

When we left the room Jim Parker went into his office and motioned for me to come in. Jim closed the door and said, "That SOB did the same thing to me one time. Don't let it bother you. It just shows what kind of guy he is."

The incident just confirmed to me that Tom Cleveland was indeed "Tiny Tim."

THE BAHAMAS AND THE LYFORD CAY CLUB

Of our three Hedwig Court neighbors we had the closest relationship with Jim and Frances Drury. Jim and I were the same age. He was a big sports fan, and we watched several sports events together. If fact, he took me to one of the first football games I saw in Houston, Rice vs. his alma mater Baylor.

Both Jim Drury and Jim Dilworth were Baylor alumni; Dilworth so enthusiastic that when he was on the Piney Point Village Water Commission he persuaded them to repaint all fire hydrants the Baylor school colors GREEN AND GOLD so "Firemen would be able to find them quickly."

Jim Drury and I were watching a football game in his den one Saturday when I noticed a *Life* magazine with a feature story about the Nassau Bay Street Gang in the Bahamas. I had already read about this small group of Canadians who had gained control of much of the business in Nassau.

In response to my query to Jim whether he had read the article, he replied, "Yes. I know some of them. I have had some business dealings with Sir *** (sorry I cannot remember his name)." This knowledge came in handy later.

The last assignment I had before I left the Coca-Cola Company was to make arrangements for a large sales meeting in Nassau hosting all Minute Maid and Hi-C Brokers throughout the United States. My good friend Bob Cords and I were working together on this project.

Bob and I had already made one trip to Nassau and were preparing to go back to finalize arrangements when Don Keogh received a call that Paul Austin, Board Chairman and CEO of Coca-Cola wanted to stay at the exclusive Lyford Cay Club in Nassau but nobody could get him in.

I phoned Jim Drury and told him about my situation and asked if he might be able to help. Jim said he needed to call Sir *** that day about something else and would get back to me. Thirty minutes later Jim called and said, "It's all set. Here is his address. All you need to do is go to his office. He will look forward to meeting you."

Upon meeting him I learned he had only one condition. He wanted to meet Paul Austin personally while he was in Nassau. Mr. & Mrs. Paul Austin became welcome guests at the Lyford Cay Club and its golf course.

PARADISE ISLAND

In 1971 Charlie Adams, a senior Coca-Cola VP with whom I had traveled for a week as a member of the Coca-Cola packaging committee came to Houston and delivered an ultimatum to the foods division: "Get your marketing department integrated or you will have trouble."

The timing of this message was very important. We were headed for Nassau for a large company meeting. The Coca-Cola Company did not have a good relationship with the franchise bottler in Nassau who was black. That was one reason Paul Austin could not get into the Lyford Cay Club. Normally the bottler in any area had connections. Not so in Nassau.

Don Keogh managed to hire a "token black" just in time before we left for the sales meeting. He was good looking and bright, with an attractive wife. My assignment was to play host to everybody and every situation that could help ease racial tensions and build a better relationship between the Coca-Cola Company and the Nassau franchise bottler.

I was well prepared for every situation. I had Dee with me and she was a conciliator. We had a suite with a bar and a stretch limo with a driver on standby; I had an unlimited expense account and was expected to entertain whomever and wherever I felt it beneficial.

Elsa Rosborough, the highly respected model who had been featured for many years as spokesperson for Maryland Club Coffee, "The coffee you'd drink if you owned all the coffee in the world," was there with her husband, an oil company executive in Houston.

After one of the evening dinners the black Coca-Cola bottler suggested we visit some night spots in Nassau tourists rarely get to see. We had the limo. We invited Elsa Rosborough, her husband, our black marketing member and his wife to be guests of Dee and me. It was a lovely experience.

Charles Duncan and I met Paul Austin and his wife at the Nassau airport and took them to the Lyford Cay Club. They invited me to stay for lunch.

I accepted of course, but was surprised that Austin, the CEO and Duncan, the second largest stockholder, discussed high level, sensitive Coca-Cola Company problems in my presence. They knew I was leaving the Company.

DON KEOGH'S COMPLEXITY

After I left the Coca-Cola Company I often made this statement about Don Keogh. "The most miserable SOB I had ever known, but a marketing genius, and I learned so much from him I should never say a bad word about him."

One observation about which I had no doubt after working for Keogh for six years: his goal was to get to the top, and he would do anything necessary to get there. He had NO loyalty to anyone under him.

He would stop at nothing to get ahead. When he became president of the Coca-Cola Company and Roberto Goizueta was chairman and CEO, I would have suggested Goizueta's security detail include a food taster and someone to watch his back at all times.

Evelyn Harding, the wife of a man who had worked for Keogh for several years, had too much to drink one time and told me how badly he had mistreated her husband. Yet, he was one of Keogh's favorite people.

Tom Cleveland was Keogh's fair haired boy. He often talked about when the two of them were in Omaha together their desks faced each other and they ran the Butter Nut operation. Keogh called him, "Tommy Boy,"

One Sunday Keogh and I flew to New York on an early afternoon flight. He suggested we meet at the airport an hour before scheduled take off so that we could go to the Braniff lounge and have a drink.

Keogh must have had three drinks before we got on the plane. Then, flying first class, the flight attendant brought us drinks as soon as our glasses were empty. Keogh was in a very talkative mood. We discussed a variety of subjects. I tried to pace myself drinking, but he just kept going.

Finally, he started to slur his words and began telling me about the power he had over men who worked for him. He bragged to me that he could be so critical of Tom Cleveland that Tom would go home and throw up. I asked myself, "What kind of man is this?" I could not believe what I was hearing, but Keogh was dead serious.

Like buying a convertible or a boat, for some people, two of the happiest days of my life were my first and last days working for Coca-Cola.

LAS VEGAS AND HOWARD HUGHES

Howard Hughes, 1939

Dick and Betsy Gray, two of our neighbors in Houston, moved to Las Vegas in 1966 so Dick could give on-the-spot legal advice to Howard Hughes as he expanded his holdings in Sin City (No, that is not misspelled). I had a trip planned to Los Angeles and San Francisco. Deenie had never been to the West Coast so I arranged to have her accompany me.

It turned out to be an eventful trip. First, we had dinner in Hollywood with Vic Hunter and Gloria Blondell who had shared that infamous late night charter flight over the Rockies with Don Keogh from Phoenix to Las Vegas. Reliving that experience dominated our entire conversation.

In San Francisco my only meeting took only about an hour so we went sight-seeing. We took a cab through Haight Ashbury, which in the 1960's had become famous as the heart of the counterculture scene.

Because of nostalgia, Haight Ashbury still remains one of San Francisco's most culturally mixed areas with radical bookstores, laid back cafes and second hand clothing boutiques recalling its days of international celebrity.

We also visited Lefty O'Doul's sports bar and rode the cable car to dinner at Joe DiMaggio's Fisherman's Wharf restaurant. From there we could see Alcatraz, the federal maximum security prison from 1934 until 1963, which was home to Al Capone and other world's famous criminals.

Our trip included a weekend in Las Vegas as guests of Dick and Betsy who, with their children, were living in an executive suite at the Sands Hotel, also owned by Hughes, a famous recluse. Vegas casino operators offered reciprocal guest privileges to each other. Bob Mayhew and Dick Gray, his two key executives could eat anywhere, see every show in town at no cost.

Jean Peters

Our weekend included front row seats to see Dean Martin, the hottest show in town, gourmet dinners at the Desert Inn, a sightseeing tour of the Hughes Ranch and a view of the secret home of Hughes's girl friend at the time, movie actress Jean Peters.

Unfortunately, the Vegas lifestyle that tourists enjoy ruined Dick and Betsy's marriage. She told us later, she did not want to raise her children in a cultural sewer. Betsy sold her Hedwig Court home after the divorce.

MY REAL ESTATE LICENSE

We had about ten or twelve other couples, or families, in First Congregational Church with whom we became very dear friends willing to support each other at all times. We prayed, worked and played together.

One of these was Glynn Slayden, a former Texas Christian University basketball star, big, bright, astute, and a true Texan. He was a banker.

After I left the Coca-Cola Company and had some free time he suggested I go to school and get my real estate license. "I have had mine for 25 years," Glynn told me, "I have used it many times. You never know when it will benefit you."

I enrolled in a real estate school with a class of 80 students that met four nights a week for two weeks. I LOVED IT! I had time during the day to read related materials. I was well prepared and looked forward to every class.

We were told that there would be a social event the next night following our final exam. Attendance was not mandatory but, if we passed, they would give us our certificates that night. Otherwise they would mail them to us.

I had not really planned to go.

Then the next morning someone from the school called and talked to Dee. All she told me was that for some reason they wanted me to be there so I agreed to go. SURPRISE. I WAS THE CLASS VALEDICTORIAN!

Who would have guessed, when Glynn Slayden advised me to take a real estate course, that three years later I would be qualified to take a real estate broker's course and exam in New Braunfels so that I could open—

GAZ GREEN REAL ESTATE

"Where Your Green Tree Quickly Becomes a Red Sold Sign"

IN NEW BRAUNFELS IST DAS LEBEN SCHÖN

In New Braunfels is the Good Life!

This developed into one of the happiest periods of my life.

CONSULTING IOWA BEEF COMPANY

Dee and I decided we would get our home spruced up so it would look good if we decided to put it on the market for sale.

I was up on a ladder with a paint brush and a roller when the phone rang. Dee answered it and told me some man from Iowa Beef Company wanted to talk with me.

It turned out to be the new president of Iowa Beef Producers, Inc. He had only been there a few months, but was looking for ways to diversify his company, which was the largest supplier of beef products to supermarket chains in the U.S.

I had handled the contracts for consultants Don Keogh had doing special assignments for him. I knew how much they were being paid, the perks they received, so it was easy for me to quote my fees without prior thought or study. I also knew I could produce the desired results.

He asked me to fly to Los Angeles the next afternoon arriving in time to have dinner with his VP of finance and a CPA from his auditing firm. At dinner I learned more details. He was considering the purchase of a meat distributor in LA who had built a substantial business selling corned beef, plus kosher and non-kosher delicatessen meat products.

We spent all of the next day touring their facilities, examining their product lines, and analyzing their distribution system. Arrangements were made for the CPA and me to stay and have access to any and all information and records we deemed important. IBP president and financial VP flew home.

After three days I went out and bought clothes, some jockey shorts and some shirts. I was being paid an excellent set fee per day, plus all expenses. If I could work seven days a week while I was away, that was fine with me.

That first assignment lasted three weeks. I came home for a weekend and went back to LA for two more weeks. Every evening we called the president, reported our findings and received our next assignment.

Finally he told me to go home for a weekend with my family and then come to the company headquarters in Dakota City, Nebraska.

DAKOTA CITY, NEBRASKA

To get to Dakota City, Nebraska, I flew from Houston to Kansas City, changed planes and continued to Sioux City, Iowa. I was treated like a king as soon as I arrived at the Hilton Hotel in Dakota City. There was a letter from the president of Iowa Beef telling me that a chauffeured car would pick me up and take me back and forth to IBP's headquarters.

His office was in a building next to possibly the world's largest slaughter house. Iowa Beef Products, Inc. was the largest purveyor of beef in the U.S., having pioneered the butchering of beef on a mass scale at one central location and then shipping frozen pre-packaged cuts to retail grocery outlets.

Upon arrival, I learned that the president's office was next to the board chairman who had left for Florida for two months. I was to use his office and have his personal secretary at my disposal at all times. What a setup!

It was obvious from the president's questions, and his instructions to me that he wanted to acquire this Los Angeles company. My job was to develop a marketing plan for him to present to get approval from the IBP board. Basically, the question was, "Could he replicate the Los Angeles experience on a national basis and have it be profitable?"

I relied heavily on my good friend Bill Bienneman, group vice president at Tatham, Laird and Kudner for help. It is routine for ad agencies to do speculative work at their own expense when they are seeking new accounts, particularly one of this potential magnitude.

Through Bill, I was able to get all the projected advertising and marketing costs for introduction into test markets, then the rollout on a national basis. I had gained practical experience at P&G and Coca-Cola plus theoretical experience preparing for the course I taught at the University of Houston.

After six weeks we were just about finished with the proposal when the president shared with me shocking news he had received. His Chairman had had been indicted in New York for offering illegal discounts.

The company terminated the project. I was paid in full, but IBP, instead of diversifying and expanding, was found guilty of other illegal trade practices and in a few short years was acquired by another company.

(USDA)

BEFORE DEPARTNG HOUSTON

During the seven years we lived in Houston our family celebrated several milestones:

♦ Adene was graduated from Vassar and married Richard Wilson, a music professor there. She called a few days before the wedding, saying she and Richard would be wed that weekend in a picturesque setting by Vassar Lake.

♦ Graham played soccer and tennis and entertained on the piano before graduating from the Kincaid School where Congressman George Bush spoke at his Commencement. He worked for the Coca-Cola Bottling Company of Houston in the summers. He then entered Depauw University, became, like me, a Fiji. I had the privilege of pinning the pin on him when he was initiated into Phi Gamma Delta.

♦ Mutti (Dee) and I celebrated our 25th wedding anniversary on January 30 1966 by having dinner with Les and Jettie Pugh at the Forest Club. Lois, the only child at home, helped me install our first stereo system.

♦ Marianne and Oscar lived a frugal, but very busy, life in Switzerland as Oscar continued his residency.

♦ Lisa Hagmann, our first grandchild was born in Switzerland. I received the word just before I conducted a sales meeting in Omaha, Nebraska. Bob Hawkes went out and bought cigars for me to distribute with an announcement at the end of the meeting.

♦ Lois grew into a lovely young lady. She made us all proud when she volunteered to spend one summer working for the American Cancer Society to honor her dear neighbor friend Steve who died that year.

♦ As a family we rejoiced in the nourishment we received from our involvement in the Congregational Church.

♦ We loved our years in Houston, developed many life-long friends there, and now looked forward to Life in New Braunfels.

HERSKOWITZ & GEORGE W. BUSH

In writing my memoirs, another surprise revelation I came across was that Mickey Herskowitz, whom I had known in Houston primarily as a sports writer, had developed a successful career as ghostwriter for the biographies of 30 prominent Americans.

Mickey Herskowitz

Russ Baker, an award winning independent journalist who has been published in the New York Times, The Nation and the Washington Post, interviewed Herskowitz for an article he published October 28, 2004 on the website gnn.tv.

He reported that two years before 9/11, Candidate George W. Bush was already talking privately about attacking Iraq, according to his former ghost writer.

In 1999 Herskowitz struck a deal with the staff of Texas Gov. George W. Bush to write his autobiography as he was preparing for his first Presidential campaign. He signed a contract stipulating that he and Bush would split the profits from the sale of the book, *A Charge to Keep. My Journey to The White House*. William Warren, publisher.

Herskowitz was given unimpeded access to Bush, and, as reported by Russ Baker, an award winning independent journalist, the two met approximately 20 times so Bush could share his thoughts.

In May 1999, within two months after he started working on the book, Herskowitz had completed and submitted 10 chapters and had four to six more in his computer. Suddenly, when Bush's handlers concluded that his views and experiences were not being cast in a positive enough light, Herskowitz was replaced by Karen Hughes.

Is it any wonder? Bush in 1999 reportedly said he had been thinking about invading Iraq and felt his father had wasted a great opportunity by not taking out Saddam Hussein when he had his chance.

If you are interested you can check this out yourself.

• Did George Bush say, as it has been claimed by Mickey Herskowitz, that one of the keys to being a great leader is to be seen as a commander in chief?

• Did George Bush feel that his father had wasted political capital by not taking Saddam Hussein?

• Bush admitted that he failed to fulfill his Vietnam era domestic National Guard service obligation, but claimed he had been "excused."

• Bush revealed that after he left his Texas National Guard unit in 1972 under murky circumstances, he never piloted a plane again. That casts doubt on the carefully choreographed moment of Bush's emergence in pilot's garb from a jet on the aircraft carrier USS Abraham Lincoln in 2003 to celebrate "Mission Accomplished in Iraq. This created the impression that Bush had played a role in landing the craft.

He also had described his own business ventures as "floundering" before campaign officials insisted on recasting them in a positive light. So, said Herskowitz, the best material was left on the cutting room floor. "He told me that as a leader, you never admit a mistake... that was one of the keys to becoming a leader."

Herskowitz, who had written biographies for such notables as Michael Deaver, John Connally and Dan Rather, gained retribution three years after being pulled off the George W. book when the President's father called him and asked him to author the biography of George W.'s Grandfather, Senator Prescott Bush, scion of this political family.

Book written by George W. Bush, Mickey Herskowitz and Karen Hughes, published by Harper Collins in 1999.

To read more, Google Mickey Herskowitz "Two Years Before 9/11" or log on to: http://www.commondreams.org/ headlines04/1028-01.htm

CHAPTER NINE

TAKING A YEAR OUT

It was June 1972. Graham was graduating from DePauw University. Lois was graduating from Memorial High School in Houston and had been accepted at the University of Texas.

Mutti (Dee) and I decided to take a year out of our lives to "see what we wanted to do." We looked into the Peace Corps and investigated lay church work. Our kids thought we were going to become hippies and applauded.

Our dear friend Les Pugh had been called to become the senior pastor of the 2,000 member First Protestant Church in New Braunfels, also the tenth largest United Church of Christ church in the United States. Les suggested we move to New Braunfels and take our year out there.

We went to New Braunfels to look around. Les was like the Chamber of Commerce showing us around. He drove us up picturesque River Road to Canyon Lake then to T-Bar-M Tennis Ranch partially owned by John Newcomb, the Australian Tennis star who lived there with his family.

We liked what we saw, went back to Houston and put our house in shape. We listed it with a real estate broker and returned to New Braunfels to look for a place to live. The second day we received a phone call from our broker saying she had an offer for full price on our home. We had to do something very quickly.

We found a small home on that portion of the Guadalupe River below town called Lake Dunlap. The other recreational lake on the river between New Braunfels and Seguin is Lake McQueeney, downstream from Lake Dunlap.

We had a New Braunfels address but actually lived in a different county and congressional district.

It took about 10 minutes to drive into New Braunfels, and we quickly became part of that community. Les Pugh was pastor of the biggest church in town and was very helpful in seeing that we met people quickly.

Harry Preston, a friend of Les and a former Houston banker owned the Guaranty State Bank. He volunteered to finance our home, so in almost no time, we had bought a lake house and made our first investment in the town which had become known as Houston's playground.

GETTING RENEWED

When we moved to New Braunfels the first thing we did was unwind completely. I was 51, Mutti 48. We had downsized from a 4,000 square foot home to a 1200 sq. ft. lake house. We added a huge deck and an extra room for the piano and library and loved living there.

It was a beautiful setting, overlooking the lake. It did not take us long to get into the spirit. From our boat dock we could go inner tubing, swimming and even have an occasional moonlight night skinny dip.

When friends from Houston came to visit us, we would get out on the lake in inner tubes with a can of beer and talk about how much money could be made in New Braunfels, a charming sleepy German community founded by settlers from the old country in 1845.

New Braunfels had two beautiful rivers running through the town. We lived on the Guadalupe and the other, the Comal, came out of springs year round at 70 degrees so you could swim all year. In the summer it cools you off, while in the cold weather it warms you up.

The town had a big summer tourist trade attracted by the lure of the rivers, especially with the opportunity to float down the Comal River in an inner tube, or to negotiate the rapids of the Guadalupe in a raft.

Camp Warneke was the largest and most famous resort on the Comal. "The Other Place," the name chosen when some local investors built a smaller overnight accommodation next to Camp Warnecke. The others were Heidelberg Lodges and Camp Landa, both further up stream from Camp Warnecke.

Bob Henry, a CPA with one of the large accounting firms in Houston, had purchased Camp Landa just before we moved there and changed the name to Landa Resort. Bob was a real idea man with great plans for the expansion of the Landa Resort and the future development of Schlitterbahn Waterpark Resort, the finest water park in the United States.

Bob Henry started by spearheading a movement to build a winter visitor program that would attract "Snowbirds" from the upper Midwest to spend part or all of their winters in the warmer climate of New Braunfels.

BEFRIENDED BY THE BIG BOYS

When we bought our home on Lake Dunlap, Harry Preston, Guaranty Bank president had his bank attorney, Bill Borchers handle the legal work for us.

This was the first time we had met Bill, who had been a leading attorney in New Braunfels for many years.

I will never forget Mr. Borchers asking me at that meeting, "Mr. Green, what do you plan to do here in New Braunfels.?"

"I don't know," I replied. "I am just taking some time out. I may be interested in getting into some investments."

"Investments! Investments!" he exclaimed!

Then he put everything down and told me that he and Harry Preston and some friends were planning to build a travel trailer park along the Comal River across from the Wursthalle. Before I knew it he, Mutti and I were out his back door getting into his car to inspect the proposed site.

Two days later I had breakfast and met more of the principals in the "Landa Trailer Park" project. They included Herb Schneider, board chairman of New Braunfels Utilities, and Claude Scruggs, owner and publisher of the New Braunfels Herald and Zeitung, the only newspaper in town.

For a modest investment all kinds of doors opened for me in New Braunfels. Our group met one morning every week for breakfast to make and receive progress reports on our project. In addition, Claude Scruggs and I were assigned the responsibility of developing marketing plans.

Claude was also one of the owners of the local radio station KNBT and highly respected in the community. He and I met at least a couple times a week to explore ideas and opportunities to promote the Landa Trailer Park as it was being built.

I had no idea that this developing relationship with Claude Scruggs would lead eventually to his recommending me for a job which guided me to a whole new career and the birth of three grandchildren in New Braunfels.

EXPLORING THE HILL COUNTRY

Mutti had always encouraged me to "Take time to smell the roses," but I was always in a rush to get there, wherever THERE might be.

As part of our unwinding, and getting renewed, we took advantage of the opportunity to take leisurely drives throughout LBJ's beloved Hill Country.

Lyndon Baines Johnson, who became the 36th President of the United States after the assassination of John Kennedy on November 22, 1963, was elected a year later to a four-year term and served until January 30, 1969. He was president when we moved from New York to Houston in 1965

Johnson was born in Stonewall, Texas, on 27th August, 1908 and died of a heart attack at San Antonio on January 22, 1973, while we were living in New Braunfels about 30 miles away.

The Johnson Ranch is on the Pedernales River between Fredericksburg and Marble Falls, less than an hour's drive from where we lived. In our exploring we visited the En-chanted Rock, picking up samples from the quarry where the marble was extracted to build the state capitol building in Austin.

Yes, the Hill Country is rugged, but the rolling hills exhibit such natural beauty it was easy to understand why Johnson loved it so much. The LBJ Ranch, is now a national shrine open to the public.

We also visited Kerrville and the upper Guadalupe River, home to many of Texas's most popular young people's camps, like the one our friend Ann Eastman's parents owned. Ann's roommate at the University of Texas, along with Ann, was a counselor at the camp when she was being courted by her husband to be, future Texas Governor John Connally.

Technically, New Braunfels, was not in the Hill Country, but rather was in the escarpment, or on the edge. The terrain changed completely when we traveled south to San Antonio, but not the charm. We explored and we loved choice of where we wanted to live. And we had never been so happy.

In New Braunfels ist das Leben schön …

In New Braunfels is The Good Life!

THE NEW CIVIC CENTER

New Braunfels was about to open a beautiful new Civic Center two blocks from the Plaza in the center of the town. Under a contract with the city, the Chamber of Commerce would move its headquarters to a building next door and be responsible for the management of the Civic Center.

New Braunfels Herald publisher Claude Scruggs told Tom Purdum, chamber manager, about my background and recommended me for the newly created position of Manager of Conventions and Tourism. The responsibilities included managing the Civic Center and being assistant Chamber manager.

Every city has its political "Ins" and "Outs," those who are currently in power and those they replaced. In my series of interviews, I soon discovered that my associates in the Landa Trailer Park, with the exception of Scruggs, were the political "outs."

Tom Purdum did not attend Rev. Pugh's church, but he was part of a men's group that met with Les for lunch each Friday and had a very high regard for him. He was aware of my long time relationship with Les and talked to him about me. Fortunately, Les gave me a good recommendation! I was hired.

I quickly learned that the Civic Center was hotly contested, had passed 51% to 49% in a bond election, and there were some very vocal critics...before it was built. Fortunately, when completed, it was so beautiful that the noise of the opposition was muted.

My primary job was to sell the Civic Center. I think I spoke to every organized group in town. Claude's newspaper gave us great support, and I was on the local radio so much people came to recognize my voice when I called on the telephone. The name Gaz Green became well known.

When we had more than 50 days occupancy booked for the first year, I told Tom Purdum we needed to have an "objective" to use as our goal. He agreed and we picked 100 days and all reports thenceforth showed we had reached 78% of objective, then 94%, now 122%.

We ended the year at 147% of objective and everybody was happy. No one ever questioned who set the objective. Let's call this Salesmanship 101.

THE GREEN AND WHITE WEDDING

F. Clifton White, the first of the big time political consultants, was the man who maneuvered the Republican nomination for Senator Barry Goldwater for President in 1956. He also is the person who brought Ronald Reagan into politics, making his first nation-wide speech, in support of Richard Nixon.

Clif managed the campaigns of Jesse Helms for the U.S. Senate from North Carolina, as a Republican. He ran the successful campaign for Conservative Jim Buckley when he became the only third party candidate ever to be elected to the U. S. Senate from New York State.

Clif had been a professor at Cornell University before he moved to Rye, NY to start his consulting career. He had served on the city council in Ithaca with Les Scott. The two couples, Clif & Bunny White and Les & Marie Scott had become very close friends in Ithaca.

As if it were preordained, all three of us couples moved to Westchester at about the same time. Les Scott accepted a position with the Rockefeller family so the Scotts & Greens settled in Pocantico Hills. We had not been there a month before we met Marie at a Sunday school teachers meeting and started a life long friendship.

The Whites had two children, Kip and Carole; the Scotts had two, Tina and Scotty. The Greens had four, Marianne, Adene, G. Graham III, and Lois.

Before Clif died in 1993 we shared four grandchildren, Tabitha, G. Graham IV, Meghann and Garrett. This was the result of a beautiful Green & White wedding in the Rye Presbyterian Church in 1974 when Carole White became the bride of G. Graham Green III. The reception was at the Rye Country Club.

There was not a dry eye in the house when Carole, accompanied by Graham at the piano, sang in her beautifully trained soprano voice, "Thank You for Letting Me in Your Life," that Graham had written for Carole, just for their wedding. Since then Carole has been asked many times to sing it, and it is just as beautiful now as it was that day in Connecticut.

After Ronald Reagan became the 40th President, Clif had a direct line to the First Lady, Nancy for any message he wanted to give to the President.

BECOMING PART OF THE TOWN

It did not take me long to realize that living in New Braunfels was very much like my small towns in Pennsylvania. Tom Purdum was a Rotarian and encouraged me to become a member of the Noon Lions Club, the largest service club in town.

The "Ins" and the "Outs," again. The "Ins" accepted me like I was a long lost brother while my friends, the "Outs" still considered me one of their own. I swear at the end of 90 days I knew where every body was buried.

The city council met bi-weekly. I attended every council meeting because the chamber was very involved. We, the "Ins" controlled the council 5 to 2. After every council meeting Tom Purdum and I drank beer with "our" mayor and "our" four council members and planned our "agenda" for the next two weeks as we prepared for the next meeting.

Jack Ohlrich, a realtor/rancher was mayor: Dr. Stanley Woodward was mayor pro-tem. Stanley was also my personal physician. He always ended every beer drinking session with the comment, "Well, I've got brain surgery scheduled for 7:00 in the morning so I had better get home." It was a joke, of course.

Dee and I became good friends with all of these people and became part of the social life in the community. We were invited to join a very exclusive dance group, the Ski Lodge at Lake McQueeney and played tennis regularly at Newk's Tennis Ranch. Church, as always, was very important to us.

Before the end of my first year in the Noon Lions Club I was chosen by the nominating committee to be the next third vice president, on the path to become president in three years. The two men ahead of me were Norm Whisenant, school superintendent, and Bob Pfeiffer, a leading attorney who became the district court judge.

When I accepted the position at the Chamber of Commerce I had no idea that I would be going into business in New Braunfels. But, I fell in love with the town and the people. The public exposure, and positive publicity I received certainly put me in a good position to capitalize on my name—Gaz Green, hard to remember, but even harder to forget when you see it and hear it repeatedly. That's why I want you to CALL ME GAZ.

BECOMING A STOCK BROKER

I had an account with the only stock broker in New Braunfels, Tom Spicer, and we had become friends. He was from Wisconsin by way of Florida.

When I was trying to decide what I wanted to do, Spicer, who represented a small member firm of the N.Y. Stock Exchange suggested I come in with him. He introduced me to the owners of his company, and they agreed. So, Gaz Green decided to become a stock broker. (It did not take me long to learn the client takes credit for any recommendation that turns out well; if it goes bad, it is the broker's fault.)

As I recall, the rules back then required that I had to work in a brokerage office three months before I could take the required examinations. They gave me a minimum stipend. Basically, all I did was answer the phone, observe Tom Spicer, and study, study, study.

First I had to pass the NASD (National Association of Securities Dealers) exam and then the NYSE (New York Stock Exchange) exam. They totaled about four hours and had to be passed in one sitting, with no break. Failing any one of the four sections of the NYSE meant failing the entire exam.

I will assume that all readers of this will have taken an examination for a driver's license, which requires memorization of legal rules, which, once the exam was completed, were never used again. That was the way the NYSE exam was structured. One part was nothing but legal rulings which had to be learned for this situation only.

Between the time I flunked out of college in my freshman year and this exam, I had nothing but great success academically. So it was a big disappointment to me when I learned I had failed one section of the NYSE and had to wait 90 days to take the exams again. Eventually I passed.

The stock market was so bad that in the year I was in this office the Dow Jones Industrial Average lost almost 40% of its value and NYSE member firms were allowed to sell insurance and real estate, plus securities.

I already had a real estate license so once I began; I took to real estate like a duck takes to water. I loved it and I KNEW FOR SURE WHAT I WANTED TO DO.

CATTLEMEN'S HALL OF FAME

Tom Spicer acted like some kind of a nut case. There is no other way for me to describe his behavior. He had been a schoolteacher but did not like that and decided to become a stockbroker, and he hated that. He lived on a farm near me and left the office every afternoon as soon as he could after the stock market closed, which was at 3:30 Central Time.

Tom had lived in Ft. Lauderdale near the International Swimming Hall of Fame which was started by, or to honor, Buster Crabbe, who won the 400 meter freestyle championship in the 1932 Olympics. Crabbe parlayed his fame into a movie career in which he appeared in more than 100 films.

Spicer had the illusion he would create and build a CATTLEMEN'S HALL OF FAME in New Braunfels. "This is the real reason I moved my family here," he told me. He wanted me to show him how to get it started.

"The first thing you do is get some letterhead stationary," I said. He had some available when the opportunity came.

There was a shortage of beef and one day the major story on the news was that a meat purveyor in Washington DC had refused to cave-in to pressure from the White House to provide some special cuts of beef for President Nixon.

"Now is the time to act," I told Tom. "The Cattleman's Hall of Fame will name the meat purveyor 'Man of the Year' and we will send out a press release to all the major newspapers, magazines, radio and TV stations, plus the Associated Press and United Press International on our stationary."

It worked so well a TV Station in San Antonio sent a live crew to interview Tom (who came across like a nut) and the *San Antonio News* had a front-page story. It was carried throughout Texas on the Texas State Radio network (including a taped interview).

The following week *Time* magazine's cover story said that the Cattleman's Hall of Fame in New Braunfels named the purveyor "Man of the Year."

It all appeared to be a HOAX; the beginning and end of Spicer's Hall of Fame.

THE STORK DELIVERS

When we were ready to open our real estate office we visited our friends in the advertising department of the New Braunfels Herald. I believe they saw immediately that our entry into the real estate business would increase the total real estate advertising they would get for their paper. That was obvious. Until my entry, the largest ad run by another real estate company in this weekly newspaper was a 2-column x 4-inch ad. Here I was asking them to help me create a one-third page ad, probably ten times the size of their regular ads. Ken Armke, the Advertising Manager created the PERFECT AD FOR US:

FIRST DAY IN BUSINESS

When you start a new real estate business, run your first advertisement and open the door for the first time, you don't know what to expect. Will anybody call? Will anyone come in? It did not take us long to find out.

We knew we had a great office location, just off the Plaza in the center of downtown New Braunfels. The island in the middle had a bandstand and several park benches. Around the traffic circle were the Comal County Courthouse, the New Braunfels Utilities, First National and Guaranty State Banks, the New Braunfels Savings and Loan and several retail stores.

Our office initially had two rooms. Mutti's desk in the reception area facing the street had two chairs for clients. My office also had two guest chairs and was separated from her office by a door and a window. Directly across the street was Naegelin's Bakery, a 75-year old institution popular with tourists.

Gaz Green
REAL ESTATE

Within two hours after we opened we had SIX people come in the office at one time and only four chairs. Mutti and I gave up our seats and sat on the window sill facing the clients who were all from out of town and had seen our ad.

One couple was interested in a home we had listed and one man was from McKinney (near Dallas). He owned property on I-35 and was just passing through town. He had his property listed for sale with another real estate firm, had no action on it and after visiting, listed it with us.

The couple looking for a home bought one of our listings during our first week in business. It was a listing I had gotten by going to the *New Braunfels Herald* and looking up FISBOS (Homes For Sale By Owner) that had been advertised six months before. I called all the owners to find out whether they had sold their homes. If not, I asked for the listing.

So, the first week I sold a home for $40,000. My listing, my sale, with a six percent commission so I earned $2,400 in the first seven days. What a shot in the arm for starting a new business!

After that first day I ordered four more chairs. I said I would not have an office where we could not all sit down. I continued buying office furniture for the next three years as we GREW and GREW. IT WAS FUN!

CHRIS REMMERT

When I took the real estate broker's course there was an attractive, very bright woman in the class named Chris Remmert. She had been in the real estate business in Corpus Christi, was experienced and knowledgeable.

One night, toward the end of our classes, I told her that I planned to open my own office and invited her to come visit me. During our second week in business she came in and talked with both Mutti and me and joined us.

Chris was exactly what we needed. She knew the real estate business, and I knew marketing. We combined our talents and the synergistic effect was that my one plus her one equaled three.

We had very attractive white signs with green lettering and graphics. GAZ GREEN REAL ESTATE. Our logo was a GREEN TREE which was the mnemonic device that made them recognizable and memorable. Thirty years later I still meet people in Sun City and Georgetown who tell me they remember seeing our signs.

Interstate 35 goes from the Mexican border to Canada and runs right through New Braunfels. In addition, Loop 337 goes around New Braunfels. I knew enough about the power of outdoor (billboard) advertising to set the goal of having our 4 ft. x 8 ft. signs dominate along these two highways.

By the time we had been in business three months, a visitor to New Braunfels would immediately think we were the biggest real estate company in town. We continued to use creativity in our newspaper ads as more agents switched from other companies to work with us.

Before we opened, NO real estate office in New Braunfels was open Wednesday afternoon, Saturday afternoon, or at all on Sunday. Then one day Bob Fox, manager of an upscale mobile home park, and a Lt. Col. friend of his who worked at Randolph AFB in San Antonio came into my office.

They both had real estate licenses and wanted to keep our office open all day every Saturday and Sunday. WE BECAME THE ONLY COMPANY OPEN SEVEN DAYS A WEEK!

GRAHAM JOINS US

After about a year Graham (GGG III) and Carole came to visit us. Graham said he would like to move to New Braunfels and come into the Business with us.

Graham had met some of our close friends, including Dr. Arlen Tieken, Assistant Superintendent in the Comal Independent School District. Arlen was responsible for the Adult Education Program, and he offered Graham a part-time job administering that program in the Canyon Lake area.

That gave Graham and Carole a minimum income so they could get by until he became licensed in real estate. This was perfect for us as we had wanted to open a branch office next to the Canyon Lake Bank, and it gave Graham an opportunity to get to know many people in that area.

When Graham and Carole were married, Graham was teaching and coaching at the Rectory School in Pomfret, Connecticut. He and Carole were also dorm parents for the boys living in their "house."

At the end of the school year Carole's father, F. Clifton White, a Republican political consultant with a lot of influence, helped them to relocate to Washington where they worked in the Department of Education.

Carole, Graham, Gaz & Mutti

Graham's boss at the Department left to become a senior executive at the Motorola Corporation and took Graham with him. So, when Graham made the decision to come to New Braunfels he was leaving a good position selling communications systems for bus fleets to school districts.

Also, Tabitha White Green had been born in Virginia, so they had an additional mouth to feed.

But it turned out to be the most wonderful move possible. After Graham arrived, our business really took off, and by the end of two more years we had a total of six offices from San Antonio to Austin and about 75 agents. We worked hard, but we also played hard and lived a wonderful life.

We worked together for ten years. We respected each other and never had a serious disagreement. I not only LOVED Graham. I LIKED HIM, TOO.

THE HONORABLE BOB KRUEGER

Arlon Krueger, prominent business man in New Braunfels, owned the largest car agency in town, the Faust Hotel and a Hosiery Mill. He had one son, Bob, Vice Provost and Dean of Arts and Science at Duke University, and a daughter whose husband worked in the auto agency.

In 1973 Arlon Krueger died of cancer, and Bob came home from Duke University to take over responsibility for the family business interests.

Bob remodeled a small private home next door to the Faust Hotel a half block from us to be his private office.

Bob was a graduate of Southern Methodist University with an MA from Duke. He received his PhD in literature at Oxford before

Bob Krueger

beginning a distinguished career in education. Nobody had any idea Bob was interested in running for public office when he returned to Texas, but Terry Sanford, former progressive governor of North Carolina was the president of Duke and told Bob he had an obligation to share his talents for the public good.

In 1974 O. C. Fisher of San Angelo, who had served in Congress for 32 years, announced he would not seek re-election. The 21st District representing mostly rural counties stretched from the suburbs of San Antonio far out into West Texas.

This open seat attracted several well-known politicians, including both former and currently serving statewide office holders, plus a political unknown—Bob Krueger. There were not many Democrats in New Braunfels, but when asked, I offered to help in any way I could in his campaign.

I made all the arrangements for Bob to make his announcement address from the gazebo on the Plaza. When we learned he would need a podium I put a KRUEGER FOR CONGRESS bumper sticker on the back of Lois's music stand. That picture then appeared in all his campaign literature.

O. C. Fisher (LB Smith)

Bob Krueger, to everyone's surprise forced a runoff and in a major upset, defeated Nelson Wolfe for the Democratic nomination. Wolfe, former state senator and mayor of San Antonio, had never lost a race before.

Bob cruised to victory in the November general election and was chosen one of the top ten freshmen in the 94th Congress by the New York Times.

THE RIVER RESTAURANT

Melvin Jochec, who owned a private accounting firm in New Braunfels, came to my office one day. He wanted me to "front" a group of private investors to buy and develop a choice piece of property to build an upscale "River Restaurant and Biergarten," overlooking the Comal River.

Melvin had his office in a professional building owned by doctors and dentists. I knew his investors and felt really privileged to have been chosen, not only to represent them, but also to become part of this select group.

I introduced the group to Gary Long, a young professor of architecture at Rice University, who was our church friend from Houston. Gary was a graduate of Rice with advance degrees from MIT. He became our architect.

Our real estate company gained an excellent reputation. The River Restaurant, when completed, became a showplace. Shortly thereafter we sold the nearby "Prince Solms" Inn, which had the lovely courtyard where Lois and Charlie Reiter were married.

One success led to another. Graham sold the land along IH-35 to the people from Houston to build the Holiday Inn and we sold the "Crystal Chandelier" where Country & Western star George Strait got his start.

The owner of another choice property, David Dye, asked us to help him build and market the first deluxe condominiums on the Comal riverfront. Unfortunately, we were TOO SUCCESSFUL—other developers copied us, and soon the market was overbuilt.

My favorite story was selling the Hotel Faust. It had been vacant for years, was in a bad state of disrepair, and had been on the market for a year with another realtor with no interest shown. Bob Krueger wanted me to sell it. I knew it would be a challenge. It had about 60 very small rooms.

Mutti and I went to Germany for the opening of Oktoberfest. We stayed in a little hotel in downtown Munich. I walked into a tiny room. Voila: the light bulb went on in my head. HERE WAS THE FAUST HOTEL, A SMALL AUTHENTIC GERMAN HOTEL. I was excited! I came home and sold THE CONCEPT AND THE FAUST HOTEL to Houston investors in less than sixty days to renovate and re-open. Ii is still popular today.

BAVARIAN VILLAGE

Jerome Nowotny, a genuine CHARACTER, was born in a rock house a block away from the New Braunfels Hospital. He wanted to be an actor, and as a young man, lived in a rooming house in Hollywood for a year trying to break into the movies.

Jerome collected beer bottles as a hobby and claimed to have the largest beer bottle collection in the world. Nobody challenged his claim. He built a covered dance floor behind his house and kept his collection in an adjacent building. I don't recall that anybody ever paid to see just the bottles.

The Biergarten at Bavarian Village was very popular. The specialty of the house was a Six Foot Long Sandwich. It was carried by two people on a six foot long board. When live music was available a fanfare accompanied its being served.

We loved Bavarian Village. Les Pugh took us there the first time, bought a pitcher of beer and said, "Now this is New Braunfels." Mutti and I were there on September 30, 1976 waiting for the stork to land at the hospital and deliver Gazexer Graham Green IV.

Accordionist Ed Kadlecek had the most popular oompah band in New Braunfels. His children played in his band while they were growing up. Rennie Guenther had been his tuba player for several years. When our Graham, a pianist, wanted to learn the accordion, Ed encouraged him, and Graham eventually became a valuable permanent member of the group.

The Kadlecek band was featured regularly at Bavarian Village. It was no surprise that when Jerome retired, his sons offered to sell the Village to us. They offered us owner-financing so Ed, Graham and I bought the establishment.

The Kadlecek Band became the Bavarian Village Band immediately and everywhere the band played, cruise ships, other festivals, they passed out flyers and invited their fans to come to Bavarian Village in New Braunfels.

Graham's wife, Carole, added her beautiful voice to the ensemble. Their children began to perform at a very young age and started their own musical careers with the Bavarian Village Band.

HEIDELBERG HALLE

When we sold the "Crystal Chandelier" the second time (to some of the same Houston investors who bought the Faust Hotel), Graham and I decided to invest our share of the selling commission and become "limited partners." We did this to learn something about the dance hall business and also how to construct and operate a limited partnership.

Within a couple of months the owners of El Conquistador, a dance hall that catered to the Mexican American population, approached us and asked us to sell their property.

El Conquistador was about 50% larger than the Crystal Chandelier and had the added advantage of being located on IH-35 with thousands of cars passing it every day. The 17,000 sq. ft. air conditioned building had a 4000 sq. ft. parquet wood dance floor and seating for more than 1,000 patrons.

It was beautiful and I was right when I ventured that probably 95% or more of the New Braunfels area Anglo residents had never been inside. Graham and I decided to form a limited partnership as the vehicle for purchasing El Conquistador, change the décor to a German theme and re-name it "Heidelberg Halle." We had no problem finding investors.

Our initial plan was to feature oompah band music every Saturday night and capitalize on the popularity of Wurstfest, but that was not successful.

After some experimenting we settled on a program of being open four nights each week. Thursday was "College Night," Friday "Rock & Roll," Saturday "Country & Western" and Sunday was "Big Band Music."

The most successful nights were the Sunday 6:00 - 10:00 PM dances. During the winter months we had a large crowd of "Snowbirds" aka "Winter Visitors" who came to New Braunfels to escape the cold of the upper Midwestern states.

The memories of Glen Miller, Tommy Dorsey, Russ Morgan, Guy Lombardo and other famous big band musicians had spawned ghost bands with excellent musicians playing their popular arrangements.

Sunday night at Heidelberg Halle became THE SOCIAL EVENT OF THE WEEK where the senior crowd could dress and wear their finest.

HEIDELBERG REFLECTIONS

As I look back, "The Agony and the Ecstasy," the name of a TV sports show probably describes my experiences at Heidelberg Halle perfectly.

If I could ever have been accused of being stubborn, it was probably appropriate here. I was absolutely determined to make Heidelberg Halle profitable. We tried everything, including BINGO two nights a week. But, we just could not generate enough income on a steady week-to-week basis to pay our mortgage and cover all our other expenses.

Often I would work in our real estate office all day and then go to Heidelberg in the evening, planning to stay only a short time, then not get home until after midnight. The agony ended when we found a prospective buyer to take over and operate it on a lease/purchase arrangement.

Let me dwell on the happy experiences. The Sunday night crowds came from long distances to dance to the big band sound. They loved us. I remember when we had the Glen Miller Band, the conductor asked if they could stay after the dance and have a rehearsal. "We seldom get to play in a dance hall as nice as this," he said. We stayed, watched, listened & enjoyed.

"Johnny Dee and the Rocket 88's" played "Fifties" music and had a large following. After moving to Georgetown I heard this group in San Gabriel Park 20 years later, and they were still going strong.

We found and promoted a country western band that became so popular we featured them every Saturday night one entire summer. The lead singer was great. But his girlfriend, about 15 years older & wealthy, a singer wannabe who could not keep a tune insisted on singing "Elvira" every night.

Our last event at Heidelberg featured CHUBBY CHECK-ER.

That one evening embraced both The Ecstasy – a fantastic performance by the rock & roll idol who introduced THE TWIST, and…

The Agony— the crowd was so poor we had to take cash from the bar at intermission to pay him so he would perform the second half of his show.

THE EVENT THAT PROVIDED THE GREATEST PER-
MANENT HAPPINESS:

Sunday night, March 29, 1981 Graham called from New
Braunfels Hospital to tell us that Garrett had just been born.
We immediately made an enthusiastic announcement to the
Heidelberg big band crowd.

Beautiful, talented Carole White Green, my only daughter-in-law had now given me two grandsons: One, she named
after me—Gazexer Graham Green IV; the second, Garrett
Stevenson Green had been born on my birthday.

What more could any daughter-in-law do than that?

EUROPEAN INVESTORS

As a member of the marketing committee of RELO, the
largest relocation service in the United States, I was invited
to a meeting in Chicago. I learned from another committee
member, the president-elect of the International Real Estate
Federation, that for $100.00 I could join IREF.

There was no other IREF member in the San Antonio–
Austin Corridor. I had no idea the benefits our company
would reap so quickly.

I received a letter from an IREF member in Seattle, Washington inviting us to present our property listings to European investors at a real estate seminar he was sponsoring in
Antwerp, Belgium. I showed the letter to Graham and said,
"Why don't we go?" Graham immediately said, "Yes."

This is the advertisement we ran for six weeks in the
Midwest edition of the Wall Street Journal in January and
February, our slowest months of the year. Our telephones
rang off the wall, energizing and exciting our agents.

EUROPEAN INVESTORS LOOKING
FOR PROPERTIES IN TEXAS
Farms, Ranches, Shopping Centers,
Apartment Complexes, Office Buildings,
Income Producing Properties.
Call Gaz Green Real Estate and Investments
1-800-289-5263

By the time we were ready to go to Europe in March, we had over ONE HUNDRED MILLION DOLLARS WORTH OF PROPERTIES LISTED, including some in several other states and a few outside the USA.

We hired Mike Sanders, a student at the University of Texas and the son of one of our agents, to be an intern in our office. He did such a great job assembling the detailed information packets for each of our 117 properties that we rewarded him by taking him with us to Europe.

Dee and I checked out this listing to celebrate our 36th Wedding anniversary: FANTASTIC PROPERTY FOR RESORT DEVELOPMENT ON AMBERGRIS CAY BELIZE approximately 35,000 acres with over 31 miles of waterfront. Protected by second longest barrier reef in the world. $5,750,000. Attractive terms.

EUROPE HERE WE COME

The day before we left for Europe we scored our company's FIRST MILLION DOLLAR SALE—a tract of land at Canyon Lake to some Canadian Investors. This property was owned by a man from Houston who never would have listed this property except for our European program.

We had worked so hard for about three months that we decided to reward ourselves by combining business with pleasure on our European trip. We started by spending two nights in London. We enjoyed a couple of shows, did touristy things and unwound. This sale validated the entire program.

We then took a hovercraft from England to Belgium. In the two days we spent in Brussels we were guests for lunch at NATO and had dinner at the home of my old and dear friends, Martha and Max Rettig, who was vice president and sales manager for Procter & Gamble in Europe.

We arrived in Antwerp with all our props in hand. Mike was responsible for the huge display case we had designed featuring John Newcomb, the No. 1 ranked tennis player in the world. He had just won the Wimbledon Championship and was very well known and respected in Europe. We had his tennis ranch located near New Braunfels for sale.

After the Antwerp expo was over, we went to Switzerland to visit Marianne, Oscar and the girls, Lisa, Heidi, Cordelia and Rebecca. Graham and Mike got in a couple days of excellent skiing while I enjoyed the extra time with Marianne and my beautiful granddaughters. On our last night in Switzerland we celebrated Fastnacht (like Fat Tuesday in New Orleans).

The Antwerp show was a major disappointment – very few prospective investors came, and nobody sold anything. WE HAD A GREAT VACATION AND WITHIN A MONTH AFTER WE RETURNED WE SOLD A $2.8 MILLION APARTMENT COMPLEX IN BAYTOWN—OUR BIGGEST SALE EVER.

Question? What's a little real estate company in New Braunfels doing selling an apartment complex in a Houston suburb to a group of CALIFORNIA INVESTORS?

A TITLE COMPANY DIRECTOR

Northcliffe Country Club Scorecard, c. 1980

What is a title company? A title insurance company is the proper name. Every time a home is sold the seller must purchase an insurance policy guaranteeing there are no liens against the title, even if the home is sold a year later. The buyer must provide similar assurance to a mortgage lender.

In New Braunfels there were two title companies, The New Braunfels Title Company owned by one group of lawyers, and the Comal Title Company owned by another group of lawyers. The two of them controlled almost all of the title company business in Comal County.

When U. S. Life Title, a national company, announced the opening of an office in New Braunfels, the owners of New Braunfels Title Co. invited the four largest real estate brokers to become stock holders and directors.

What they offered each of us was stock in a very prosperous and profitable organization. They loaned us the money to buy the stock, and our directors' fees paid for the stock. I wish I could find more deals like that. The board met quarterly, and we were paid $300.00 for attending a half hour business meeting and then enjoying a social hour or so after.

Unless you were a close personal friend of a lawyer, real estate brokers and members of the legal profession rarely got along well. There was feeling among brokers that lawyers rarely helped make a deal, but they sure could kill deals for you in a hurry.

Being on the same board with them, and sharing the rewards of working together, helped to develop a friendlier and more cooperative attitude on the part of most. And our title company flourished. I remember one year we made so much money that our accountant said we should have four weekly board meetings paying us $300.00 each to distribute the profit.

Later, when I had a leisurely moment with my former neighbor and friend Jim Drury, one of Howard Hughes's top lawyers, I asked him, "Jim, is a title company a license to steal?"

"What do you mean?" he asked me.

"Do they ever pay off?" I countered.

"I'm sure they do sometimes," Jim said and continued, "I have never thought of it that way. But, you may be right."

SHARING GRAHAM'S HUMOR

When Graham left Motorola in Washington to come to New Braunfels to join his mother and me in our real estate company, I talked with him about the importance of being on time and of developing a good work ethic. I told him the office opened at 8:00, and he and I were both expected to be there.

New Braunfels was a small town of about 25,000. Graham lived about five minutes from the office. One day he came in late and immediately came to my office to apologize.

"Sorry, I'm late, Dad," he said. "THE TRAFFIC LIGHT WAS RED!"

Our good friend Dr. Arlen Tieken, Assistant Superintendent of Schools liked Graham and offered him a job to supplement his income. He would supervise the evening adult education classes at Canyon Lake.

When the two of them went to a two-day conference they shared a twin bed room in a College Station motel. Graham claimed that he had never heard anyone snore so loudly as Arlen.

The result: Graham ended up sleeping in the bathtub all night with the door closed just to escape.

* * *

Graham and I were at the Texas State Realtor's Convention in Houston. At one of the social events I spotted a young woman from Corsicana who had been in a real estate class with me a few months earlier. I took Graham over to meet her.

After visiting for a few minutes I asked, very innocently, "When are you expecting?"

Looking quite surprised she replied emphatically, "WHAT?"

After it was determined it was the new style dress, I apologized to her.

As we walked away, Graham turned to me and said, "Dad. I can't take you anywhere."

FOUNDING HOSPICE

Liz Urban, the energetic director of the New Braunfels Community Resource Center was a real go-getter. Dee was member of the board and asked me to help find a location for their new headquarters.

My ophthalmologist and good friend, Dr. David Way, was going to build a new office building and offered the house free to the Resource Center if a site could be found and money raised to move the house to the new location.

I found her a great location, across from the Eagles Hall and only five minutes from downtown. As soon as she got settled, Liz began a campaign to start a hospice organization in New Braunfels. Dee volunteered me (as we had often done to or for each other.) Then we worked together on one of the most worthwhile and successful projects I have ever been involved in.

Hospice mission is to give support for a terminally ill patient to live comfortably and die with dignity. Hospice aims to give the best quality of care and support the needs of families, friends and their care givers.

When we started our hospice I expected a group of senior citizens to volunteer. I was totally surprised when several beautiful young women came forth. Why? Because, each of them had recently lost a parent in some other city or community and hospice had helped them through their struggle.

Hospice was new and not well known. As president my major role was to raise money and public awareness. I took two lovely young women, a nurse and a volunteer coordinator, to speak at Rotary, Lions and other clubs. I introduced them, then sat back and watch men pull out their handkerchiefs and wipe their eyes.

Our first patient was a nine-year-old black girl suffering from congenital heart failure. Graham took his accordion and Tabitha, then age 12, to play and sing by her bedside... She was at home, in a coma and had shown no sign of any recognition. All of the sudden her mother pointed to her daughter's little feet. She was wiggling her toes in rhythm to the music.

After this experience, Graham told his mother how difficult it was for him to play when, "All I wanted to do was cry." The child died a within a few days.

FINDING UNITY

Les Pugh accepted the call to become Senior Minister of the Mayflower Church in Minneapolis. So our dear friends, Les and Jettie, moved to the frigid north to continue their ministry. Dee and I liked his successor personally, but found his sermons non-stimulating and negative.

After deciding we could not be happy staying in the First Protestant Church, we visited several other churches in New Braunfels. Failing to find a church we both liked we decided to check out the Unity Church in San Antonio.

I did not know anything about Unity, but Dee's mother subscribed to *Daily Word*, a devotional magazine published by Unity since 1924. Dee had read it in her home as a child growing up.

We both were delighted when we visited the Unity Church. So much was new to us that we also attended a weekly Wednesday night class to learn more about the history of Unity, the prayer and healing on which the movement was founded, and meditation, which seemed mystical to me.

The minister, Rev. Norman Olsson, had been a buyer for a major food chain so by our backgrounds we had much in common. He was a prolific writer and a frequent contributor to Unity publications. I must confess we had not made a complete commitment to the church while he was there.

We had purchased a home facing the tenth tee of the Northcliffe Country Club golf course and the couple's tournament they held every Sunday morning was very tempting. We were preparing to leave for Switzerland for a month to visit Marianne and her family when we attended a retirement celebration for Rev. Olsson at which time they introduced his successors, a husband and wife ministerial couple, Robert and Kim Hudson.

The Sunday after we returned from Switzerland we decided to go to Unity Church instead of playing golf. It was one of our best decisions ever.

We could not believe the excitement Robert and Kim had built in such a short time. We knew we had found a church home. Every Sunday thereafter as we left for church and passed our friends playing golf I would say—

"THERE, BUT FOR THE GRACE OF GOD, GO WE."

UNITY VILLAGE

In the 1880s, Charles and Myrtle Fillmore met in Denison, Texas, where Myrtle was a schoolteacher and Charles worked for the railroad. Myrtle Fillmore had been given very little time to live, but she healed herself of tuberculosis through prayer and meditation and lived many more decades.

After they were married they moved to Kansas City where Charles became a real estate developer, watched Myrtle in amazement and set out to learn how her spiritual healing had worked.

Initially Unity's teachings were also somewhat similar to the Christian Science movement which still today adheres very closely to the church dogma established by Mary Baker Eddy much earlier.

The basic difference was that when Charles and Myrtle started Unity, it was a study group and was never meant to become a church. One of Charles Fillmore's most famous statements was, "This I believe now, but I reserve the right to change my mind." This has kept Unity relevant.

What appealed to us when we first found Unity was the POSITIVE attitude of the people who attended the Unity Church. There was no preaching of guilt. The emphasis was to live our lives in accordance with Jesus's teachings. No dogma, no liturgy. Jesus was our WAY-SHOWER.

Dee and I became very involved in the Unity Church and, at our first opportunity, went to Unity Village in Missouri for a retreat. Charles and Myrtle had lived on a farm near Lee's Summit, a Kansas City suburban community. This became the world headquarters for the Unity Movement.

We met more wonderful, inspiring people and started each day outside in "Greeting the Sun" group exercises. At the end of that session we each selected someone we did not know to be "Our Special Person for the Day."

We ate our meals with that person and exchanged hugs each time we met.

The most special person I chose was a Catholic nun who also was there for the first time. This one week experience had such a positive influence on Dee and me that before returning home we went to the Unity School of Christianity to get information so we could enroll in the program to become licensed teachers.

BEING TOO SUCCESSFUL

Yes, it is possible to be TOO SUCCESSFUL and have it become the start of your company going downhill.

I mentioned this briefly when David Dye asked us to help him develop his choice piece of property overlooking the Comal River near the River Restaurant. This was directly across the river from Camp Warnecke, the famous resort that had been a favorite tourist destination for Houstonians for more than 50 years.

It was a perfect location for our first development. We planned to build four buildings, each to contain four 2-Bedroom, 2-Bath condos with about 1200 sq. ft. We built one four-plex at a time. Then, as soon as we sold two condos, we started another building. It was a perfect strategy.

While our Comal Condos were under construction, thousands of tubers passed by, floating down the Comal River. The popular exit at Camp Warnecke was less than 25 feet away, directly across from where our guests entered and exited the refreshing water of the Comal River for their own use.

All of our Comal Condos sold quickly and that signaled the start of several other large condominium projects on the Comal and Guadalupe Rivers.

Bob Krueger had gone with us to look at an 18-acre tract of land on a high bluff overlooking a tranquil stretch of the Guadalupe River just above the dam immediately upriver from the old Rt. 81 bridge crossing. There was a gentle slope down to the 100 ft. plus river front. Bob told us this was his favorite canoeing area from his family home on up the river.

We decided to build 24 more condos of approximately 1500 to 1600 sq ft. each. With an established record, and with former Congressman Krueger as a partner, we had no trouble getting attractive financing, and there were major economies by building the whole project. Early sales were excellent.

Until, when we were just over 50% sold, word came out of Washington that the government was considering eliminating the income tax deduction for second homes.

Sales for everything in the New Braunfels came to a screeching halt.

A YEAR TO FORGET

Graham and I were the general partners in the Riverside Condominiums. As a limited partner, Bob Krueger was able to work out an agreement with the savings and loan that had financed the project. He paid a substantial amount of cash to be relieved of all liability for the project.

That was OK with Graham and me. We made the mortgage payments on the eleven unsold condos until our reserve funds ran out after about a year. We owed about $800,000 for the condos appraised at $130,000 each, or a total of $1,430,000. Our equity (potential profit) was $640,000. IRS did not change the rules, so we felt sure the market would improve. IT DID NOT.

Because we could no longer make the payments, we asked, in lieu of foreclosure, to get new appraisals, and if the total value was determined to be less than what we owed, we would agree to pay the S&L the difference.

We met with the S&L president. a good friend, and reached an agreement.

We were SHOCKED a few days later when we received a NOTICE OF FORECLOSURE. We knew the S&L had been sold to a large financial institution in Dallas, but had not been told that local management no longer had any authority. Nor, that our friend, the president, was already looking for another job and left within a few weeks. The damage was done.

Graham and I both had other good investments and we began liquidating. I sold my stock in N.B. Title Co., and we refinanced some other real estate investments. Graham had been an organizing director of the new Executive Banc in New Braunfels. Other directors agreed to buy his and my stock.

We cut expenses to the bone and closed all but one of our real estate offices. Finally we knew the end was in sight, and we could no longer keep going. Graham and Carole came down to our home at Northcliffe. We sat and talked and cried because it was the end of a beautiful dream, the wonderful relationship we had working together and having grandchildren so near.

At the end of the evening we all felt relieved. We realized they had been worrying about what would happen to us, and we were equally concerned about what they would do. It turned out we, both couples, knew exactly what our next moves would be.

CHAPTER TEN

KANSAS CITY PLAZA

Contrary to what some people may think, Kansas City is not out in the middle of a cornfield. Instead, it is a very sophisticated metropolitan community. While it is a sprawling city, KC's heart is in the Country Club Plaza, several miles from the original "downtown."

Robert Hudson, before he and Kim came to San Antonio, had been associate minister at Unity on the Plaza, aka the Founders Church in honor of Charles and Myrtle Fillmore who selected the site for their first Unity Church.

Robert had made several phone calls to his friends asking them to look out for us, then suggested we look first to see if we could find an apartment on or near the Plaza. We were most fortunate. We found a lovely 2-bedroom garden apartment about a block from the church.

On our first visit to the church we saw a familiar face, Duke Tufti, who had been a classmate of ours at Unity Village the previous year. Duke was in his early 40's, looked like TV's Ted Danson, with a great heart, imagination and a wonderful sense of humor. His application to ministerial school was rejected with the suggestion he gain more experience in Unity and re-apply.

Recently divorced, Duke had sold his automobile agency and was eager to start a new life. Financially secure, he had volunteered his services to work for a year without salary as assistant to the new minister at the Plaza Church, Max Lafser, who had just completed his one-year term as president of the Association of Unity Churches.

With help from Duke, Max Lafser and other of Robert Hudson's friends, Dee and I became involved immediately. On Thanksgiving Day the Lafsers invited us, along with a few others, to their home for dinner. That was when we first met Duke's beautiful redheaded girlfriend, Leesa.

Duke was accepted at Unity School and began his two-year course to become a minister. Duke, Leesa, Dee and I enjoyed each other so much that it soon became apparent they had "adopted" us as their surrogate parents. Two years later they invited us their wedding as part of their real family.

We had begun a beautiful friendship which flourished until Dee's death fifteen years later.

ENJOYING A FRUGAL LIFE

An advantage of having grown up during the Great Depression is that you knew how to become frugal when necessary and not have it ruin your life. Our apartment was not air conditioned so we went to the Sears warehouse store. I bought and installed a window AC unit for $125.00. It worked fine.

Dee and I had serious classes at Unity Village for two weeks every couple of months. Graham's Carole suggested we take a travel agent course since we liked traveling so much. We enjoyed that thoroughly. Then I got my first computer and enrolled in a free class at the nearby junior college.

We visited the senior citizen center and were amazed to learn how many opportunities existed for FREE entertainment and education. We could attend rehearsals or special children's performances by the symphony, ballet, opera and various theatre groups.

Duke's Leesa had her master's degree in art history and was pursuing her PhD which she received after we left Kansas City. She introduced us to the famous Kansas City Art Museum and kept us current on their free programs.

Duke had really buckled down to his seminary studies. But, come Friday afternoon he and Leesa were ready to relax. It became our ritual that Friday afternoon the four of us would go to a movie matinee, have a drink at our apartment or Duke's, less than two locks away, then enjoy dinner at one of the many moderately priced restaurants in the area.

We had enough money to get along. The Good Lord really smiled on us. After liquidating assets, we no longer owned any shares of publicly held stock. So on October 19, 1987 we were not affected by the largest one-day stock market crash in history. The Dow lost 22.6% of its value or $500 billion dollars, but we lost nothing.

While we kept hoping the Texas real estate economy would rebound, it got continually worse. John Connally, former Governor of Texas, former Secretary of the Treasury, and probably the most respected man in Texas went broke and had to declare bankruptcy.

I will confess I began to worry for the first time.

GOD HAD ANOTHER PLAN

Before we moved to Kansas City, Robert Hudson had urged the president of Unity, to take advantage of my marketing background. Her responsibility included the Unity School of Christianity and all publications.

Max Lafser followed up and invited me, as the only layperson to meet with the marketing committee for the Association of Unity Churches, an organization completely separate from Unity. This committee consisted of about five or six ministers from the biggest and most successful churches.

For several months I was led to believe that they were going to create a position in the "Association" where I would become director of development, charged to spread the word about the Unity movement, referred to by many as the "World's Best Kept Secret."

So it came as a real surprise to me when I was asked to come to the "Association headquarters" to be interviewed by a special committee appointed to hire the new director of development.

Imagine my further shock when, just before I went in for the interview, the executive director came out and told me that they had changed to the criteria for the position, and since I had not been informed, it was not necessary for me to take the interview.

The "bolt out of the blue" came the next day when I learned the position had been filled by a friend of someone on the committee who had agreed to take it on a part-time basis which arrangement would save the "Association" several thousand dollars.

I wrote to my friend, Jack Boland, who had built his Unity church in the Detroit suburb of Warren, Michigan, to be the second largest in the Unity movement. His response, "Dear Gaz, God has another plan for you."

A few nights later, without knowing anything about what had happened to me, my brother, Bill who had no children, called to tell me he wanted me to move to Florida to be near him. He was concerned about his failing health.

YES, GOD DID HAVE ANOTHER PLAN IN MIND FOR US.

THE GHOST OF HARRY TRUMAN

Harry Truman was born in Lamar, Missouri, in 1884, so he was the same age as my mother and father. He grew up in Independence, a suburb of Kansas City and for 12 years prospered as a Missouri farmer.

He went to France during World War I and was highly regarded as a captain in the field artillery. Returning, he married Elizabeth Virginia Wallace and opened a haberdashery in Kansas City.

Elected Vice President in 1944 he scarcely saw President Roosevelt, and received no briefing on the development of the atomic bomb or the unfolding difficulties with Soviet Russia.

Suddenly these and a host of other wartime problems became Truman's to solve when, on Roosevelt's death April 12, 1945, he became President. He told reporters, "I felt like the moon, the stars, and all the planets had fallen on me."

Atomic Bomb dropped on Nagasaki, Japan, August 9, 1945.

Truman had no formal education beyond high school and was looked down on by many of the intellectuals Roosevelt had brought into the government during his 12-year administration. But Truman had a voracious appetite for reading, particularly history. The more I learned about him as I got older, the more respect I had for him.

As President, Truman made some of the most crucial decisions in history. Soon after V-E Day, the war against Japan had reached its final stage. An urgent plea to Japan to surrender was rejected.

Truman, after consultations with his advisers, ordered atomic bombs dropped on two cities devoted to war work, Hiroshima and Nagasaki. Japanese surrender followed quickly. There is no question in my mind that his was the right decision. Millions of lives, American and Japanese, were saved by eliminating the need to invade Japan.

During the year we were in Kansas City everyone who came to visit us was taken on a tour of the Truman Library and the home of Truman's mother in law, Mrs. Wallace. This is where Truman and his wife Bess lived after the Presidency. Both this home and the library were in Independence, a few short miles from where we lived.

KANSAS CITY FAREWELL

William Stevenson Green, my only brother, lived on the west coast of Florida, between Tampa Bay and the Gulf of Mexico just north of St. Petersburg. Bill's first wife, Dot, had died of cancer and his second wife, Edith, was nine years older than he.

Unless she was handled with kid gloves, Edith could be difficult. For that reason we wanted to live near enough so that we could be available when Bill needed us, but not so close that it might impinge on our privacy.

Our sister, Adelaide, lived in Sun City Center, about half way between Tampa and Bradenton. Dee and I stayed with her. She gave us good advice and suggested we look in the Wildewood Springs area of Bradenton. We did and found exactly what we wanted, a 2-bedroom, 2-bathroom condo with two tennis courts right out our back door.

Before we signed a lease I called Bill to make sure it was near enough to suit him. I felt he gave me a reluctant "Yes," but he certainly did not say "No." We went to the Unity Church in Bradenton that Sunday announcing to the congregation that we would soon be joining them.

We went back to Kansas City to complete another set of two-week classes. In the men's room between classes the first day I heard this booming voice in a southern accent say, "I'm here from Sarasota Florida. I'm in the Minister by Exception program."

I introduced myself immediately to Don Jackson, discovered he lived a few blocks from our condo in Bradenton, and that he and his wife, Dorothy Ann were taking some of the same classes as Dee and I and would be there for two weeks. The four of us became almost inseparable before they left.

Before we departed Kansas City, Duke and Leesa and others gave us a surprise farewell party. Guests included our friends, Tim Cook, former minister of Unity of Austin and his wife Barbara, who were back in Kansas City and were destined to play a major role in our lives 15 years later.

A MINISTER DILEMMA

Which church should we attend when we move to Florida?

We had told the minister and congregation at the Bradenton Unity Church we would be joining them when we moved into our rented condo in Wildewood Springs, Bradenton. Then, we met Don and Dorothy Ann Jackson and bonded over a two-week period.

Dee and I had both taken counseling courses as part of our training at Unity School of Christianity. We decided to seek help from the head of the counseling department at the school and made an appointment to talk with him. He listened patiently and then told us not to worry, "You will know."

We wrote the same letter to each minister in Bradenton and Sarasota, giving our date of arrival, our new address and phone number. We stopped for a couple of nights to visit Lois, Charlie and their children in Florence, Alabama.

We were really excited about our new home in Wildewood Springs, one of the most beautiful condominium developments I have ever seen. It was a dedicated wild life refuge, with lakes, and ponds, lots of birds and animals in their natural habitat.

Each cluster of condos had its own swimming pool and, in our case, our own tennis courts. Most of the owners in our cluster were, fortunately, year-round residents, which meant we had more stability and a better opportunity to know our neighbors.

Also, most of our residents were from the upper Midwest—Illinois, Wisconsin, and Minnesota. In fact, it was interesting that most New Yorkers and people from the Mid-Atlantic states were attracted to Florida's East Coast.

The same letter to both ministers! What were their responses? Don and Dorothy Ann Jackson came over to our condo with food and beverages while we were still unloading. The other minister contacted us three weeks later. We became happy members of the Unity Church of Sarasota.

Our counseling professor was right. He said we would KNOW.

NICK BOLLETTIERI

Don and Dorothy Ann Jackson's condo was about eight blocks from our home in Wildewood Springs. Midway between us was the most famous tennis academy in the world run by the legendary coach Nick Bollettieri.

The academy grounds were always open and occasionally we would stop in just to watch future tennis stars, still just kids, from all over the world develop their skills to prepare them to become the future champions.

I had seen Nick Bollettieri on television and knew that the Rockefeller family had brought him to Pocantico Hills to give lessons to their children.

Some of the future stars who were there during the years we lived in Bradenton were Andre Agassi and Jim Courier from the U. S., Tommy Haas from Germany, Monica Seles from Yugoslavia, Mary Pierce from France *www.nickbollettieri.com* and the Russian, Anna Kournikova, who became better known throughout the world for her beauty than for success on the championship tour.

The Bollettieri Tennis Academy is now owned by IMG, the world's premier sports, entertainment and media company, founded by the late Mark McCormack, who in 1990 was named by Sports Illustrated as the most powerful man in sports.

McCormack, an attorney, was propelled into prominence when he signed contracts to represent Arnold Palmer, Gary Player and Jack Nicklaus, who became the Big Three of Golf.

IMG now represents many of the major sports stars who have been signed to 100 million dollar contracts. Their alumni are starring at the collegiate or professional level in football, baseball, basketball, soccer and golf, as well as in their pioneer sport, tennis.

Having my hair cut one day in a salon near our home, the young woman shearing my locks had an autographed picture of Andre Agassi on her stand. Yes, the future all-time tennis great and I shared the same hairdresser. And, yes, he had a full head of flowing hair as a teenager.

SOCIAL TENNIS

Mutti and I loved both tennis and golf. When we lived at Northcliffe we had the golf course out our back door. Now in Bradenton we could walk out our back door and have two beautiful hardtop tennis courts available for play at almost anytime year around. Even in summer early morning play was great.

We also met some wonderful men and women through tennis and had many delightful games. We even had a tennis pro from England who had been teaching for Bollettieri but left there to spend more time grooming his teenage daughter for a professional carecr. They helped us get better.

One of my favorite memories was of an older man, Carl Warmington, who played everyday with us when he was not playing in local, regional or national championships in the 80-and-over, then the 85-and-over age brackets.

Carl was a most interesting person. He was very polite, but a stickler for the rules and very serious when he played. He did not want any idle chatter.

We helped him celebrate his 90th birthday. I remember how happy he was that he could now move up into another age bracket where his chances of winning became infinitely better.

Carl and his wife had us over for dinner one evening, and we learned that he also was a musician. As a student at the University of Minnesota in 1930 he had organized a college dance band that played for fraternity dances and other social occasions. The band was so good they played one entire summer on a cruise ship in the Pacific Ocean.

His favorite tennis story was about four men in their 80's playing in a men's doubles championship match. In the climatic tiebreaker the score was 4-to-3, but they could not remember who had the four and who had the three. So they decided to go have drinks, eat and start all over the next day.

Mutti was having increasing difficulty with her knees. The pain finally became so bad she had to stop playing. She consulted with a top orthopedic surgeon and decided to have both knees replaced at the same time. Six months later she was back playing with my men friends and me.

When it was all over Mutti said she would have exactly the same procedure again—both knees at the same time.

NEAL & NEAL

The developer of Wildewood Springs was the father and son combination of Neal & Neal. They were also building another large complex and owned the largest real estate company, Neal & Neal, in Bradenton.

The senior Neal had made his fortune and was practically retired from the business. The broker and general manager for the seven real estate offices was Bill Davidson. The junior Neal had been a POWERFUL member of the Florida State Senate until voted out of office.

The State of Florida had no reciprocal agreements with other states for professional licenses. Even though I held a valid real estate brokers license in Texas, I could not sell real estate in Florida until I took the required courses and passed the examinations.

I could, however, be paid as a consultant to a real estate company. I approached Bill Davidson. He was interested immediately. He wanted to have the biggest real estate company between Tampa and Miami and wanted me to develop and help him implement plans to achieve this.

The only catch was that he wanted Neal & Neal Development to split the cost to hire me. He said Neal Junior was so bitter about his defeat by an unknown that all he wanted to do was get back in the Florida Senate.

I developed a plan for Neal that Davidson loved. He introduced me to their executive assistant in Tallahassee, now back in Bradenton with him. She loved the plan, and said her office could handle everything I had proposed.

My Plan: Neal Junior would become volunteer head of United Fund for Manatee County. He could be guest speaker for every organization in the area. Once a Senator, he would retain the title. All the publicity would be: Senator Neal does this; Senator Neal does that, all for charity. Make him a hero before he runs again.

Guess what he told me. There were only seven people he cared about – the county commissioners who approve the projects where he makes his money. He did not give a damn about anybody else!

Was it any surprise he lost his bid for re-election?

LIVE IN SARASOTA, SLEEP IN BRADENTON

This was Mutti's description of our life in Florida. We slept in Bradenton but we LIVED in Sarasota. That was true, literally.

We pitched in and became part of the Unity Church of Sarasota. We could drive out of our condo and our car would automatically head down the Tamiami Trail (Tampa to Miami) to Unity of Sarasota.

To get to the Unity Church we passed the Sarasota Airport on the line separating Manatee and Sarasota Counties. We also passed the world famous Ringling Bros., Barnum and Bailey Circus Museum and the renowned Asolo Theatre which is part of the Florida State Theatre Program.

The Unity Church was at 800 Cocoanut Avenue, one block from the famous Tamiami Trail and part of the vibrant downtown Sarasota community.

Location. Location. Location. That is what a real estate person looks for. Unity Church had it in spades. The building was old, but there was room to expand, and we had the energetic leadership to make that happen. The Sarasota Women's Club and the Player's Theatre were our neighbors.

Don and Dorothy Ann Jackson provided spark and the imagination. Mutti and I were happy to have arrived there when we did so that we could add our energy to their efforts.

I had been part of a group at Unity on the Plaza Church in Kansas City that had formed a speaker's bureau. The goal was to bring outstanding speakers to the church to raise money for the building fund.

Don Jackson was aware of what we had planned to do and helped me get such a group started at Unity of Sarasota. Fifteen of us each contributed $100.00 as seed money to make sure the church would not lose money if our first attempt was a failure. It was not!

We rented the 1800-seat Van Wezel Performing Arts Center, signed a contract with Dr. Wayne Dyer, estimated our expenses would be about $3,000 and went to work selling tickets.

It was the beginning of an interesting and exciting program.

CHURCH EXPANSION

The Board of Trustees at Unity of Sarasota had already approved architectural plans to add an addition to the church and was just waiting until they had enough money pledged to start construction.

By this time Don and I had become very, very close friends. Don had been a Baptist Minister for 16 years until one day he decided he could no longer say from the pulpit what the Baptist Church required. With an outgoing sales personality, he became regional sales manager for a couple of different companies, and later taught psychology at the college level.

His best friend from high school, Jim Marsh also had been a Baptist minister and left the denomination to become the pastor of the Community Church on Longboat Key. This fashionable peninsula extends from Sarasota to Bradenton along the Gulf. Don was quarterback and Jim the star end on the Hueytown, Alabama high school football team.

Jim had encouraged Don to come to Florida and then recommended him as a summer replacement for the vacationing Sarasota Unity Minister. This led to Don's becoming the full-time minister for this church.

In looking at the plans for the new building, I saw that we would have a long, well-

Sarasota Unity Church

lighted corridor connecting a large social hall to the addition. "Perfect for art exhibits," I said to Don. We then told Don and Dorothy Ann about the success Marianne's husband Oscar Hagmann had with the art exhibits he established in his medical practice in Switzerland.

Oscar helped "unknown" artists be successful by hosting a four-week exhibit of the artist's works. He kicked off the event by sponsoring a wine and cheese party with entertainment to introduce the artist to an invited clientele, including the press, art critics, connoisseurs and patrons.

What did Oscar get in return? He received a percentage of the gross sale for every painting sold in the four weeks. PLUS, he got to pick one painting for his own private collection. Word spread. Oscar was so successful that after a few months GALLERIE IM DOCTORHAUS was booked three years in advance with additional artists placed on a waiting list.

SARASOTA'S UNITY ART GALLERY WAS ABOUT TO BE BORN.

OUR NEW UNITY BOOK STORE

One of the most important features of our church addition was the large, roomy, attractive bookstore located just inside the new main entrance.

You may recall my having said earlier that when Charles and Myrtle Fillmore founded Unity they never meant it to be a church. The basic mission was education, the fostering of study groups. As a result, Unity members and followers tend to be avid readers. Every Unity church or study group, no matter how large or small, has a bookstore.

Mutti was always reading something having to do with the New Thought Movement, a magazine, a book, or a course of study. We even taught classes and led discussion groups. So, it was only natural for her to get involved in the planning and management of the new book store.

These years were among the happiest of our lives. The book store was a huge success. I was the church business manager, Mutti the bookstore manager. We worked together every day in an endeavor close to our heart.

Our church was growing. We were contributing. Every guest speaker we scheduled had books, often several, for us to feature and sell. We also sold reserved seat tickets in the bookstore for all our programs. This built traffic, brought new *Deepak Chopra* people into our church and it was not long before we had to add a second service on Sundays. It was EXCITING!

One of the most popular speakers we sponsored was Dr. Deepak Chopra, who was born in India and trained in both Eastern and Western Medicine. We also had Dr. Bernie Siegel, the famed cancer surgeon, and Og Mandino whose "Success" books sold over 50 million copies throughout the world.

One of my friends at Unity on the Plaza was a retired *Reader's Digest* editor who had hired Alex Haley when he completed his 20-year stint in the Coast Guard. The author of "Roots" had begun his writing career.

Alex was a gracious and a wonderful man. Through this connection we were able to get this master storyteller to let us host a reception in his honor and raise extra funds to support a school project in the inner city. Sadly, he died suddenly of a heart attack shortly after his Sarasota visit with us in 1992

Alex Haley

THREE FACES OF EVE

In 1957 Joanne Woodward, along with David Wayne and Lee J. Cobb, starred in the hit movie about a young woman who suffered from Multiple Personality Disorder. The film, THE THREE FACES OF EVE," was based on the true case of Chris Costner-Sizemore who later wrote the book, *I'm Eve*, about her multiple personality problems.

We were surprised to learn that Chris Sizemore, by now cured of her terrible disorder, was married and living happily in Bradenton just a few blocks from where we had our condo.

After we became acquainted, we found Chris Sizemore to be a truly delightful person, totally cooperative, and eager to work with us. She was almost like a gift from Heaven. We had three venues to feature her Three Faces.

The Unity Book Store to sell her book, *I'm Eve.*

The Unity Speakers Bureau to provide a place to tell her story.

The Unity Art Gallery to exhibit and sell her paintings.

Each one of these helped promote the other, and, even though Chris Sizemore was the least well known speaker we ever had at Van Wezel, it was a successful event. Her story was memorable.

We were able to present the most amazing part of her life in our art gallery where we exhibited paintings she had created left handed in one of her lives, and others painted with her right hand which was dominant in what eventually became her natural life.

Her major source of income, I learned from Chris, was as an expert witness in court cases throughout the United States when a defense lawyer chose to use multiple personality disorder as a defense for a client.

She was totally credible and available to either the defense in a legitimate case or for the prosecution if there was suspicion of fraud.

Chris Sizemore, *"I'M EVE,"* was an amazing story. And person.

INTRODUCTION TO CHAUTAUQUA

One of the strongest supporters of our Speaker's Bureau was Jo Ann Webb, who spent her winters in Bradenton/Sarasota where she owned several apartments facing the Gulf and her summers in her home at the Chautauqua Institute in upstate New York between Buffalo and Erie, PA.

My grandmother had taken me to a traveling Chautauqua tent show in Lock Haven, PA when I was very young. So, I had known about Chautauqua all my life, but had never been there. We were excited when Jo Ann offered to make a slide presentation about Chautauqua one evening at our church.

That was all we needed. Jo Ann had made an arrangement with Joan Piper, owner of the Englewood Guest House at Chautauqua also to call it "UNITY HOUSE." One large bedroom with a private bath would be made available for visiting Unity ministers each week. In return, Jo Ann would promote this guesthouse throughout the Unity movement. This was in the early 1990's.

It was an ideal setup. The location was perfect, less than one block from the 5,000-seat Amphitheatre where all the major events take place and literally across the street from the food court.

We arrived in Jamestown on a Saturday night and stayed at the Holiday Inn. We turned on the TV Sunday morning and found, to our amazement, that CBS's "On the Road with Charles Kuralt" was featuring Chautauqua.

Two hours later we saw in person what we had just watched on TV.

Our first year we stayed one week, the next few years a month, and eventually the entire nine-weeks of the Chautauqua Institute's Summer Program.

Chautauqua was, and is, an educational and cultural paradise. Each week had a theme, such as "How can education in the United States be better?" Every morning in the 5,000 seat amphitheatre you could attend a lecture by a prominent educator or government official.

In the afternoon there would be more lectures and discussions available. The evening would be entertainment, by one of the two symphony orchestras, the ballet company, the resident theater group, or professional entertainers from all over the world. Yes, it was "A Cultural Paradise."

GARRETT, JAMIE & BASEBALL

Almost all of the major league baseball teams begin spring training about the first of February and then hold exhibition games open to the public almost until the end of March.

We invited two of our grandsons, Jamie Wilson from Poughkeepsie, New York, and Garrett Green from Fredericksburg, Virginia, to visit us so I could take them to some ball games. They were both terrific kids, but quite different in temperament. Jamie was quiet and reserved. Garrett was very outgoing.

Other than the obvious blood line they had one very important trait in common. THEY WERE ENTHUSIASTIC NEW YORK YANKEE FANS. Each arrived at the Tampa Airport wearing his New York Yankee cap and a baseball glove prepared to catch foul balls.

Jamie Wilson & Garrett Green at Spring Training.

Mutti and I had bought new baseballs for them so that

they could get autographs, and I had purchased good reserved seats in the stands behind the Yankee dugout for two games to be played in Sarasota against the Chicago White Sox who made their winter home there.

The games started at 1:00, but, of course, we had to be there at 11:00 when they opened the gates. I took reading material along so that I could pass the time while they were pursuing autographs before the game. It was a wonderful family atmosphere with lots of young kids present.

We had not even gotten to our seats for the first game before a foul ball came our way, took one bounce and was grabbed by Garrett with his glove in the air. What a propitious beginning!

They both were successful in getting autographs. One of the first that Garrett got was that of Steve Howe, an outstanding Yankee pitcher who had been suspended from baseball for substance abuse for the seventh time on June 8, 1992 and then reinstated for the seventh time November 12 of the same year.

When Garrett showed the ball to his cousin, Jamie's only comment was, "What do you want that druggie's autograph for?

It was an entirely different matter the next day when Jamie had an opportunity to get the same autograph.

The one autograph they tried, but could not get, was that of George Steinbrenner, owner of the Yankees who was sitting in a box a few rows in front of us.

But, they did get the Baltimore Orioles' Hall of Fame third baseman Brooks Robinson, who was in St. Petersburg for an Old Timers Game.

MY 70th BIRTHDAY

One of the last times my brother Bill, sister Adelaide, niece Jennie Locke and I were all together for a special occasion was on March 29, 1990 for my 70th birthday. It was a very special day.

Our dear Pocantico Hills friends, Les and Marie Scott, came to Bradenton from Cape Coral. Evelyne Hale, the veteran radio soap opera actress who had become a very special

friend to both Dee and me was there, as were Don and Dorothy Ann Jackson, along with other family members.

The biggest surprise came when I started to unwrap what
I thought was a card table. Lo and behold, it was one of the
biggest surprises and most wonderful presents I had ever
received in my life.

It was a large framed watercolor painting of me relaxing
on a porch swing on our front porch back in State College
when I was about twelve years old. The artist was Blanchard
Gummo. There is a tag on the back proving that it was on
exhibit at the prestigious Chicago Museum of Art in 1934.

Blanchard knew that I was a very active, fidgety kid. So
he made me get comfortable on the porch swing by playing
"Idiot's Delight," a card game.

Blanchard Gummo, head of the art department at Bucknell University, was from Lock Haven. His parents, close
friends of our mother
and dad, had asked per-
mission for Blanchard to
live with us during the
summer of 1932, while
he was doing graduate
work at Penn State. He
was a serious diabetic and
needed to use our kitchen
to weigh his food as he
prepared his meals.

*Watercolor of Gaz Green, 14, painted by Blanchard
Gummo, was shown at the Chicago Art Museum.*

I had not seen this
painting for nearly 60 years and never thought it possible
that we might own it. Adelaide learned that Blanchard had
died and contacted his only living relative, his sister, who
inherited his paintings.

After Blanchard's sister agreed to sell this painting to
Adelaide and Bill, my favorite niece Jennie, a graduate of
Bucknell, drove to Lock Haven, got the painting and brought
it to Florida. She was present at the party and can confirm the
unbridled joy I expressed upon receiving it as a gift.

It has been in a prominent spot in our home ever since.
Am I proud of the painting? Absolutely, and eternally grateful to Adelaide, Bill and Jennie.

GOODBYES TO FLORIDA

While we were living in Florida Lois's Charlie had completed Southwestern Medical School in Dallas, his residency in Memphis, a stint in Florence, Alabama and become a cardio-thoracic surgeon at Scott & White Hospital, aka in the Southwest as "the little Mayo Clinic," in Temple, Texas.

Lois had played in the Austin Symphony Orchestra while she was an undergraduate and graduate student at the University of Texas, where she received her master's degree in violin performance.

When she arrived in Temple there was no symphony orchestra. So she, Tom Fairlie, head of the music department at Temple College, and Dr. Clyde Goodnight, a physician, started the Temple Symphony Orchestra in 1993. In addition to performing in the orchestra, Lois also served as its first president.

Dee and I had come back to Texas to hear the orchestra several times and were so proud of Lois. In the fall of 1996, Lois invited us to come for Thanksgiving and wanted us to see the new retirement community Del Webb was building in Georgetown, midway between Temple and Austin.

We flew into San Antonio, spent a couple of nights at the Marriott on the Riverwalk, and drove toward Temple. We saw signs for Sun City, noted that we were early, and decided to go look. We stopped at a real estate office where an accommodating agent showed us some of the earliest homes built.

When we arrived at Lois's home Mutti announced in a positive voice that she wanted no part of Sun City and would not even consider moving there.

Lois replied very smartly, "Oh, Mother, don't make any decision until you see downtown Georgetown. Wait until after Thanksgiving."

On a bright and sunny Friday morning we left Temple with our first stop the Georgetown Chamber of Commerce to secure literature, then a tour of the picturesque campus of Southwestern, the oldest university in Texas, and our final destination, the historic downtown with its Courthouse Square.

THAT DID IT! On Sunday, before we returned to Florida we signed a contract with Del Webb to purchase a new home under construction. Bill and Edith had passed away. Adelaide was going to California to live near Jennie. We knew it was the right move, and we never looked back.

Marianne, Lois, Graham, Mutti, Gaz & Dee

CHAPTER ELEVEN

ARRIVING IN SUN CITY

There is an old story about a couple who drove into a town and thought it looked like a place where they want to live. They stopped a gentleman on the street, expressed their interest and asked him, "What are the people like in this town?"

"What are the people like where you live now? He countered.

"Oh, they are wonderful, caring, friendly, loving people," was their answer.

"Well, that is exactly the same kind of people you will find here," he said.

There is more truth than poetry in this story. We have found people every where we have lived have been wonderful. As much as we knew we would miss our friends in Pocantico Hills we felt we would make great friends in Houston, then New Braunfels, Kansas City, Florida and now in Sun City.

When we closed on our house February 1, 1997, our new back neighbor, John Cielo, a retired IBM employee, came over and walked through with us to make sure we caught every possible defect on the final builder inspection.

When that was completed, John looked up the street and said, "There is Bill Doggett. Let me take you up to meet him."

There we learned that Bill Doggett, PhD had retired as the number two man in the State of Texas Mental Health and Retardation Department and was affable and outgoing. When we started to walk away, Bill said, "If there is anything I can do to 'HEP' you, just let me know." Dee, with a big smile said, "Boy, we sure know we are back in Texas now."

We moved onto Falcon Cove, a cul-de-sac with eleven homes. Everyone on the "Cove" has been friendly, though in a retirement community you lose your friends too frequently. The husband of Susan Schroeder, our neighbor across the street, died while their home was under construction.

In the nine years we have lived here we have lost Raz Landry, Bill Coonrod, Bill Doggett, Mary Barringer, and Dee.

DON'T MESS WITH OLD PEOPLE

Old Harold's in the Hospital

Harold was an old man. He was sick and in the hospital.

There was a young nurse who drove him crazy.

Every time she came in she would talk to him like he was a little child. She would say in a patronizing tone of voice, "And how are we doing this morning, or are we ready for a bath, or, are we hungry?"

Old Harold had enough of this particular nurse. One day, Old Harold had breakfast, pulled the juice off the tray and put it on his bed stand. He had been given a urine bottle to fill for testing.

The juice was apple juice. So…you know where the juice went.

The nurse came in a little later, picked up the urine bottle and looked at it. "My, but it seems we are a little cloudy today."

At this Old Harold snatched the bottle out of her hand, popped off the top, and drank it down, saying, "Well, I'll run it through again. Maybe I can filter it better this time."

The nurse fainted! …Old Harold just smiled!

MOVING IN

Our furniture was shipped from Bradenton in time to arrive at 103 Falcon Cove by March 1. We drove our Chrysler van and shipped our second car, a small Ford coupe.

We had arranged to have some lovely cabinets crafted for Dee's music room and library, and we were eager to see them. The result was just what we had hoped for.

We loved our new home, right from the start. First, we were on a quiet street with no through traffic. Second, the developer, Del Webb, had done a wonderful job of preserving the live oak trees on our own and the adjacent properties. The Ciello's, for example, have a huge perhaps 100-year old tree, one half of which provides beautiful shade over OUR back yard.

We experienced all the joys of a new home, and almost none of the problems. We had all new appliances, a wonderful gas fireplace in the living room, ceiling fans everywhere and both front and back porches.

The view from our spacious back porch was one of the features that attracted us to this house in the beginning. We made plans immediately and had it screened in. We found a fireplace and patio store in Georgetown that enabled us to match and expand the outdoor furniture we owned and loved.

The first few months were busy, fun filled and satisfying. We joined the Sun City Tennis Club, immediately made new friends with a like interest and continued our love of playing mixed doubles almost every day.

On the day after Cinco de Mayo (May 5, 1997, a holiday in Texas to honor the Mexican-American heritage), Dee and I had appointments at the Scott & White Clinic in Sun City to meet our new doctors.

On the way we stopped by the Legacy Hills Golf Course Pro Shop to pay our dues and join the Golf Associations. I then made the mistake of bragging to my new doctor that I had never spent a night in a hospital.

The next morning I tripped playing tennis and fell. I could not get up and knew I was really hurt. My partners scraped me off the court and took me back to Scott & White where X-rays showed that my right hip was broken.

A BROKEN HIP

After the X-ray determined that my right hip was broken an ambulance was called from Temple to take me to the Scott & White Hospital.

While I was sitting in my wheelchair waiting for the ambulance, a tall good-looking young man, Kevin Bell, introduced himself to me as the business manager of the Scott & White Clinic. He did not want any money, nor was he checking credentials. He just wanted to make sure I was being cared for.

He asked where I lived before moving to Sun City. When I said Sarasota Florida, he lit up like a Christmas tree. "I loved Sarasota," he said. "I was down there with the Kansas City Royals baseball team in spring training."

When daughter Dee heard that story, she said, "Only my father could break his hip and find a baseball player to talk to."

Kevin Bell came to visit me in the hospital in Temple and we became good friends. When we started the Rotary Club of Sun City it was decided we would strive for a mix of Sun City residents (older men and women) and some really fine younger people from the Greater Georgetown Community.

I recommended Kevin, who not only accepted but found our first permanent meeting place for us: the conference room in the beautiful new S&W Clinic which became our Rotary home for the next three years.

One day while our meeting was in progress Kevin was accompanying the president of Scott and White on a tour of the new facilities. "What group is meeting in there?" Kevin was asked. When told it was the new Sun City Rotary Club Dr. Montgomery replied, "Wonderful." Would you expect any different answer from a past president of the Temple Rotary Club?

I must comment on our first meeting to organize this new Rotary Club. There were about seven or eight of us. I had broken my hip and was using a walker. The only person entering ahead of me was Hal Downey who had been in an automobile accident. He, too, was using a walker.

All I could think was how my son, Past District Governor Graham, would burst laughing if he saw a picture of these two old cripples starting a Rotary Club.

THE JARRELL TORNADO

I stayed in the Scott & White Hospital in Temple for about ten days after Dr. Robert Probe, Orthopedic Surgeon, operated on my hip. I could say he really screwed me—in fact when I saw on the X-ray the size of metal bolt, I could say he screwed me royally, in the good humorous sense, of course.

A week or so after I returned home Graham and Carole came from Virginia to visit. I was using a walker, but could be up and around. Other than coming home from the hospital, I had not gone out of the house at all.

Graham and Carole wanted to drive to New Braunfels to see some of their friends, and Mutti went along. The weather in May in this part of Texas is usually beautiful, and this day was no exception.

On May 27, 1997 I felt no concern when I remained alone at home as the three of them left in the morning for the roughly two-hour drive to New Braunfels. They said they would be home in time for supper. The weather forecast offered no unusual warnings.

Then in the early afternoon the skies turned increasingly dark and looked threatening. I moved nervously from looking south through front windows to peering north to the rear. Shortly before 3:45 pm a violent tornado struck portions of Jarrell, TX, less than ten miles north of Sun City.

This storm killed 27 people directly and caused such damage it was officially rated F5 on the Fujita Scale—the most extreme level of tornado. This tornado blew some houses completely off the foundations, killed and dismembered hundreds of cattle, and bounced vehicles for up to half a mile from their parking places.

As the storm headed south, miraculously it went around—not through—Sun City, but then it generated another tornado near Cedar Park, which destroyed an Albertson's Supermarket. Additional tornadoes hit northwest Austin causing property damage and injuries. Hail was reported all the way to the Mexican border.

Phone service between New Braunfels and Sun City was out for several hours. I was relieved when Graham, Carole and Mutti finally got word to me and arrived home some time past 9:00, four hours later than scheduled.

SPORTS CAREER ENDS

I felt so fortunate to have a fitness center with an Olympic size pool in Sun City that opened at 7:00 AM every day to accommodate my rehab program. I was waiting in line with some other "faithfuls" who were there every morning.

The beauty of an early start was that I could gain immediate access to a lap lane. Walking with limited weight bearing was the number one exercise my doctor wanted me to do. After that I could get into a hot tub and direct the powerful jets onto my healing muscles.

The surgery left my right leg one-half inch shorter than the left, and I knew I my tennis days were over. I had hopes that I could resume golf, but found that when I finally got my ball in the hole it was painful just to reach over to retrieve the ball from the cup.

I have always believed that some good comes from everything, so it was no surprise to me that when my physical activity was limited, other opportunities arose that proved very fulfilling.

A "Learning in Retirement" program—Senior University Georgetown—was started in Sun City with Dee and me as two of the first students.

We were in a class studying and discussing "Great Decisions in Foreign Policy" moderated by Jack Kelly who had brought the idea for Senior University from Emory University when he moved here from Atlanta.

The semester was for six weeks. You had your choice of one of several classes from 9:00 to 10:00, and then students from all classes came together for a lecture at 10:30.

At the end of six weeks we were asked to complete a questionnaire. I rated four lectures excellent, one fair, and one poor. I commented that the program was too good to have a lecture less than excellent.

Linda Watkins, one Senior University's founders agreed with my critique and invited me to serve on the Board of Directors. My new career began.

SENIOR UNIVERSITY GEORGETOWN

Linda Watkins was an ordained Methodist minister, having earned her Doctor of Divinity degree at the Perkins School of Religion at Southern Methodist University. She had also studied at the Jung Institute in Switzerland.

By the end of the second semester Linda had assembled a fine group of volunteers willing to serve on the board of directors of Senior University. A two-day retreat was held at the Stagecoach Inn in Salado so we could get to know each other and plan for the future.

Linda was also a great believer in the Briggs-Myers personality tests to help determine where each of us board members might fit and make the best contribution.

A list of all the possible positions was put up on a chart. We were asked to volunteer for those jobs we would be willing to fill. I said I was willing to do anything, except serve as secretary.

As we moved into the second and final afternoon, Vic Figurelli and I were the only ones left to fill the jobs of president and vice president. I repeated that I had offered to be anything except secretary. Vic said he had offered to be anything except president so that made it very simple: Gaz would be the president and he would be the vice president.

It was so interesting how that turned out because I was president for three years, and then Vic succeeded me and served for the next three years. Except for some corporate background similarities (Vic-Colgate Palmolive and Shell Oil and me P&G and Coca-Cola) we were distinct opposites, but we complemented each other.

The retreat was a huge success. Vic's corporate background was developing and implementing training programs and training guides. In fact he is still in much demand as a consultant in these areas. His leadership in the first and subsequent retreats was invaluable to us.

My marketing experience enabled me to provide leadership in building membership and in selling the exciting programs we offered, both so critical for the success of a new organization.

FIRST SYMPHONY CONCERT

When we moved from Florida to Sun City, one of the first things Lois said to me was, "OK, Daddy. Now you have to help us market the Temple Symphony Orchestra."

Lois was not only one of the founders of the orchestra with Tom Fairlie in 1994 but served as the first president. I was happy to help and designed their first season brochure. I became a member of their board and tried to provide additional assistance.

By 1999 they had expanded to a four-concert season, with most performances at Temple College. They wanted to present a concert in Sun City or Georgetown but we had no suitable auditorium.

Then in the fall of 1999 the Performing Arts Center at Georgetown High School was completed and turned out to be one of the most beautiful high school auditoriums in the United States. It is state of the art, one level with 1200 cushioned seats sloping down to the stage in a hall with perfect acoustics.

We reached agreement to bring the Temple Symphony Orchestra to play a concert at 4:00 PM on a Sunday afternoon in late January 2000. We estimated our total cost would be $8,000 and agreed all tickets would be $5.00 each.

The Senior University Board agreed to buy 200 tickets @ $5.00 to give to the first 200 people who came to our early January annual meeting. (238 actually came and we sold 38 additional tickets.)

Then I set out to raise money to help underwrite the cost of the concert. After Ken Hull, Del Webb VP gave me a check for $1,000, I began calling "cold turkey" on business prospects, presenting a letter of appeal asking for $100 to $1,000, "whatever you feel comfortable with."

We ended up with an enthusiastic audience of more than 1,000 people that gave the Temple Symphony two standing ovations and us a $2,000 profit.

Then I started receiving telephone calls, e-mails and letters from people asking us if we could have more concerts.

SYMPHONY CONCERT COMMENTS

"The Temple Symphony was simply wonderful. Providing the impetus for bringing the orchestra to Georgetown may be the singularly best thing our Senior University has been involved with." —Dr. Linda Watkins, Chair of Programs and Curriculum.

"Congratulations on your fine work in bringing the Temple Symphony to Georgetown. We really enjoyed yesterday's concert and were tickled to see so many friends and neighbors from Sun City. I would like to make a donation to help the Georgetown Symphony Society…do I send the check to you? Whom do I make it out to?" —Ron Lockhart, Sun City Resident.

"I enjoyed the music very much. I hope it is just the first of many." —Janet Russell, Chairman-elect for student activities, Austin District Music Teachers Association and member of the Georgetown Music Study Club.

"We host out of town sales prospects for Sun City in our Vacation Getaway Villas. Last weekend we invited them to be our guests at the Temple Symphony Concert. One couple from North Texas said this music was as good as anything they can hear in Dallas…and to think they can have it right here in Georgetown." —Terri Edson, Marketing Director, Del Webb Corporation, Sun City Georgetown.

"A word of appreciation for the wonderful turnout at the Sunday performance of the Temple Symphony. Another full house and great event as a product of your dedication, enthusiasm and interest in our community." —Maj. Gen. (Ret)) Sandy Meloy, former Commanding General, 82nd Airborne Division.

Temple Symphony Orchestra, Tom Fairlie conducting

"Congrats! You must be very pleased with the Temple Symphony outcome. A fine program; a full house; an enthusiastic response from the audience—the culmination of many months of hard work—a dream come true." —Ron Stinson, Treasurer of Senior University.

"We were happy to have been a sponsor for the first concert. It was great. Just tell us what you want us to do to help with the future programs." —Ken Hull, VP and General Manager, Del Webb, Sun City.

"YOUNG PEOPLES CONCERT"
TEMPLE SYMPHONY ORCHESTRA, January 23, 2000
"A Program for Young People of All Ages."
"Carnival of the Animals," by Saint-Saens.

This is a letter I received from a mother after this concert:

"I want to thank you for your hard work and perseverance in getting the Temple Symphony Orchestra to perform in Georgetown. The new facility was wonderful and the seating was great.

"We attended with four young ladies, ages 8—12, who are all musicians. They were enchanted! One was pleased to learn that the orchestra 'tunes' to the oboe (her instrument). Another loved the string bass 'resonating' as her favorite animal, the elephant, 'walked' across the stage.

"Our daughter, a violin player, was especially pleased to see the orchestra 'start-and-stop all at the same time' and 'make the same bow strokes together.'

"We all were excited and grateful to enjoy such fine music. We look forward to their return." —Dana Reno Coyle, Mother of a budding Violinist.

Author's note:

Jennifer Coyle is now (in the fall of 2006) a senior at Georgetown High School. No longer a "budding violinist," she is concertmaster and president of the outstanding Georgetown High School Orchestra. She also is a member of the Austin Youth Orchestra and has a very bright future ahead.

Jennifer is a beautiful violinist. She was particularly outstanding when we watched her play first violin in a string quartet in a masterclass at Mary Hardin Baylor College last year presented by our daughter, Lois Reiter, and our Swiss granddaughter, Cordelia Hagmann.

GEORGETOWN SYMPHONY SOCIETY FORMED

We put one item in the *Williamson County Sun* inviting people interested in forming a Symphony Society in Georgetown to a meeting and thirty-eight people came.

We were privileged to have daughter Lois and Tom Fairlie present representing the Temple Symphony Orchestra; Dr Jo Ann Ford, retired Middle School Principal who had started the school orchestra program in the Georgetown schools; Linda Scarbrough, co-publisher of the *Sun,* and Sondra Carlton, head of public relations for Del Webb, developer of Sun City.

I introduced Tom and Lois. They talked about their willingness to work with us to develop a series of concerts here in Georgetown.

After that, all I did was go around the room and ask everyone present what his or her background or interests in music were that caused them to come. It turned out to be an unbelievable group.

We had one woman, Marge Mirkin, who had served as president of the Kalamazoo Michigan Symphony Board. Another, Gerry Giddings had been president of the Omaha Nebraska Symphony Board. Numerous other enthusiastic persons had served on symphony boards all across the United States.

It was clearly obvious that everyone there wanted to see this movement go forward.

I volunteered to serve as president to get it started and then asked for volunteers. Dr. George Biggs, a Dartmouth graduate with a PhD from the Indiana University Conservatory, offered to serve as vice president; Barbara Konetchy, secretary and Lynn Duvall, treasurer.

Before the evening was over we had enough enthusiastic volunteers, representing both Sun City and other parts of Georgetown to establish an outstanding, experienced board of directors and an excellent advisory board.

The Georgetown Symphony Society was born March 8, 2000.

MUTTI'S HEALTH CHALLENGES

In January 2002, we planned a trip to Florida, first to visit friends in Bradenton and Sarasota, then to re-visit Sanibel Island where we had enjoyed several vacations.

We flew Southwest from Austin to Houston, and then changed planes for a non-stop trip to Tampa. Everything was going along fine, until about an hour after we left Houston, Mutti told me she did not feel well. I called a flight attendant immediately, but before she could get there Mutti had fainted. Our seatmate and I got up so Mutti could lie down across the three seats.

The flight attendant was very professional and well trained. A medical doctor from California, sitting a few rows behind us volunteered his services, as did a registered nurse nearby. Mutti's face felt clammy, and everyone was alarmed when her pulse dropped to 50.

The pilots were alerted, and preliminary plans made for an emergency unscheduled landing in Jackson, Mississippi, the nearest airport.

Suddenly, the Doctor monitoring her blood pressure and pulse gave us some encouraging news. I asked if it would be safe to continue to Tampa, arranging to take her to a hospital immediately upon arrival. The doctor, nurse and flight attendant all agreed to that plan.

Tampa EMS personnel were waiting at the gate when we arrived. All passengers waited respectfully while she was carried by litter from the plane and taken by ambulance to the hospital.

An airline representative helped me get our luggage and the rental car we had reserved. Then, he made sure I had complete directions from the airport to the hospital.

Mutti had had a complete medical examination at Scott & White in Temple less than a month before which disclosed nothing of concern. The Tampa doctors gave her many of the same tests, also found nothing, but kept her overnight for observation.

SARASOTA AND SANIBEL ISLAND

Don and Dorothy Ann Jackson, our ministers and dear friends at the Unity Church of Sarasota, had invited us to stay with them for the weekend upon arrival in Tampa, an hour away. I called them from the hospital and told them we would arrive a day late.

After all the tests had been completed at the hospital, the doctors had assured me Mutti was in no danger, I found a room in a nearby motel for the night.

Mutti was released from the hospital late Saturday morning. We had lunch and a relaxed visit with Don and Dorothy Ann in the afternoon before attending, with them, a fundraising dinner for the church. Many of our dearest friends were at the dinner, others we saw at the church services Sunday morning.

On Monday we drove to Sanibel Island just north of Ft. Myers and west of Cape Coral where our dear friends Les and Marie Scott, from Pocantico Hills lived in retirement. Sanibel, which contains a huge nature preserve and a pristine beach, was made famous by Ann Morrow Lindberg who authored her "Gifts of the Sea" books there.

We had visited Sanibel almost every year after our real estate business in New Braunfels became successful. Other favorite friends from our Pocantico Hills days, Dottie and John Baverstock, who retired in Greenville North Carolina, and Jim and Gay Wooding, then living in Salem Ohio all came to Sanibel or nearby Ft. Myers Beach.

We had a wonderful reunion, but realized we were all beginning to age and that we should cherish every moment we had together. In addition to Mutti's scare on the plane, Gay Wooding required an oxygen tank at all times and her husband Jim had already had at least one heart attack.

We had no way of knowing this was the last time the eight of us would all be together, Mutti, Gay and Jim having passed on first, and then Les and Marie. We have never had a group of closer, more loyal and fun friends.

MUTTI'S STROKE

Before we made our final plans to return to Texas we solicited advice from Lois's husband, Charlie, a highly respected Cardio-Thoracic surgeon at Scott & White. He felt it would be better if we could take a train, but it was probably safe to fly.

We investigated the train option, discovered it would take one day to get to Chicago, then another day from Chicago to Temple, the nearest station in Texas to our home. Also, we were told the service was unreliable and often ran several hours late.

Instead, we secured a room in the Marriott Hotel in the Tampa Airport. That way we could have dinner, a good night's rest and a leisurely breakfast before boarding a Southwest plane in mid-morning that would get us home that afternoon. It was a relaxing return trip.

Mutti handled it well and seemed fine. Then, two weeks later on a Sunday, she said, "I don't feel well. I think I will just take it easy today."

I checked on her regularly, and she responded with no change until late in the afternoon she said, "I wonder if I might be having a stroke."

There was no slurring of words or other outward indications. I phoned Lois immediately and she said, "Bring her immediately to the Scott & White emergency room in Temple, and I will meet you there."

Lois was waiting when we arrived and had already alerted the emergency room personnel. Mutti was admitted immediately and after about five hours of exhaustive testing the Doctors confirmed that, yes, she had suffered a cerebral hemorrhage, the severity of which could be determined only after continued testing.

Lois and Charlie were wonderful in watching out for Mutti. She received the best possible treatment from a team of doctors led by Charlie's best friend, David Lindzey, Chief Medical Officer for the Scott & White Hospital who became her personal physician.

At the end of three weeks Mutti had improved enough to move into a wonderful assisted living facility, The Temple Meridian.

MERIDIAN HEALTH CARE

Daughter Lois knew the wonderful reputation the Meridian enjoyed before she took me to visit the facility a few blocks from Scott & White. It offered three levels of support: 24-hour nursing care, assisted care and independent living.

The facility operates at, or near, capacity all the time. We were very lucky to get Mutti into a semi-private room with a real sparkplug of a woman in her 90's who had been there for quite some time. She and Mutti became friends immediately.

Located on a 21-acre site, the Meridian features a beautifully landscaped circle drive with cottages on the exterior. The apartment buildings, community building and health center are in the interior.

I never dreamed I would find a facility like this. First, the managers, Keith and Mary Rayl, were so special. Keith is one of the brightest men I have ever known and an excellent administrator. His wife Mary, an RN who had been head of the health programs also was a fine executive, and they had an experienced staff.

After Mutti had been in residence for about a month, and we saw the outstanding care she was receiving, I leased a 2-bedroom apartment in the independent living section to give Mutti encouragement to get well enough to move in with me. It worked.

Occasionally I could bring her in a wheelchair up to the main dining room for lunch or dinner, but usually we had dinner together in the special dining room for the health center. Mutti had no speech impairment, nor paralysis from her stroke. She did have some confusion in her mind, which she laughed about when it happened.

One evening we were having dinner with a man with Alzheimer's disease. He kept asking me where I lived over and over again. Suddenly, Mutti said to him, "You have a beautiful nose."

She reached over, took his hand and held his fingers up for me to view, and said, "See. He has a beautiful nose. Look at them."

MUTTI HAS VISITORS

The Meridian maintained a guest suite which could be rented for a nominal charge when out of town guests came. Plus, Lois and Charlie had a guest apartment at their Owl Creek Ranch, about 20 minutes away.

What pleased Mutti most was when one or more of her family entertained the guests for dinner in the main dining room. Graham, on the grand piano, and Carole singing, performed several times.

Granddaughter Cordelia Hagmann, after finishing at the Swiss Conservatory in Winterthur, had moved to New York. Cordelia is such an outstanding violinist and plays so beautifully. Everybody loved her when she visited Mutti and played for them. Cordelia since has performed in a feature role twice with the Temple Symphony Orchestra.

Ft. Hood, one of the largest military bases in the United States, is located in Killeen, TX, about 15 miles from Temple and easily accessible from the Meridian. Because of the large military base, American Airlines has commuter flights to and from Dallas.

I remember meeting Cordelia, a world traveler, arriving in Killeen. She was literally shaking when I greeted her, saying she had never been as frightened as she was on this flight. Turned out she had never flown before on a propeller plane which has much more vibration than a jet.

Mutti was so delighted with the visits by her children and grandchildren who came from near and far to visit her in the last months she was alive. Daughter Dee and I were with her when she suffered a massive stroke while taking a shower.

David Lindzey, her personal physician, was so wonderful. He came to see her almost every night on his way home after he had completed his rounds at the hospital. We had a ground floor apartment and he could park his car and come in through our patio door.

Although she never regained consciousness, all of our children came, stayed and were at her bedside when she made her transition July 23, 2002.

RETURN TO FALCON COVE

Fortunately, our home in Sun City had not been sold during the couple of months I had it on the market. Marianne stayed and helped me get everything ready for the mover to take our belongings back to 103 Falcon Cove from the Temple Meridian.

I had taken Mutti's two Himalayan cats, Mike and Michelle, to be with her at the Meridian, so on moving day, Marianne stayed with the mover while I left to take some rental equipment back to the Cable company.

With the two cats in a big kennel-like cage in the back of my van loaded with personal belongings, I set out to find the Cable company office in an unfamiliar area of Temple to return the leased equipment. Suddenly, as I squinted to read a street address, the traffic in front of me stopped, but I could NOT.

I had never heard such screaming in my life as came from those two cats. I don't blame them. They were probably scared to death. Fortunately, no one was injured, and the cats were OK, but I smashed the front of the van and had to be towed to a body shop.

Daughter Lois came to my rescue. She arrived in her van, helped me transfer all the contents of my car, including the now subdued Mike and Michelle, and drove us to Sun City. Marianne followed a little later, and we all arrived home safe and sound.

Graham had already said the first thing I needed to get was a big screen (60-inch) TV to watch football. He took me out to an appliance store and we ordered one.

Then, he and Carole said I needed to move my computer out of the utility room. They took me to Austin where we found a perfect piece of modern furniture for my computer that would fit space in the living room previously occupied by Mutti's grand piano that she wanted grandson Jamie Wilson to inherit.

After the children returned to their homes, Mutti's absence created a huge void. I knew I would have to keep busy to be able to adjust.

A CELEBRATION OF HER LIFE

I cannot imagine a more wonderful tribute to Dee than the memorial service held in the Sun City Ballroom and attended by more than 400 of her family and friends who knew her and loved her so deeply.

Leading the service was Dr. W. Leslie Pugh, our pastor and dear friend in Houston and New Braunfels, who along with his wife Jettie, were the only people who helped Dee and me celebrate all three of our 25th, 50th and 55th Wedding Anniversaries.

We arranged to have Dee's grand piano transported to the ballroom and tuned, as music would be at the center of the Celebration.

Son Graham played the piano; daughters Dee and Lois, violinists, joined sister Marianne on the cello to present beautiful music for string trios; Graham accompanied his wife Carole whose lovely soprano voice Mutti loved so much. Marianne shared some poetry led a guided Meditation and added mystique with her Spherical Improvisations.

Mutti was always so proud of her grandchildren who continued on with her music tradition. Two of the most talented, violinist Cordelia Hagmann, a graduate of the Swiss Conservatory at Wintertur, and Jamie Wilson, recipient of the outstanding pianist award upon graduation from Vassar College, both performed.

Meghann Green represented the grandchildren in expressing the love they had for Mutti, and I was fortunate enough to maintain my composure to tell the story of how we met after the Daily Collegian identified her as one of the most beautiful girls in the Penn State freshman class of 1944.

The closing hymn and prayer were Dee's favorites, "Let there be peace on earth" and the service concluded with The Unity Prayer of Protection as the Benediction:

The Light of God Surrounds You,
The Love of God Enfolds You
The Power of God Protects You
The Presence of God Watches Over You
Wherever you are, God Is.

CHAPTER TWELVE

STARTING MY NEW LIFE

All of my children were so thoughtful and supportive of me after the Memorial Service. Rarely a day went by that Graham did not call me.

And the girls were just as attentive.

Fortunately, I was still president of the Georgetown Symphony Society and we were busy preparing for our third season. Also, I was still involved with Senior University and the Sun City Rotary Club. I kept busy and time went by quickly.

I had the wonderful computer setup so that I could be at my desk, watch TV and enjoy the views across the green space to the rear and out through the oak trees in the front yard.

I began a routine that I still have to this day. The *Austin American-Statesman* is delivered to my front door. Then, after checking my e-mail each morning, I read the online *New York Times*, *Washington Post*, and the *Centre Daily Times* from my hometown of State College, Pennsylvania.

When I started to write my memoirs I discovered how helpful it was to have the research sources of the internet available to check names, dates, and facts pertaining to specific periods of my life.

What I discovered was almost unbelievable.

As well as I knew Nelson Rockefeller, I had never been aware of the supposed conspiracy theory that Nelson had placed Henry Kissinger and General Haig in Nixon's inner circle to keep tabs on him, and that these two were responsible for disclosure of the Watergate break-in.

And what a surprise I got when I looked up Mickey Herskowitz, Houston sports writer, just to check the spelling of his name. I learned that Mickey had been commissioned to "ghost write" the autobiography of Governor George Bush for his Presidential Campaign and then was fired because he included information, told to him by Bush, that the campaign staff felt would be detrimental.

Karen Hughes reportedly edited and completed the book so that it contained only the positive contents they desired.

PENN STATE SOCCER REUNION

Along with the excitement of the start of the college football season I received an invitation to return to State College to celebrate the 90th anniversary of the birth of the Penn State soccer program.

I called Graham immediately. He said he would love to go with me so we made our plans and reservations. It would be the weekend of October 10 & 11. We would be honored guests for the Friday night soccer game between Penn State and the defending National Champion University of Indiana.

Saturday afternoon we would be guests at the Penn State-Purdue football game before 107,000 fans in Beaver Stadium. Purdue was favored on the strength its All-American Quarterback Drew Brees, who went on to become a huge star in the National Football League with the San Diego Chargers and the New Orleans Saints.

Penn State's upset victory set the mood for a festive reunion dinner and evening in the ballroom of the Penn State Convocation Center.

While Penn State had additional National Champion Soccer teams in the 1950's, the Golden Age of Soccer for the Nittany Lions was from 1933 to 1940 when the team was UNDEFEATED FOR EIGHT YEARS IN A ROW. I was fortunate to have played left halfback on the 1939 and 1940 teams, both of which were designated National Champion.

There were only four of us back from the pre-World War II era and the present Penn State coach, Barry Gorman, asked me to represent the group and speak briefly at the banquet and share some memories of the legendary Coach Bill Jeffrey, who built all those winning teams.

I told the story of how, the night before the last game of the season, he called for a team meeting in our hotel in Philadelphia. He had never done this before. He urged us to stop worrying about the unbeaten streak. "Just go out and have fun and you will be OK."

WE DID, WE WON, AND WE REMAINED UNDEFEATED!

WICKERSHAM FAMILY GRAVES

Luther Wickersham, Mary Ann Sutton Wickersham, and Winifred Wickersham, Dee's parents and sister, were all natives of the Harrisburg area.

Luther grew up in Harrisburg and then was graduated from Penn State in 1913 with a degree in sanitary engineering. After college he worked for the Pennsylvanian Department of Health for several years in Harrisburg and Pittsburgh before joining the American Water Works Company at their headquarters in New York.

When Dee (Lois Adene Wickersham, born August 22, 1923 in Harrisburg) was in elementary school the family moved to Rutherford, NJ, a commuter town to Manhattan.

Dee's sister, Winnie, was seven years older and never married. She lived at home almost her entire life and moved with her parents to their new Wynnewood home when Luther's company moved its headquarters to Philadelphia a few years before he retired.

Dee's mother's father was a blacksmith in New Cumberland, a small town on the west shore of the Susquehanna River across from Harrisburg. She was the second oldest in a family of five girls and one boy. Their father died quite young and all the girls worked while going to school to help support the family.

Mary was lovely. She was beautiful and every inch a lady. I always said I fell in love with Dee's mother before I fell in love with her. She had all the qualities I wanted in a wife and the mother of our children.

Early on, Luther and Mary had purchased a section in a beautiful cemetery in New Cumberland with space for four adult caskets, and they, along with Winnie, were buried there. Dee was steadfast in her desire to be cremated.

So Graham and I, as part of our trip to State College, scheduled a visit to the cemetery to spread Dee's ashes among the graves of her parents and sister whom she loved so much. Dee is now with them in Spirit.

INTRODUCING PAT MUSE

I have written about Bob Cords, my good friend with whom I worked at the Coca-Cola Company. Bob's wife, Ruth, had a gorgeous soprano voice and was a soloist at the Memorial Drive Methodist Church. Ruth sang at the wedding when our Marianne and the Swiss Doctor Oscar Hagmann were married in Houston in 1965. Sadly, Ruth suffered a heart attack and died not long after that.

Several years after we moved to New Braunfels I received a surprise phone call from Bob informing me that he had married a very attractive younger woman, Pat Wylie, head of the Cost Accounting Department at the Coca-Cola Foods Division.

Bob and Pat had retired and moved into a golf course retirement community at Walden on Lake Conroe north of Houston. Dee and I also had moved into our golf course home at Northcliffe so it was only fitting that the best way for us to get to know Pat was to exchange "golfing" visits to each other's home.

We liked Pat right from the start. Bob had gotten her started in golf. She had natural ability, worked hard and was tenacious. It was no surprise that she kept moving up the ladder until she reached the Championship Flight.

Dee and I moved to Kansas City and on to Florida for ten years. We lost track of Bob and Pat until one Sunday night in 2000 in Sun City the phone rang and a woman on the other end of the line said, "I am reading a column in the Stacy Letter 'Gaz Green Recommends' ... Is this MY Gaz Green?" It was Pat Muse, who brought me up to date.

After a very happy 23 years together, Bob Cords had died. Pat then was pursued by another of Bob's friends, Lamar Muse, founder of Southwest Airlines, and they were united in a marriage that did not work out.

So here was Pat Muse at the Holiday Inn in Georgetown looking at Sun City. I said I would tell Don Stacy first thing in the morning to take care of her.

His office did. She bought a home and moved here.

DINNER WITH PAT MUSE

Dee and I had been to Pat's home for dinner and she became a season ticket holder to our symphony concerts so we saw her occasionally there.

However, Pat's two main interests were golf and bridge. She was in the Sun City Women's Golf Association Championship Flight and played regularly two or three times a week. I think she might have been just as devoted to Bridge.

After Dee died I wrote to Pat, as I did to other friends that I knew were gone from Sun City for the summer and told her what had happened. When she returned in September she wrote me a lovely note suggesting that if I ever wanted a sympathetic ear to call her.

I invited her to go to dinner at the Outback Steak House in Round Rock. She was not in the car five minutes until I realized that she was hurting, and I was hurting.

We ordered a drink and started to talk. Pat opened up and told me about the very difficult period she had been through when she realized that her life with Lamar Muse was so unpleasant it was destined to end in divorce.

Certain aspects of the marriage were glamorous. Their winter home was on Saint Simon Island, Georgia and their summers were spent on the *Holy Moses*, Lamar's 65-ft. yacht that he kept in La Conner, Washington, north of Seattle for easy access to the open waters to Vancouver, British Columbia and Alaska.

The *Holy Moses* had three staterooms to accommodate six persons comfortably and Lamar, who had become quite wealthy after starting the most successful new airline in the United States in the last half century, loved to entertain.

Glamorous is not the way Pat would have described her role aboard the Holy Moses. She was the CREW. She was the chief cook and bottle washer, expected to do all the work yet still help entertain.

And, when the Captain was ungrateful that was *Too Much*!

TASTE OF THE WURST

Graham and Carole wanted to come from Virginia for Wurstfest, which starts the first weekend in November. A member of the Wurstfest Association since 1973, I am now a Senior Opa which means I am entitled to all the privileges without having to work at Wurstfest.

Our Sun City Rotary Club had sponsored charter buses to Wurstfest and this was very popular. So this year we decided we would bring entertainers from Wurstfest to Sun City and give Sun City residents "A Taste of the Wurst."

Graham, who had been one of the featured accordionists at Wurstfest when he lived in New Braunfels, enlisted the support of Ed Kadlecek and Rennie Guenther.

The three of them were the nucleus of the Bavarian Village Band where they performed regularly at New Braunfels's most popular Biergarten. They also represented the Bavarian Village when they performed at other festivals in Texas and on cruise ships.

By scheduling our "Taste of Texas" for the night before the opening of Wurstfest, Graham knew he could attract other Wurstfest headline performers. And he got two of the most popular, Paul McLaughlin (violin/trumpet, humorist) and Mike Barker, whose own band is the headliner at Houston's most popular German restaurant.

By this time, Pat and I had realized we enjoyed each other's company. We had been to a couple of movies and out to dinner several times. So I invited Pat and her long time best friend, Helen Bradley who lives about an hour away at Horseshoe Falls to join me at the private table I had setup for the entertainers and their guests.

I wanted Graham and Carole to meet Pat, but I did not want to be too obvious about how close our friendship had become. I did not realize until several months later how successful I had been.

Eventually, when I told Graham that Pat and I had become serious, he said, "Gosh, Dad. Why did you not tell us when we were down for Wurstfest? We would really have tried to get to know her."

TAROT CARD

In Marianne's own words:

"Daddy came to visit me in Boulder, October, 2002. I had moved there 2 months before, Mother had passed on in July, and I was enrolled in a few courses at Naropa University.

"One was on the Tarot. (Carl Jung regarded the tarot cards as representing archetypes: fundamental types of persons or situations embedded in the subconscious of all human beings. The images and symbols on the cards facilitate these energies to rise to the surface to be integrated consciously in our present life).

"When Daddy arrived, he said that he wanted me to tell him all about this course. I, in turn, asked him how he was getting along with all the widows in Sun City.

"He got a funny look on his face! The next morning, I suggested that the best way to approach his understand about the Tarot would be for him to just pick a card. He promptly picked the card: 'THE LOVERS'.....and this is when he began to tell me about Pat for the first time."

I told Marianne how well Pat and I got along, how fond we had become of each other, but I was concerned about how she and her siblings, Dee, Graham and Lois, might feel knowing that I was dating someone so soon after their mother had passed away,

Without hesitation, Marianne, whom I have admired all my life for her own values and her levelheaded approach to everything, stated very positively,

"DADDY, GO FOR IT!

"MOTHER WOULD NOT WANT YOU SITTING AT HOME BY YOUR-SELF."

That was all the encouragement I needed.

MEETING PAT'S FAMILY

At Christmas time Marianne and her daughter Rebecca Hagmann, visiting from Switzerland, went with Pat and me to San Antonio to attend Rudy Harst's Church.

Then, as pre-arranged, we met Pat's identical twin sister Dee Erwin, her husband, Frank and middle sister, Jonnie Hall, to stay overnight and enjoy the Riverwalk.

Consider the confusion. Mutti was also known as Dee. Daughter Adene was always called Dee which was no problem within our own family until her mother, at about age 35 decided her nickname, Deenie, from when we met in college was not mature enough. So now we had "Big Dee" and "Little Dee".

When we joined the Congregational church in Houston and our minister Les Pugh introduced "Big Dee" the congregation burst out laughing. Mutti was embarrassed. She thought it was personal and did not realize the reference "Big D" was for DALLAS.

But, back to Pat's twin sister Dee. Even after being married to Pat for four years we often must clarify "Is it Sister Dee or Daughter Dee?"

Since I first met "Sister Dee" I have loved to see these wonderful identical twins together. They are always holding hands or showing each other unmatched affection. It is beautiful to behold.

My favorite story about mistaken identity was the time Frank came into the bathroom to brush his teeth while Pat was sitting on the john. He thought it was Dee, patted her on the head as he left the bathroom, walked out into the hall and bumped into his wife!

Dee and Jonnie were very friendly to me from the first time we met. About a month later we stayed overnight with Jonnie at her home in Rockwall, near Dallas en-route to Honey Grove to meet her father.

Jonnie heard me ask Pat to help me on with my socks, and the word quickly spread. "Why, Pat even has to help him put on his socks!"

Jonnie has never lived that one down.

HONEY GROVE, TEXAS

Pat was born in the small East Texas town of Cooper but grew up on a farm near Honey Grove, another small community of about 2,000 population, between Paris and Bonham.

Bonham was well known as the hometown of the Honorable Sam Rayburn, powerful Speaker of the U. S. House of Representatives from 1940 until he died in 1961. Sam Rayburn taught school in Honey Grove before he began his distinguished political career.

Pat's parents had been married for almost 70 years before her mother, Hazel, died. She was very artistic and, like the legendary Grandma Moses, became an accomplished painter in her latter years. I am sorry I never knew her because I have always heard what a wonderful woman she was and how everybody loved her.

Pat's father Ray moved his family to Dallas and took a job in a defense plant after being forced to move off their farm during World War II because of a drought. A vengeful draft board cancelled his deferment, and this 37-year old father of four children was drafted into the U. S Army and served in the Philippines.

Her mother Hazel kept the family fed and clothed by also working in a defense plant so she could save all of Ray's army pay. This gave the family the nest egg they needed for a new start.

Justice prevailed when Ray returned from the Pacific a war veteran and thereby eligible for a Veteran's Administration loan, which he used to purchase a 183-acre farm within four miles of Honey Grove.

Ray and I became great friends in the three years that I knew him before he died at age 97. He loved playing cards with his family. He had a keen mind, read extensively and had a great sense of humor. And he was politically correct. (Translation: he and I agreed.)

When Pat and I decided to get married, I told him I would get down on my knee and ask for her hand, except I might not be able to get back up. He laughed and gave us his blessing.

ANDY, SANDY AND THE GRANDKIDS

There was one more test to pass. Pat's daughter Sandy, husband Andy and three children Courtney, 14, Brittany, 10, and Kyle, 5, lived near Richmond, a western suburb of Houston.

I had not met any of them yet, but Pat had told them about us. Courtney, the oldest child, began sending me the cutest e-mails. Finally she got around to asking me what she should call me.

She asked if she should call me Mr. Green. I told her, "No, Mr. Green was my son."

Then she e-mailed back to me. "If his name is Mr. Green, wouldn't you be Mr. Green, too?" Good logic, but I did not want her to be so formal. I believe I told her all my kids and grandkids call me Bumi, but suggested if she wanted to call me Gaz, that would be fine, too. She was so adorable through this process I was really eager to meet her.

Finally the day came for Pat and me to drive to Richmond to meet the Cordova Family. Pat's daughter, Sandy, is a slim, very attractive young mother with a lot of pep and enthusiasm. Andy, her husband, is a tall, well built, about six-foot-two, very athletic looking young man.

We went in two cars. I asked Sandy to ride with me to Luby's Cafeteria, the first of three short trips we would take, so I could first get acquainted with her. We all went through the buffet line and ordered. When we sat down at the table to eat, Andy began a surprising INQUISITION. He wanted to know all about me, in effect, "What are my background, and my intentions?"

Every time I took a bite, he would ask me another question. It was irritating to me, but it also was obvious Andy was looking out for his Mother-in-law, and that I appreciated. Finally, Pat came to my rescue!

They were preparing to build their new home in River Forest, a super lovely new area. Courtney and I bonded as we rode together to their new home site.

All I needed to do now was start to build the relationship with Andy, my new son-in-law to be, as together us rode back to his home.

OUR TRIP TO NEW YORK

Pat and I planned a trip to Poughkeepsie and New York City after Christmas, which turned out to be almost perfect for developing the relationship I wanted Pat to have with all other members of the Green Family.

We visited Dee and Richard in Poughkeepsie. Dee took us up to Bard College in Annandale on the Hudson for a preview tour of the new Performing Arts Center designed by internationally acclaimed architect Frank Gehry. This had added significance because our architect granddaughter Katherine Wilson had spent the previous summer as an intern with Gehry's firm on this project.

I knew Dee and Richard would bond with Pat, and they did so immediately.

Then it was on to New York where we stayed in a small Suites Hotel between Grand Central Station and the United Nations headquarters. Graham and Carole came up from Fredericksburg, and we spent the weekend together.

We experienced New York City after a snowfall, toured the U. N. Building, saw a couple of Broadway shows and live TV programs, attended an American Symphony Orchestra concert in Lincoln Center and enjoyed Richard's pre-concert lecture.

We visited the hallowed site of "Ground Zero" where the 9/11 attack took place, had lunch with concert pianist Rui Shi near the Julliard School and celebrated our last night in the city by having dinner in the Rainbow Room above Rockefeller Center.

Pat, not having ever lived in New York, insisted on picking up the tab for the Rainbow Room. She was a gracious hostess even though she almost fainted when she paid the bill, which was almost $700.00 for five of us. (Carole's nephew Cameron White, a budding young sports TV executive joined us for dinner.)

Yes, my family loved Pat, and the feeling was obviously mutual.

PLANNING FOR OUR WEDDING

March and April are normally lovely months in Texas. Our love for each other grew stronger so we set the date, Saturday, May 17, and decided it would be a wedding shared by our families, with only a few other friends in attendance.

We began by inviting our combined 22 grandchildren to come to our wedding, to bring their spouses or significant others and their parents.

About 46 was the final count of those who came to share the festivities with us.

We reserved the open air Sun City Pavilion, a beautiful setting that overlooks a small lake. We also reserved guest rooms at a luxurious Suites Hotel in Round Rock, less than 30 minutes from Sun City.

This hotel had a most cooperative young woman salesmanager who helped us in every way. She arranged for us to bring our own caterer, use their corporate meeting room for our Happy Hour and the entire lobby dining area for our rehearsal dinner. Featured performers of the Graham Green Oompah Band, namely, Graham III on accordion, Graham IV on tuba, and Carole, voice provided music that put everyone in a festive mood.

Those who arrived early were encouraged to join a pool party hosted by my favorite niece, Jenny Locke of San Diego. Our weekend goal was to meld two families into one in a three-day period.

Our caterer from Rotary, Alycia Heeneman, "Do Yourself a Flavor!" prepared and served a wonderful dinner. We appreciated beautiful toasts from family members on both sides of the aisle.

Pat's "baby sister" Ann was the only member of her immediate family I had not met. I immediately recognized her as one of the warmest, friendliest persons I had ever known.

She made me feel right at home as part of the "Wylie" family. It was a glorious and memorable evening.

THE CORDS FAMILY REPRESENTED

It was especially gratifying to welcome so many members of the Cords family who came from Kansas, Arizona and Nevada to help us celebrate.

Remember the important role that my good friend Bob Cords played in my life. First, we had memorable experiences working together for six years at the Coca-Cola Company. Also he was so knowledgeable about advertising that I learned so much from him.

Second, it was his first wife, Ruth, who sang at Marianne's wedding when she and Oscar were married in 1965 by Dr. W. Leslie Pugh at the First Congregational Church in Houston. Bob and Ruth had two children, twins Robert and Nancy. They were both away in college so I barely got to know them as Ruth died suddenly in about 1969.

Then, if Bob had not married Pat in 1973 I would never have met her. She joined the Coca-Cola Company Foods Division before I resigned in 1971 but, as head of the Cost Accounting Department, her office was at another location.

Here is the part of the story I love. Nancy married Bill Maxwell and they had four daughters, two of whom were born after Ruth, their natural grandmother had died. They grew up loving Pat as the only maternal grandmother they had known.

And, as grown-ups, I have never seen four more beautiful sisters. Andrea, the oldest, came to our wedding from Las Vegas where she was an executive at the famous Hotel Bellagio. The middle two, Melinda and Carrie came from the Phoenix area. The one who could not attend, Pam, had just been blessed with a set of twins.

It was such fun to hear these three beautiful young women laugh as the reminisced about crawling into bed with Grandpa Bob and Pat when they were little.

It was also great to renew friendships with Robert and Nancy and to get to know their lovely life partners, Robert's Margy and Nancy's Bill, who roots for Nebraska as enthusiastically as I do for Penn State.

WHO'S WHO AT OUR WEDDING—
ON THE GREEN SIDE

Gaz Green (GGGJr.) Happy Groom
Marianne Green, daughter from Boulder (CO) read poem.
Cordelia Hagmann, Marianne's Swiss daughter – violinist
Adene (Dee) Wilson, daughter from Poughkeepsie NY
Graham Green (GGG3) Gaz's son & best man & accordion-
  ist (VA)
Carole Green, Graham's wife sang at wedding (VA).
Tabitha Barr, Graham's daughter (VA)
Robb Barr, Tabitha's husband (VA)
Cleopatra Barr, Tabitha and Robb's daughter. (VA)
Graham Green (GGG4) --- GGG3's son (VA)
Alexis Green, GGG4's wife. (VA)
Quint Green (GGG5) Gaz's great-grandson and namesake.
  (VA)
Meghann Green, GGG3's daughter, George Mason Univ.
  (VA)
David Abramson, Meghann's significant other (VA)
Garrett Green, GGG3's son, Longwood College (VA)
Amber Duffy, Garrett's significant other (VA)
Lois Reiter, Gaz's daughter, Temple (TX).
Julia Reiter, Lois's daughter, Southwestern University (TX)
Emily Reiter, Lois' daughter, Baylor University (TX)
A. G. Agee, Emily's friend (TX)
Leslie Reiter, Lois' daughter (TX)
Pat Hodges, Leslie's friend (TX)
Jennifer Locke, Gaz's favorite niece, San Diego (CA)
SPECIAL GUESTS
Jettie & Dr. W. Leslie Pugh who performed Marianne's
  wedding where Ruth Cords sang. Midland (TX)

WHO'S WHO AT THE WEDDING—
ON THE WYLIE SIDE

Pat Wylie Muse – Happy Bride
Sandy Cordova, Pat's daughter & matron of honor, Houston (TX)
Andy Cordova, Sandy's husband, Houston
Courtney Cordova, Sandy's daughter, Houston
Brittany Cordova, Sandy's daughter, Houston
Kyle Cordova, Sandy's son, Houston
Dee Erwin, Pat's twin sister, Honey Grove (TX)
Frank Erwin, Dee's husband, Honey Grove
Jonnie Hall, Pat's sister, Rockwall (TX)
Ann Larue, Pat's sister, Rockwall
Jerry Larue, Ann's husband, Rockwall
Nancy Maxwell, Pat's stepdaughter, Phoenix (AZ)
Bill Maxwell, Nancy's husband, Phoenix
Andrea Maxwell, Nancy's daughter, Las Vegas (NV)
Melinda Shuckhart, Nancy's daughter, Phoenix
Carrie Todd, Nancy's daughter, Phoenix
Robert Cords, Pat's stepson, Derby KS
Margy Cords, Robert's wife, Derby
SPECIAL GUESTS
Dr. Linda Watkins, Methodist minister who performed the ceremony.
Dr. George and Jeanne Biggs, Georgetown (TX). George sang.
Dr. Bud and Lynn Duvall (lady-in-waiting) Sun City
Helen Bradley, Horseshoe Bend TX, Pat's longtime best friend.
Warren Fontenot, Helen's friend, Houston (TX)

OUR WEDDING

We could not have asked for a more perfect day. We knew it was going to be a glorious day when, at the break of dawn, a beautiful sunrise greeted our visitors who had traveled so far to be with us.

We had made arrangements through the Sun City Community Association to decorate the tables in the Pavilion Friday afternoon for our wedding ceremony at 11:00 Saturday morning. Also we had the florist, Rose Hill Designs, bring in a floral arch to serve as a backdrop when we stated our vows.

Dr. George Biggs, a musicologist and good friend who helped me so much in forming the Georgetown Symphony Society, sang, "For the Beauty of the Earth" to start the ceremony.

Pat chose her daughter, Sandy Cordova, to be her matron of honor. My son, Graham, did double duty. He served me well as best man and also played his accordion to accompany his wife, Carole, in the beautiful song she sang later in the ceremony.

Pat and I asked our friend Dr. Linda Watkins, associate minister of the Wellspring Methodist Church to perform the ceremony, and she did it with class.

In addition to our formal wedding vows, Pat and I made personal pledges to each other as we formed the new P&G Team, Pat and Gaz:

Pat: "I will put away all childish thoughts, and my life with Gaz will be the most fulfilling of my life. Those that I love will have peace, contentment and happiness. Gaz's and my families will become one filled with love. Thank God for giving me Gaz."

Gaz: "I promise to love and cherish Pat so that the dreams that we both have will come true. This is my solemn pledge."

Now, years later, we begin every day with a prayer to thank God for having given us the opportunity to live our lives together.

THE WEDDING RECEPTION

One of the advantages of living in one locale for a length of time and being involved in the community is to know the right people. I knew all the key people in Sun City, especially those in the community association and the restaurants.

Katie Sutton, manager of the catering service was especially helpful in our planning for the reception. She had her staff prepare a wonderful spread: chicken salad, shrimp salad; cheese, fruit and vegetable trays; and finger sandwiches. To quench the thirst we offered ice tea, beer, and a choice of wines and champagne.

Also, my friend Tina Asklund from the ballroom supplied us with the most wonderful bartender, Ray Diaz, a take-charge person who took full responsibility for making sure everyone had a good time.

Once again, the Legacy Hills Park Pavilion's natural setting overlooking the lake, combined with perfect weather, made for a perfect setting for us to be surrounded by 48 family members and friends.

We had not realized that granddaughter Meghann Green and her "significant other," David Abramson had gone for a stroll on one of the nature paths.

We had concluded the reception "toasts"

Gaz & Pat after their marriage, May 7, 2003.

when they returned and told us they would like to make an announcement. David had just given her an engagement ring and they wanted us to share their joy.

On my 87th birthday four years later and I was given a beautiful remembrance album, Meghann wrote, "The second reason I love Bumi (my nickname) is because he allowed David to propose to me at his wedding to Pat. It was such a special day, one that I will always treasure, so thank you Bumi and Pat for letting us share your joy that day."

Tragically, less than three months later, David died suddenly. That made the joy of their announcement on our wedding day even more important to Meghann and to all of us who were present to share her joy and happiness.

OUR HONEYMOON

We celebrated our honeymoon with a month at Chautauqua and three weeks in Europe, highlighted by visits to Switzerland with our four granddaughters, four great-grandsons and the Christening of the first of our three great-granddaughters born in 2003.

Pat's sister, Jonnie Hall, went with us, not as chaperone but as a fun loving friend to share the traveling experience. We flew to Paris, rented a car and spent a relaxing first weekend in the French wine country at a lovely chateau before going to Switzerland.

Marianne had lived for 30+ years in the near vicinity of Solothurn, a walled city dating back, I believe, to about the ninth century. I have always described the location of Solothurn this way. If you make a triangle to Basel, Bern and Zurich, Solothurn is inside that triangle with Bern, the capital, only 30 minutes away by car or by train.

Lisa, Marianne's oldest daughter and her husband, Ueli, a mountain climbing guide, lawyer and now a judge, have two sons, Julian and Lionel. Heidi, the second daughter and her husband Peter also have two sons, Jonathan and Niccolo. It was their daughter Livia who was christened in the natural setting of a small mountain stream.

Marianne's youngest daughter, Rebecca, is a travel agent and lives inside the old walled city of Solothurn. Marianne, who now lives near Boulder, Colorado, and her third daughter Cordelia, who, at the time of the wedding was concertmaster of the Indiana University Music Conservatory Orchestra, and now lives in New York, were both visiting in Switzerland.

By train we went to Budapest to visit grandson Jamie Wilson who was spending the summer as an intern at the

Open Society Archives founded by George Soros. Jamie is now at the University of Virginia pursuing a PhD in the history of American foreign relations.

By car we visited Vienna, Salzburg, and Munich, traversed the legendary Romantik Road to Heidelberg, and spent quality time in small towns in Germany and France, plus four days in Paris, including a Seine River cruise, before coming home.

HEALTH CHALLENGES

I had not spent a night in a hospital from the time I was born until May 1997 when I fell and broke my hip playing tennis. When I recovered, my sports activity was limited, I was still very active.

And, if you had seen Pat anytime from May 2003 to perhaps the end of 2006 you would have said she looked like the picture of health. She did not smoke, drank moderately, exercised regularly and kept her weight in check. She was in the Championship Flight in the Sun City Women's Golf Association.

So it came as a real shock to both of us that seventeen months after we were married, our health challenges began. Here is a summary:

October 6, 2004—Pat had sudden onset of chest pain resulting in a stent being placed in her heart.

May 10, 2005—a lung biopsy revealed a malignant squamous cell cancer in Pat's right lung requiring surgery on May 24 to remove the upper lobe, followed by radiation treatments 5 days per week for 5 weeks, then chemotherapy every 3 weeks for 14 weeks.

March 20, 2006—a tumor was discovered in her lower left lung. Chemo treatment was attempted, but her blood count fell too low, and surgery was required June 16 to remove this cancer.

December 11, 2006—My turn—I had some suspicious symptoms that my physician, Dr. David Lindzey, quickly recognized as cardiac related. He was right. I had a blocked main artery, and a stent was inserted.

December 22, 2006—Another tumor, Pat's third, was

discovered in her right lung which was removed by radio frequency ablation January 29, 2007.

January 30, 2007—Colonoscopy examinations revealed I had colon cancer. Surgery was scheduled for February 5, 2007. Six weeks after successful surgery, I was 20 pounds lighter, had a healthy semi-colon, and felt great

March 2, 2007—Pat had trouble breathing. We alerted our doctors in Temple.

March 5, 2007—Dr. Mott had already made arrangements for her to be admitted to the hospital. He had several tests done and examined her, felt it was OK for her to go back home. Pat had an episode at about 11:30 PM in bed where she could not get enough oxygen.

March 6, 2007—I called Dr. Mott's office first thing in the morning and reported the episode of the night before. They called back and said to bring her to the hospital. They would be waiting for us and would admit her as soon as we arrived.

Pat was admitted to the Scott & White Hospital at about 11:30 and they began tests immediately. Late the next afternoon, March 7, they told us that early the next morning Dr. Dominic de Keratry, a specialist in Interventional Pulmonology would examine her trachea (windpipe).

March 8, 2007—Dr. de Keratry showed us a picture of a tumor inside Pat's windpipe, saying that he would prefer to wait 24 hours before operating. He kept her in intensive care breathing a combination of oxygen and helium. They would watch her very carefully. If she had any problem breathing they would operate immediately. At about 8:00 PM Dr. de Keratry came back from his home to perform emergency surgery.

After the tumor was removed, Dr. de Keratry told us it was miracle that Pat had not died in any one of the three "episodes" she had survived when she could not get her breath. The tumor was "floating" up and down in her windpipe when she breathed in and out. Then, when she coughed, the muscles in her throat contracted and cut off the intake of oxygen altogether.

March 21, 2007—Dr. de Keratry performed a second operation on her trachea to remove a small remnant particle, which he described as a "pedestal" to which the tumor had been attached.

The End. (We hope and pray.)

CHAPTER THIRTEEN

CHAUTAUQUA EXPERIENCES

The first year Dee and I attended Chautauqua we stayed for one week; the second year, two weeks and the third year, a month. By the fourth year, we were ready to book our room for the entire nine-week season.

Our friend Jo-Ann Webb at Unity of Sarasota, who introduced us to Chautauqua, grew up near Chautauqua and had a summer home there. She also was a leader in the Unity Church of Chautauqua and had made arrangements with her friend Joan Piper for the visiting Unity minister each week to stay at Joan's Englewood Guest House.

The location of the Englewood is perfect. It is literally two buildings away from the 5000-seat Amphitheatre venue for all the major programs, lectures and concerts.

The Englewood also is directly across the street from the Food Court and Bestor Plaza the beautiful open-air mall, which extends from the Administration Building on one end to the Library on the other. It was on Bestor Plaza that John Phillip Sousa conducted outdoor concerts in the early years of the 20th Century.

One of the guest rooms at the Englewood is the Paul Newman Room, recognizing the private room with bath where Newman and his wife, Joanne Woodward, lived for a week when their teen-ager was enrolled in the Chautauqua Theatre Program. The Newmans had moved over from the Athenaeum Hotel because the other hotel guests would not allow them to have any privacy.

The following summer Joanne Woodward's secretary phoned and said that Miss Woodward would like to come back the following week and needed a room with private bath. When told a room was available but no private bath, the secretary said that would never do and hung up. Five minutes later she called back and said, "Miss Woodward said that would be fine."

A week later, one of the male guests came down stairs and asked, "Is that who I thought it was standing outside the bathroom waiting to get in?" All reports were that she was a great sport.

JIM ROSELLE'S GUESTS

Jim Roselle, a veteran and very popular local radio talk show host in Jamestown, NY, has been broadcasting live every weekday for nine weeks each summer for 33 years from Chautauqua.

A group of us sat across the table from Jim each morning as he interviewed politicians, writers, scientists, theologians, historians, philosophers, artists, conductors, and educators – leaders from all walks of life who were to be the featured speakers or performers at Chautauqua that day.

It was a very informal setting. When the interview stopped for a commercial break, we could ask the guests direct questions and receive immediate answers.

We met the cream of the crop of political reporters, including David Broder and E. J. Dionne from the *Washington Post*; presidential historians Doris Kearns Goodwin and Michael Beschloss; former Senator Alan Simpson of Wyoming and future New York Governor Elliott Spitzer.

I remember asking *Time* magazine Senior Editor Hugh Morrow, Jr. if he had ever been to Centre Hall, PA. He looked at me in total surprise and said, "Yes, but why do you ask me?"

"Because I knew your father, I replied."

After the broadcast ended I told him that when I was just a high school kid working at the *Centre Daily Times* in State College, his dad, who went on to become a distinguished chief of the Washington Bureau for the Associated Press, was just getting his career started after having graduated from Bucknell University.

He then told me that, at his father's request, he had taken him back for "one last time" to Centre Hall a small town about 20 miles from State College and how much he appreciated my coming over to the broadcast to tell him that story.

On another occasion the, the president of Planned Parenthood, a grandson of Margaret Sanger, the founder, was the featured speaker.

At Jim's broadcast, I asked him if he had ever been to State College PA and did he know any of Bob Higgins' family.

His answer, "Yes, and everywhere else in the world, wherever I go, I am known as Margaret Sanger's grandson, except in State College. There I am known as Bob Higgins' grand nephew."

Bob Higgins is one of THE ONLY FOUR head football coaches Penn State has had in my 87-year lifetime. The other three are Hugo Bezdek, Rip Engle and Joe Paterno.

All four are in the College Football Hall of Fame. Bob Higgins also was an all–America end at Penn State in 1919. I went to school with his two daughters who were just a few years younger than I.

MY 15 MINUTES OF FAME

I knew that the feature lecturer at Chautauqua, former Maine Governor John R. McKernan, Jr., was CEO of the Hathaway Shirt Company, and I wanted to meet him.

From the time when I was about eight or nine years old, and my brother Bill introduced me to puns, I had enjoyed creating them myself.

I thought When Man Hath the Will; Man Hathaway would make a great slogan for the Hathaway premium quality shirts. All I needed was an opportunity to present my idea to the right person.

So during Jim Roselle's radio interview with Gov. McKernan, when the commercial break came, I had my chance. "I like it, I like it!" said the Governor. At the conclusion of the broadcast I handed him my personal card which included my name, address, and the notation "Size 17 x 33."

Lo, and behold, an hour later during his speech before 5,000 people in the Amphitheatre he said that everywhere he went somebody asks him for a free sample of a Hathaway shirt.

McKernan then said, "It happened just this morning at the radio broadcast. Gaz Green from Texas asked me for one, and I am going to send it to him. He has given us a new slogan that I will give to our advertising people in New York tomorrow, 'When Man Hath the Will; Man Hathaway.'"

Sure enough, when we arrived home a beautiful white Hathaway shirt was waiting for me with a note of appreciation. And, he also gave me my 15 minutes of fame—at Chautauqua.

As Governor of Maine, McKernan tried to do everything possible to stem the loss of manufacturing jobs to overseas plants. He felt that after he was Governor, the only way he could save Hathaway was to form an investor group, purchase the company and keep it in Maine.

I don't read much about Gov. McKernan but we all hear lots about his wife, U. S. Senator Olympia Snowe of Maine. They had served in Congress together and later, after both had become widowed, they were married.

ALTERNATIVE MEDICINE

I remember one summer when one entire week was devoted to the subject of alternative medicine.

One of the great strengths of Chautauqua was that its staff knew how and where to get the most attractive speakers for any subject they wanted to investigate in depth.

For alternative medicine they had support from the National Institute of Health and presented an imposing lineup, which included two of the most popular speakers in the field, Dr. Deepak Chopra and Dr. Dean Ornish.

DR. DEEPAK CHOPRA is the author of more than 35 books and more than 100 audio, video and CD-Rom titles. Published in every continent and in dozens of languages, more than 20 million copies of Dr. Chopra's books have been sold.

Trained in both Eastern and Western medicine, and acknowledged as a pioneer in the field of mind/body medicine, Chopra has transformed the prevailing understanding of the meaning of health. Since establishing the Chopra Center for Well Being in 1995, Chopra's mission has been "bridging the technological miracles of the West with the wisdom of the East."

DR. DEAN ORNISH for more than 25 years has directed clinical research demonstrating, for the first time, that comprehensive lifestyle changes may begin to reverse even severe coronary heart disease, without drugs or surgery.

The research that Dean Ornish and his colleagues conducted has been reported in all the major Medical Association publications, and their work has been featured in virtually all major media, including cover stories in *Newsweek*, *Time* and *U.S. News and World Report*.

A one-hour documentary of his work was broadcast on "NOVA," the PBS Science Series, and was featured on Bill Moyers' PBS series, "Healing and The Mind."

BISHOP JOHN SHELBY SPONG

Every afternoon for five days in the Hall of Philosophy at Chautauqua a guest lecturer holds forth for one hour, followed by 30 minutes Q&A.

For one whole week, we had the privilege of hearing John Shelby Spong, the most published member of the House of Bishops of the Episcopal Church in the United States. He is the author of fourteen books and some 90 published articles. He has conducted worldwide lecture tours and been featured on every major TV interview program in the United States.

Spong grew up Catholic in segregated North Carolina. His alcoholic father died when Spong was 12 years old. A Catholic alter boy, Spong immersed himself in religion, and his Parish Priest became his surrogate father, encouraging him to be the first in his family to attend college.

After graduating Phi Beta Kappa from the University of North Carolina in three years, he married his college sweetheart and entered the Protestant Episcopal Theological Seminary in Virginia. He served as rector of various parishes in North Carolina and Virginia before being consecrated Bishop of the Newark Diocese in 1976, a position he held for 24 years.

I had read his autobiography and knew that he had worked as a sports broadcaster to help defray his educational expenses. His favorite sport was basketball, an enthusiasm engendered in part by the great teams at North Carolina developed by the legendary coach Dean Smith.

In the morning before Spong was scheduled to be the guest on Jim Roselle's radio broadcast, Jim said to me, "Gaz, what is a good question for me to ask Bishop Spong?"

I had just heard on the news that North Carolina (Spong's school) had hired Matt Doherty, the basketball coach at Notre Dame (Roselle's school). I suggested Jim ask Spong what he thought of the ethics of North Carolina stealing the basketball coach from Notre Dame.

Without batting an eye Bishop Spong replied, "We did not steal him. He was one of our own. We sent him there as a missionary, and now we have called him home."

MORMON TABERNACLE CHOIR

Among the other most unexpected experiences in my life was receiving an invitation to sing with the Mormon Tabernacle Choir in their first Amphitheatre performance at Chautauqua in many years.

After Pat and I were married I was eager to introduce her to the Chautauqua experience and for her to meet some of my friends there. I scheduled our visit to include the Saturday when the world famous Mormon Tabernacle Choir from Salt Lake City would present matinee and evening performances in the 5,000 plus seat Amphitheater.

We stayed, as I had always done, at the Englewood, which gave us a wonderful opportunity to meet and visit with members of the choir when they strolled the grounds of Chautauqua between performances. We gained an otherwise impossible insight into their tour when two beautiful young women choir members came up on the Englewood porch, sat down and visited with us.

We learned, for example, that the following year they were planning a visit to several European countries on their summer world tour. They even invited us to join them on the tour as "groupies".

We also learned that Chautauqua was the only location on the tour that would have two performances, and after they arrived they learned why this was necessary. They had more than 11,500 attend the two performances in their first appearance at Chautauqua in 36 years.

The highlight had to be the evening performance in the Amphitheater. Just imagine this fabulous 360-member Tabernacle Choir, accompanied by the Massey Memorial Organ, the largest outdoor pipe organ in the world, with 5640 pipes, an overflow performance before a standing room only audience.

The awe-inspiring program included traditional choral pieces, well-known sacred hymns, and patriotic music. At the start of the concluding number, the conductor invited us to sing-along.

"Now you can go home and tell your friends you were invited to sing with the Mormon Tabernacle Choir," he said.

Yes, Yes. Pat and I did. It was a thrill.

MARK RUSSELL

For more than 25 years Mark Russell, comedian, pianist and singer appeared on the American public broadcasting network PBS at least four times a year. He is well known for playing the piano and singing in-between periods of talking, and for satirical songs – making new words for popular melodies, which are meant to express the political situation that he is talking about.

Born in Buffalo, NY, the nearest large city to Chautauqua, Mark has been a big favorite with the summer visitors and has appeared there regularly on an alternate year basis. Pat and I have been his guests for dinner in the lake home he and his wife, Allie, now own there.

I met Mark several years ago through Jim Roselle and have had the privilege of sitting on the Englewood porch just visiting and talking. One day I asked him how he prepared his 30-minute TV show. After he answered, he told me that, for his out of town 90-minute shows, he reads local newspapers for several weeks so his humor will be topical.

That conversation resulted, a year later, in our bringing Mark Russell to Georgetown to present a program as a fundraiser for an organization that Clark Thurmond, publisher of the *Williamson County Sun* created to help school children with special needs.

When Mark came out on the stage for his show his first question to the audience was, "Do you know whose statue is on top of the Courthouse in Georgetown?" After a pause, he said, "Del Webb," creator of Sun City where most of his audience that day lives.

Also, he knew I was "selling" piano keys to raise money, so his second item warned everyone to be cautious around me since there are only 88 keys on the piano and I had already sold 110.

I knew that he and Liz Carpenter, former press secretary for Lady Bird Johnson, and Cactus Pryor, Austin humorist and TV personality were longtime friends so we had a hilarious private dinner with them after the show. Does he have writers? "Yes," he says, "535; 100 in the Senate and 435 in the House of Representatives."

CHAUTAUQUA MEETS PAT

Before we were married I had told Pat about the wonderful experiences I had enjoyed over the years at Chautauqua.

So, for the summer of 2003 I asked Joan Piper, owner of the Englewood Guest House to reserve the first floor room which had been occupied by the Unity Minister of the Week for several years.

I am guessing that the Englewood is about as old as I am and I am not sure Pat was quite prepared for that.

The room we had was large, had a king size bed and its own lavatory, toilet and shower. Otherwise it was sparse, with no closet or bureau and minimal places to hang clothes. It had one old wicker chair we sat on until one of its kind on the front porch was broken and was replaced by our chair.

Wood Starr, a former banker in Jamestown, New York, the nearest city, had "dropped out" of his accepted lifestyle and become part of a counter culture. He lived at Chautauqua year around doing some carpentry or otherwise menial tasks for his livelihood.

Woody helped Joan in the summers by doing odd jobs, but also prepared the complimentary breakfast that was served each morning beginning at 8:00. Only Woody's favorites could get a cup of coffee before breakfast was served. Pat was one of several guests who resented that treatment.

Pat loves to play golf and has been in the Women's championship flight ever since she moved to Sun City in 2000.

Pat and Gaz at Chautauqua, 2003.

Chautauqua has a picturesque 18-hole course and I had made arrangements before we left home for her to play there. I knew she would meet interesting people. Also, my good friend Jane Washington's son-in-law Larry Tindle, who coached an Evansville Indiana state high school champion-ship golf team, would be there. Pat enjoyed playing a few rounds with him, also.

When I introduced Pat to my friend Jim Roselle, the radio talk show host, he invited her to some sit down next to him. She had no idea he had paused for a recorded com-mercial. She sat down. Then very quietly, Jim handed her a microphone with no advance warning and she was on the air talking to a live audience who tuned in every day to listen to Chautauqua guest speakers.

Pat's arrival at Chautauqua began with a "welcome back" party at the summer home of Jo-Ann Webb, followed quickly as a guest on the Jim Roselle radio program and a sing-along with the Mormon Tabernacle Choir.

Could anything top that? How about a cheerful greeting from Senator Alan Simpson or a hug from Ken Starr, the prosecutor in the President Clinton impeachment trial?

If that would not do it, picture her having dinner on the front porch of the Chautauqua Lake home of Mark and Ellie Russell. Yes, we spent a delightful evening with them just a few days after Mark had received a standing ovation for his performance before a standing room only audience in the 5,000 seat Amphitheatre.

And we have a wonderful picture of Pat and Mark to-gether to remember the evening.

Pat with humorist Mark Russell after we had dinner at Mark & Allie's home on Lake Chautauqua in 2004.

CHAPTER FOURTEEN

FACING HEALTH CHALLENGES— LIVING WITH CANCER

In Sarasota I had the privilege of introducing Dr. Bernie Siegel to a large audience as part of our Unity Church Speakers Program.

Dr. Siegel is a physician who has cared for and counseled innumerable patients. He embraces a philosophy that is at the forefront of a society grappling with medical ethics and spiritual issues. His best-selling books include: *Love, Medicine & Miracles*; *Peace, Love & Healing*; and *How to Live Between Office Visits*.

One of Bernie Siegel's basic tenets that he tells audiences is, *"Don't let any doctor tell you how long you have to live."* Also, you can begin to heal yourself by following the paths others have followed.

Forgive yourself and others, live with hope, faith and love and watch the results in your life and in the lives you touch. Remember that success and healing refer to *what you do with your life*, not to how long you avoid death.

This is exactly what Pat has done, and I followed when I was diagnosed.

Pat's own words described the *Friday the 13th of April, 2007* visit to her oncologist: "I had an appointment with Dr. Frank Mott this afternoon after having a CT scan yesterday. They had thought there was a shadow on my right lung, which has meant for the past two years another tumor. Today, when Gaz and I went into Dr. Mott's office he had a big smile on his face.

"The shadow was gone and the last tumor I had in my air passage and had removed was clear, the left lung was clear and for the first time since I was first diagnosed he said 'Pat you are in remission and I think you should work on your golf game and forget about cancer.'

"This is the best possible news and I am sure it is because of the prayers of my friends and family. Thank you.

"Monday, I am going to the driving range, and ready or not I want to start back playing in the next week or two."

We sent the following e-mail to family and friends on October 7, 2007:

Dear Family and Friends,

Today, Dr. Mott our oncologist said he had to do something he had never done before, give bad news to both a husband and a wife at the same time. We both got bad reports from our CT scans and MRI's.

First—Gaz. His cancer of the colon has spread to his liver and to his lungs in several places. There is actually nothing that can be done except give him a low dose of chemo which hopefully will slow the inevitable. He is feeling fine except a pain in his rib cage which he thought was a broken rib but turns out to be cancer. He has also had trouble breathing which may be caused by fluid in the lining of the lung. He is going to re-pace his schedule so we have more time to do things together, for him to finish his book and for us not be under any pressure.

Pat—For sometime has had trouble swallowing and felt a pressure in her throat. She has a tumor which is pressing against her trachea and next Monday her Radiologist Dr. Boyle will start radiation therapy to try and shrink the tumor. She will have chemotherapy and next Monday they will do CT scans of her lungs to make sure nothing else is involved.

The prognosis for both of us is not very good. God has blessed us both beyond anything we could possibly be entitled to so we will face this together knowing that God is with us and He (or She) will see us through whatever we now face. Please keep us in your prayers.

We send our love.

The P&G Team, Pat & Gaz

CHAPTER FIFTEEN

REVIVING A WRITING CAREER AT AGE 87

When I returned home from duty aboard the *USS MANA-TEE* (AO58) during the winter of 1945-1946 the newly elected Executive Director of the Penn State Alumni Association, Ridge Riley hired me for four months to be Editor of the *Alumni News* magazine.

In May, 1946, I drew the last pay-check I would receive for writing until **51** years later when Clark Thurmond and Linda Scarbrough, owners and co-publishers, of the *Williamson County Sun* hired me to write a weekly column in the newly launched CITY WEEK a Special Section for Sun City which had now grown to more than 10,000 population.

I said I would commit to a weekly column if I could choose my subject: PROFILES OF INTERESTING PEOPLE. I got the idea from reading obituary notices in the newspaper about interesting people living in Sun City who had died and I would say to myself, "I wish I had known that person." I wanted to write their obituary notices while the person was still alive.

Also, I knew there were so many interesting people living in Sun City that I would never run out of subjects for my columns.

SOME INTERESTING PROFILES

Bennie Davis, under the legendary Coach Red Blaik became an All-America football player at West-Point. He also was Unlimited Heavyweight Wrestling Champion. Davis rose to four-star General and Commander in Chief, of the Strategic Air Command.

I wanted to show the other side of Bennie Davis, the man who loved opera and how, in addition to supporting us financially, he and his wife Pat ushered at our concerts and were willing to help with almost anything we asked of them.

Another profile was of a young Mexican immigrant who dropped out of ninth grade at age 17 to enlist in the Marines during World War II and then went on to become Gonzalo

Garza, PhD. When he retired as Acting Superintendent of
Schools the Garza High School in Austin was named for
him.

"Chub" Meeker showed me the letter of commendation
he received from the President of Braniff Air; complimenting
him on how calm he remained when the plane on which he
was a passenger had been hijacked.

Dr. Dan Bonner was returning to New Haven, Connecticut from Princeton, New Jersey on a Pennsylvania Railroad
train after having addressed the graduation class at Princeton
Theological Seminary. As the train entered the Newark Station all passengers were ordered to leave the train immediately and remain on the station platforms. Across the river
smoke billowed from the World Trade Center. It was 9/11
and Dan arrived just in time to see the SECOND high-jacked
plane fly into the Twin-Towers.

I hate to leave anyone out, it was such a privilege for me
to write every profile; Jim Romine, Betty Jukes, Jack Noble,
Alicia Griffin, Ron Lockhart, George Flynn, Bill White, Coun-
cilman Bill Saddler, Pulte President Dino Longi, Acting GISD
Superintendent Dr. George Garver, Jarrel ISD Superintendent Jamie Mattison, Vic Figurelli, Tom and Lori Minor and
football Hall of Famer Bob Lilly.

And who could forget Bob Kelety, who, as a mid-shipman
told Pope Pius XII, a little white lie in a Private Audience?

I could go on, and on.

But, I can't.

IN MEMORIUM

LOSING A SON

G. GRAHAM GREEN III
December 8, 1948 – February 22, 2006

I had always said that losing a child had to be the most heart wrenching experience a person could have. Our son Graham was killed in a plane crash in Stafford, Virginia on February 22, 2006, at age 57. At his Memorial Service, I wanted everyone to celebrate the wonderful life he lived and what he gave back to his family and the Community.

Graham was a loving husband, father and grandfather; son, brother, cousin and friend. He was a leader, having served as President and District Governor in Rotary International. He was a solid businessman having built his own successful Real Estate Company. Above all, he was giving—of his time, his talent and his resources.

He and I were in business together for ten years in New Braunfels Texas... Without hesitation, I would tell everyone I not only loved him, I liked him. We worked together and we played together. He had a great sense of humor.

I remember how proud I was the first time he beat me in tennis. I am not sure I ever won again, but that was OK. We had many spirited games, playing doubles with Graham and his mother against his wife, Carole, and me.

Graham and I also played a lot of golf together. We made huge bets—$500 on a putt, $1,000 on a hole. One day playing with an older couple I missed my putt and Graham said, "OK Dad. You now owe me $10,500." A few days later the woman in the couple said to me, "Gaz, I can't believe you and your son bet so much money." I answered; "Why? We NEVER PAY OFF so it is NO problem."

When Graham was about 30 years old he and Carol helped us start a Hospice Program. The very first patient we had was a beautiful little ten year old black girl with a congenital heart problem. She was lying in bed at home in a coma when Graham brought his accordion and his daughter, Tabitha, to play and sing for her. All of the sudden the little girl began to wiggle her toes in time with the music.

I remember Graham, after that experience, saying to his mother there are times that all you want to do is cry, but you can't. They did not. They kept on singing. That is what I want all of us to do—remember how Graham brought joy and happiness into each of our lives.

When he and Carole were to be married he wrote a song for her that she sang and he accompanied her on the piano at the Reception. It was entitled, "Thank You, For Letting Me in Your Life."

Today I say to Graham, Thank You for Letting Me in Your Life, and Thank You for all the happiness you brought to us in our lives.

*   *   *

(I choked up before I could end my remarks with these last two lines. I am sure that when Graham gets to Heaven he will find a piano, or an accordion. If not, he will learn to play the harp and continue to make lovely music.)

G. GRAHAM GREEN III
December 8, 1948 – February 22, 2006

Armadillo Publishing
Corporation

See online the fine books we sell:
www.FineLiterature.com